KIPS Publishing LLC
Rochester, PA

I believe it's important to point out that I, like all humans, am not exempt from making mistakes, and they have humbled me in the face of the vast knowledge that still awaits my collective understanding.

So, as you read through my work, I would like you to view it as a testament to diligent effort and human fallibility. I'm excited to share the polished outcomes of my research and the raw and imperfect process that underlies it. Together, we can appreciate the evolution of ideas and the remarkable journey that is the pursuit of knowledge.

With gratitude and humility,
Robin

Your Words Have Power
Be Careful How You
Use Them

"I don't study to know more but to ignore less."

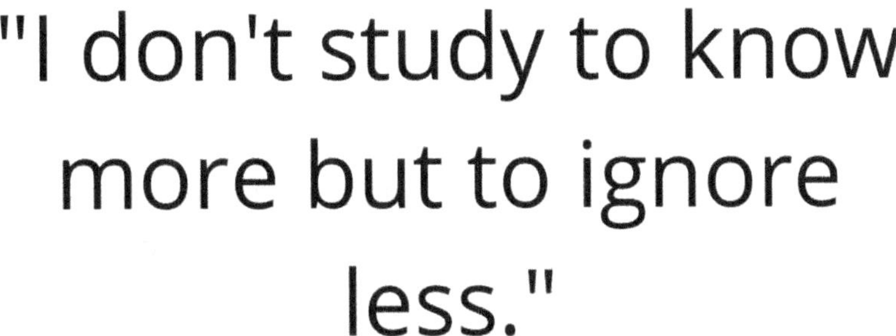

- Juana Inés de la Cruz

We all have our own unique ways of doing amazing things that speak to our hearts, regardless of others' opinions. I believe that everyone's interpretation of what they see, hear, and feel is subjective. My books aim to provide a solid foundation for your own research or exploration of new and exciting things. I'm not perfect and don't have all the answers, but every journey should involve learning and personal growth. As I continue to research, I'm grateful to be learning with you. Therefore, I believe that everyone is on their own path to enlightenment, and you are not alone.

As Always,
Blessings to You and Yours

Acknowledgments

Since embarking on this journey a year ago, I've been blessed to have so many wonderful people come into my life. Your love, friendship, kindness, and guidance have enriched my life in so many ways, and for that, I'm incredibly grateful.

Each of you holds a special place in my heart, and I wish you all the very best in return. Thank you for being a part of my journey!

I'd also like to express my gratitude to my editor, who meticulously reviewed my notes and helped make this book more polished.

As aways,
Blessings to You and Yours
from Me and Mine

CHAPTER 1

Wheel of the Year

Sabbat Dates

Sabbat	Northern Hemisphere Date	Southern Hemisphere Date
Imbolc	February 1-2	August 1-2
Ostara	March 19-21	September 20-23
Beltane	May 1	October 31
Litha	June 20-22	December 20-23
Lammas	August 1-2	February 1-2
Mabon	September 21-24	March 20-22
Samhain	October 31	April 30
Yule	December 20-23	June 20-22

Sabbats: The Wheel of the Year

Yule - Winter Solstice

God as Oak King is born of the Goddess.
God as Holly King prepares to depart.
Goddess is the Mother of the Sun God.
Goddess is the Crone of Winter.

Imbolc - Purification and Fire

Goddess is cleansed and purified.
Milk flows for lambs and for the baby God.
The quickening of the Earth.
Goddess is preparing to return to Maiden.

Ostara - Spring Equinox

Goddess is Maiden/brings Spring.
God and Goddess encourage animal fertility.

Beltane - Fertility and Fire

God Youth and Goddess Maiden unite in love.
May Day flowers, romps, and bonfires.

Litha - Summer Solstice

God turns from Youth to Sage.
Marriage of God to Goddess.

Lughnassadh - Bread Harvest

God enters the Earth in marriage, giving his energy into the grain, now his body.
First Harvest/Bread Harvest-grains.

Mabon - Autumn Equinox

God gives his spirit into the vines, fruit, and barleycorn;
wine, cider, whiskey, beer, and mead are now his blood.
He rules the Underworld.
Goddess alone and pregnant with the God.

Samhain - Death and Rebirth

God within the Goddess, yet also Leader of the Wild Hunt.
The veil between the worlds at its thinnest,
Crone and Hunter [Lord of Shadows] reign together.

The Wheel of the Year Explained

The Wheel of the Year, also known as the Wheel of Life, symbolizes the Earth's cycles and the cycle of life itself. Our ancestors used it to mark the turning of the seasons and years, for farmers to plan their work, and for modern pagans to reconnect with nature's rhythms.

The Wheel of the Year consists of eight holidays or festivals, also known as holy days. These festivals follow the cyclical calendar of the sun and moon and the natural world's rhythms. Four of them are solar festivals or lesser Sabbats, which are associated with the sun and God. The other four are season-change festivals, or Grand Sabbats, related to the Earth and Goddess.

The Wheel of the Year has two halves: a dark half marking Autumn/Winter and a light half marking Spring/Summer. Each half has two lesser Sabbats and two Grand Sabbats. The lesser Sabbats are Yule, the Winter Solstice; Ostara, the Spring Equinox; Litha, the Midsummer Solstice and Equinox; Litha, the Midsummer Solstice, and Mabon, the Autumn Equinox. The two annual equinox solstices are the solar festivals or lesser Sabbats. The equinoxes occur when we have a day and night of almost equal length because the sun is directly over the equator. The solstices occur when we have the shortest day (June) and the longest day (December), related to the Earth's tilt. The exact date varies each year by a few days due to the Earth's rotation around the sun in 365.25 days, while our calendar is set for 365 days. Hence, we have a leap year every four years to balance out the calendar.

The Wheel of the Year Explained

The four significant season changes for the year are the seasonal festivals or Grand Sabbats, also known as cross-quarter days or fire festivals.

The Wheel of the Year is divided into the dark half (Autumn/Winter) and the light half (Spring/Summer). Each half has two lesser Sabbats and two Grand Sabbats. We mark this division at the equinoxes. The Autumn Equinox (Mabon) marks the beginning of the dark half of the year, while the Spring Equinox (Ostara) marks the beginning of the light half of the year.

During the dark half of the year, we turn inward. It is the cold, hibernating months when we focus on inner work, contemplation, and meditation. We use this time to rest, recover from the hustle and bustle of the light half of the year, and focus on our homes and hearths.

In contrast, the light half of the year is about looking outward. It is the warm, lively spring and summer months when life abounds everywhere. During this time, we work with our communities, traditionally planting fields, tending newborns, and gathering food for the winter store. Births, weddings, harvest feasts, and general merriment are common during this time.

The light half of the year starts with the Lesser Sabbat at the Spring Equinox, Ostara, in September, followed by the Grand Sabbat of Beltane at the start of summer in October. The Lesser Sabbat at the Mid-summer Solstice, Litha, is in December, and finally, Llamas is at the beginning of autumn in February.

While the Wheel of the Year is rooted in Celtic and European cultures, its symbolism and concepts can be found in many ancient cultures worldwide.

Quarter and Cross-Quarters

The eight seasonal festivals celebrated in Pagan and Wiccan traditions are divided into quarters and cross-quarters. The quarters, also known as the solstices and equinoxes, mark the four major points of the solar year. These include Yule (winter solstice), Ostara (spring equinox), Litha (summer solstice), and Mabon (autumn equinox). On the other hand, the cross-quarter sabbats occur midway between the quarters and symbolize the shifting seasons. They are Imbolc (around February 1st), Beltane (around May 1st), Lammas (around August 1st), and Samhain (around October 31st). These cross-quarter sabbats hold spiritual significance and often commemorate the agricultural cycles or ancestral connections.

Dividing the sabbats into quarters and cross-quarters provides a balanced representation of life's changing seasons and cyclical nature.
The quarters align with the solstices and equinoxes, emphasizing the sun's influence on the Earth. At the same time, the cross-quarters highlight the subtle transitions between the seasons and the interconnectedness of all living beings. This way, they honor the Earth's natural rhythms.

Overall, the eight seasonal festivals are important in Pagan and Wiccan traditions. They help people connect with the Earth, its seasons, and the spiritual significance they hold. They also remind us of the cyclical nature of life and the interconnectedness of all things.

Quarters - Green [lesser] Sabbats
Yule - Winter Solstice
God is born of the Goddess.
Goddess is both Mother and Crone of Winter.

Ostara - Spring Equinox
Goddess is Maiden/brings Spring to Earth.
God and Goddess encourage the fertility of Earth.

Litha - Summer Solstice
God turns from Youth to Sage/Oak to Holly King.
Marriage of God to Goddess.
Holly King impregnates Goddess with Oak King.

Mabon - Autumn Equinox
God gives his blood into the vines.
Goddess alone and pregnant with the God.

Cross-Quarters - White [Greater] Sabbats

Samhain - Death and Rebirth
God within the Goddess/tomb becomes the womb.
The veil between the worlds is thinnest.

Imbolc - Purification and Fire
Milk flows for the baby God as Oak King.
The quickening of the Earth.

Beltane - Fertility and Fire
God and Goddess unite in love.
May Day romps and bonfires/fertility encouraged.

Lughnasadh - Bread Harvest
God enters the Earth in marriage, giving his body to be the grain.
First Harvest- grains.

Winter?

Is the Winter Solstice really the start of winter?

There is not a black-and-white answer to this question; it depends on which definition of "winter" you follow:
Astronomical winter begins at the winter solstice and ends at the spring equinox. Astronomical seasons are based on the position of Earth in relation to the Sun.

Meteorological winter (in the Northern Hemisphere) starts on December 1 and ends on February 28 (or 29). Meteorological seasons are based on the annual temperature cycle and climatological patterns observed on Earth.

CHAPTER 2

Yule at a Glance

Yule - December 21 - January 1
Pronounced: yo͞ol

Yule (also called Jul, Jul blot, joulu, "Yule time," or "Yule season" is a festival historically observed by the Germanic peoples. Scholars have connected the original celebrations of Yule to the Wild Hunt, the god Odin, and the pagan Anglo-Saxon Modraniht ("Mothers' Night"). Also called Yuletide, Yulefest. Yule, Festival of Lights, Alban Arthan, and Christmas

Yule is an ancient tradition celebrated around December 20-23 during the Winter Solstice. It is a time to celebrate the victory of light over darkness and honor the spirit of new beginnings. Rich in symbolism and rituals, it embodies rebirth, introspection, hope, setting intentions, and the sacred celebration of light.

Its roots span various cultures and civilizations from Ancient Rome to early Christianity. In Wiccan belief systems, Yule marks the reawakening of the God who had fallen during Samhain and honored a resting Goddess who has just given birth. Greeks, Persians, and Early Christians also have ancestral connections to this festival.

Enchanting decorations like evergreen branches and holly and radiant sun imagery in red, green, white, and gold amplify its mystical atmosphere. Traditional Christmas customs such as decorating trees or burning logs have pagan origins dating back centuries.

They are honoring this profound juncture by immersing yourself in ceremonies that connect you with deities like the Green Man of English folklore, who symbolizes life and fertility in nature. Similarly, appreciate St. Nicholas, Santa Claus, Jesus' birth, Saturnalia rituals of gift-giving, caroling, mistletoe, fruitcake offerings, greenery decorations, and a mock sacrifice of Saturn performed in some temples.

So live and let live!

Quicky Yule Correspondences

Goddesses
Amaterasu
Baba Yaga
Befana
Bona Dea
Brimo
Cailleach
Carlin
Carravogue
Ceres
Decima
Fauna
Holda
Koliada
Lachesis
Marzana, aka Moranna
Rind
Skadi
Snegurochka
Tonan

Gods
Bacchus (*Roman; often linked to winter via feasting and drinking*)
Hodhr (*aka Hod, Hoder, Hodur; Norse*)
Saturn or Saturnus (*Roman; Lord of Capricorn*)

Magical Beings
Cert (aka Krampus)
Dilis Varsvlavi (Georgian mythos)
Elves
Gawain the Green Knight (Arthurian legend)
the Green Man
the Holly King, who is said to surrender to the Oak King at the Winter Solstice
Karkantzaros (Greek)
Knecht Ruprecht (German)
Lucka (Bohemia)
the Lutzelfrau (German)
the Pelznichol, Perchta (aka Bertha; German)
Samichlaus (Swiss)
the Stallo (Sami
Tomten (including the Nisse and theTonttu; Scandinavian)
Weihnachtsmann (German; the "gift man")
Egregores: Santa Claus!

Archaeoastronomical Sites
Almendres Cromlech (Portugal)
Cahokia Mounds (Missouri, US)
Chaco Canyon (New Mexico, US)
Chichen Itza (Mexico, Yucatán peninsula)
Easter Island (Polynesia)

Flowers
Christmas rose and poinsettia

Trees
Evergreens, cedar, fir, pine, spruce, holly, and pecan

Crystals
Onyx, tanzanite, turquoise, and zircon

Metals
Gold and lead

Scents for Oils, Incense, Potpourri, or just Floating in the Air
Cardamom, cinnamon, clove, evergreens (fir, pine, spruce, and cedar), frankincense, myrrh, and wood smoke

Herbs
Cardamom, cinnamon, cloves, ivy, mistletoe, nutmeg, peppermint, rosemary, sage (culinary), and saffron

Animals, Totems, and Mythical Creatures
Bear, cows and oxen, flying reindeer, horse, pigs, raven, reindeer, and stag

Acts of Service
Giving to those less fortunate, feeding birds and wildlife (while following sustainable practices), furnishing warm clothing for those in need, sending packages to military personnel overseas, working in food banks and soup kitchens

Symbols
Cauldron, darkness evergreens/greenery, light, mother and child, trees, wreaths, and yule log

Food
Buche de Noel (roasts of meat and poultry), citrus fruits, fruitcake, homemade baked goods, scalloped/ mashed/ roasted/ au gratin root vegetables (potatoes, rutabagas, turnips, parsnips, and sweet potatoes)

Drinks
Drinking vinegars, eggnog, glug, hot buttered rum, hot coffee drinks, hot chocolate, hot toddy, mulled wine, tea, Tom and Jerry, and wassail

Colors
Green, gold, red, and white

Traditions
Decorating the homestead, making and giving gifts, baking soul cakes, attending live performances and concerts (traditional: Mummer plays and Morris dancing), watching the Gemini meteor showers (December 12-14), game playing, caroling, bonfires and fire circles, storytelling, ringing of bells, "first footing
(on New Year's), and all varieties of rituals (solo and communal) and "high celebration."

Alternate Names for Yule in Other Traditions and Cultures

Alban Arthan ("druidic" per the writings of Iola Morganwyg; although most of Morganwyg's works have been found to be self-created, many still follow his teachings)
December solstice (used to clarify Northern/ Southern Hemisphere meanings)
Dongzhi Festival (December 22; China and other Asian countries)
Goru (December 21; Mali)
Inti Raymi June 21-24; Peru)
Midvinterblot (December 21; Norse)
Midwinter
Natalis Sol Invictus -Birth of the Unconquered Sun (December 21; Etruscan, Roman)
Soyal (December 21; Zuni and Hopi)
We Tripantu June 21-24; Chile)
Winter Solstice (December 21-22; marks the time of the longest night and shortest day in the Northern Hemisphere)
Winternights
Yalda (December 21; Iran)
Yulefest, Yuletide
Ziemassvetki (December 22; ancient Latvia)

Holidays or Traditions Occurring During Yule in the Northern Hemisphere: RELIGIOUS

Brumalia (Often began at the end of November and extended into January)
Sanghamitta (First full moon in December; Sri Lanka)
Chalica (First week in December; Unitarian Universalists)
St. Barbara's Day (December 4. Christian; once a church-sponsored holiday, the day is now celebrated by a number of traditions)
Advent (Christian; date varies but involves the four Sundays before Christmas)
Chanukah/Hanukkah (variable date; Jewish)
St. Nicholas' Day (December 6)
Bodhi Day (December 8; Buddha's enlightenment)
Our Lady of Guadalupe (December 12; Mexican)
St. Lucia's Day (December 13; Swedish)
Las Posadas (December 16-24; Mexico)
Saturnalia (December 17-23; Roman)
Koruchan (December 21; Eastern European- Slavic)
Pancha Ganapati (December 21-25; US Hindus)
Koliada (aka Koleda; once ancient but now celebrated around December 24 in modern Slavic countries)
Christmas (December 25)
Mother's Night or Modranicht (December 27; Saxon)
Twelvetide (Twelve Days of Christmas)
Twelfth Night (night of January 5)
Epiphany January 6)

Secular
Deuorius Riuri (Ancient Gaul)
Krampusnacht (December 6; Alpine
Europe)
Feast of Fools (Variable times beginning in
mid-December; wild communal parties
sprouting up around the time of the
Winter Solstice; medieval Europe)
Burning of the Clocks (December 21-22;
Brighton, United Kingdom)
Festivus (December 23; United States)
Kwanzaa (December 26; Pan-African
holiday celebrated in North America)
Boxing Day (December 26; United
Kingdom, Australia, Canada, and New
Zealand)
Junkanoo (December 26; Caribbean
countries)
Wren Day or La an Dreoilin (December
26; Ireland, the Isle of Man, and Wales)
Watch Night (December 31)
Hogmanay and "First Footing" (Night of
December 31 to dawn on January 1;
Scotland)
New Year's Eve and Day (December 31
and January 1)
Distaff Day (January 7; also called Roc
Day; European nations)

**Holidays or Traditions Occurring
During Yule in the Southern
Hemisphere: RELIGIOUS**
Vestalia, the Festival of Vesta June 7-15)
St. Alban's Day June 20 or 22)
Gwyl o Cerridwen (Feast of Cerridwen;
modern Welsh witchcraft, July 13)

Secular
Fete de la Musique (World Music
Day; June 21)
Indians Day or Peasants Day June 24;
Peru)
Canada Day (July 1)
US Independence Day (July 4)
French Bastille Day (July 14)

Winter Solstice Blessing

May you find peace in the promise of the Solstice night. I hope that each day henceforth is blessed with more light. May the cycle of nature remain unbroken and true, bringing faith to your soul and well-being to you. Rejoice in the darkness, find rest in the silence, and may the following days be abundantly blessed.

CHAPTER 3

Introduction to Deities

Worshiping and dedicating to gods and goddesses is an important aspect of many pagan traditions, including those celebrating the Litha Sabbat. The honored and revered deities can vary greatly depending on the individual or group's beliefs and practices. Some may worship a pantheon of gods and goddesses, while others may focus their devotion on a single deity. Regardless of the approach, dedicating oneself to these powerful spiritual forces can be a significant and transformative experience.

Many pagans see their relationship with the divine as a two-way street. They believe they can receive blessings, guidance, and protection in return by offering devotion and reverence to the gods and goddesses. This energy exchange is often seen as a way to maintain balance in the world and one's life. Some also view the deities as archetypes or personifications of natural forces, such as the sun or the moon, and may seek to align themselves with these energies through worship.

There are many ways to worship and dedicate oneself to the gods and goddesses. Some may perform rituals or ceremonies, make food or drink offerings, or create sacred spaces in their homes or outdoor areas. Others may meditate, pray, or engage in personal acts of devotion. Whatever form it takes, this connection with the divine can be a source of inspiration, comfort, and spiritual growth for those who seek it.

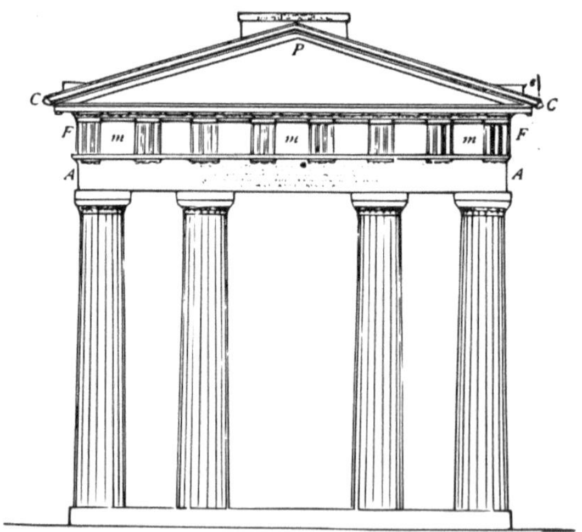

Baba Yaga (Slavic)

Baba Yaga, a formidable figure in Slavic folklore, embodies the enigmatic and often chilling essence of ancient tales. Renowned as an ogress with a taste for theft, cooking, and consuming her victims—frequently children—her presence in the folklore is shrouded in a mystique that transcends ordinary imagination. As a guardian of the fountains that hold the sacred water of life, she dwells in a peculiar forest hut that defies reality, perched upon birds' legs and spinning incessantly. An eerie fence adorned with human skulls encapsulates her dwelling, a testament to her intimidating persona.

The imagery surrounding Baba Yaga is both captivating and haunting. She extraordinarily traverses the skies, riding in an iron kettle or a mortar propelled by a pestle, leaving tempests in her wake. Her association with Death adds to her ominous reputation, as she accompanies the harbinger of the afterlife, consuming the souls newly released into the world beyond. Her presence evokes an unsettling blend of fear and fascination, woven intricately into the tapestry of Slavic folklore.

However, within the depths of her terrifying nature lies a complexity that transcends mere malevolence. Despite her ominous deeds, Baba Yaga is often considered a guardian of profound wisdom and arcane knowledge. She challenges seekers who approach her hut, testing their wit and resilience. Those who prove worthy may receive her aid or acquire the wisdom sought, revealing a nuanced aspect of her character that extends beyond the surface of terror, showcasing her as a guardian of hidden truths and esoteric wisdom in the ancient Slavic world.

Bona Dea (Roman)

Bona Dea (Roman)
This fertility goddess was worshiped in a secret temple on the Aventine hill in Rome, and only women were permitted to attend her rites. Her annual festival was held early in December. High-ranking women would gather at the house of Rome's most prominent magistrates, the Pontifex Maximus. While there, the magistrate's wife led secret rituals at which men were forbidden. It was even prohibited to discuss men or anything masculine at the ritual.

Demeter (Greek)

Through her daughter, Persephone, Demeter is linked strongly to the changing of the seasons and is often connected to the image of the Dark Mother in winter. When Persephone was abducted by Hades, Demeter's grief caused the earth to die for six months, until her daughter's return.

Dionysus (Greek)

A festival called Brumalia was held every December in honor of Dionysus and his fermented grape wine. The event proved so popular that the Romans also adopted it in their celebrations of Bacchus.

Frigga (Norse)

Frigga honored her son, Baldur, by asking all of nature not to harm him, but in her haste overlooked the mistletoe plant. Loki fooled Baldur's blind twin, Hodr, into killing him with a spear made of mistletoe but Odin later restored him to life. As thanks, Frigga declared that mistletoe must be regarded as a plant of love, rather than death.

Baldur (Norse)

Baldur (Norse)
Baldur is associated with the legend of the mistletoe. His mother, Frigga, honored Baldur and asked all of nature to promise not to harm him. Unfortunately, in her haste, Frigga overlooked the mistletoe plant, so Loki - the resident trickster - took advantage of the opportunity and fooled Baldur's blind twin, Hodr, into killing him with a spear made of mistletoe. Baldur was later restored to life.

Hodr (Norse)

Hodr, sometimes called Hod, was the twin brother of Baldur and the Norse god of darkness and winter. He also happened to be blind and appears a few times in the Norse Skaldic poetry. When he kills his brother, Hodr sets in motion the string of events leading to Ragnarok, the end of the world.

Odin (Norse)

In some legends, Odin bestowed gifts at Yuletide upon his people, riding a magical flying horse across the sky. This legend may have combined with that of St. Nicholas to create the modern Santa Claus.

Saturn (Roman)

Every December, the Romans threw a week-long celebration of debauchery and fun, called Saturnalia in honor of their agricultural god, Saturn. Roles were reversed, and slaves became the masters, at least temporarily. This is where the tradition of the Lord of Misrule originated.

Holly King (British/Celtic)

The Holly King is a figure found in British tales and folklore. He is similar to the Green Man, the archetype of the forest. In modern Pagan religion, the Holly King battles the Oak King for supremacy throughout the year. At the winter solstice, the Holly King is defeated.

Horus (Egyptian)

Horus was one of the solar deities of the ancient Egyptians. He rose and set every day and is often associated with Nut, the sky god. Horus later became connected with another sun god, Ra.

Lord of Misrule (British)

The custom of appointing a Lord of Misrule to preside over winter holiday festivities actually has its roots in antiquity, during the Roman week of Saturnalia. Typically, the Lord of Misrule was someone of a lower social status than the homeowner and his guests, which made it acceptable for them to poke fun at him during drunken revelries. In some parts of England, this custom overlapped with the Feast of Fools – with the Lord of Misrule being the Fool. There was often a great deal of feasting and drinking going on, and in many areas, there was a complete reversal of traditional social roles, albeit a temporary one.

Mithras (Roman)

Mithras was celebrated as part of a mystery religion in ancient Rome. He was a god of the sun, who was born around the time of the winter solstice and then experienced a resurrection around the spring equinox.

CHAPTER 4

Magical Figures

As the winter solstice approaches and the world embraces the quiet majesty of Yule, we are beckoned into a realm where the veils between worlds grow thin, allowing glimpses of fantastical creatures from diverse cultures to grace our presence. Beyond the well-known figure of Santa Claus lies a tapestry woven with an array of mystical beings, each carrying the essence of their unique traditions and folklore. In this chapter, we embark on a wondrous expedition through the global mosaic of Yuletide magic, encountering an array of mystical entities that have long held sway over the festive season. From the mischievous yet endearing spirits to the guardians of ancient wisdom, these magical beings transcend borders and time, embodying the spirit of Yule in ways that captivate hearts and spark the imagination.

Samichlaus (Swiss)

On December 5th, parades known as Klausjagen occur throughout Switzerland to celebrate the arrival of Samichlaus and Schmutzli. Children recite a poem called a spruchli to Samichlaus and are rewarded with treats for their good behavior. Zurich has a Samichlaus-themed Märlitram, which makes a loop around the city. On the evening of December 5th, children place their shoes by the front door. If they behaved well, they will find a Samichlaus bag placed in their shoes in the morning, otherwise, they may find a lump of coal or sticks delivered by Schmutzli.

the Stallo (Sami)

Stallo is a terrifying figure in Sami mythology. Often depicted as half-human or troll-like, Stallo steal from and eat people. They can also serve as demons created by Shamans to take down their enemies. Although wealthy, Stallo are quite foolish and always lose to humans in fairy tales. To obtain their riches, humans must kill Stallo, but the wealth is not always worth the risk.

Stallo dress in dark clothes and carry a dog and a sack. They may have a whistle with a cruel sound and use an iron pipe to suck the breath out of people. They often trick humans into using their own knives against themselves. Stallo were used to scare children during upbringing, especially during Christmas. If children made noise, Stallo would come and slaughter them. Good order in the house was essential during Christmas, and a water bucket needed to be kept outside to quench Stallo's thirst. If Stallo got his water, he would go away, but if not, it meant trouble.

Weihnachtsmann (German)

On December 5th, parades known as Klausjagen occur throughout Switzerland to celebrate the arrival of Samichlaus and Schmutzli. Children recite a poem called a spruchli to Samichlaus and are rewarded with treats for their good behavior. Zurich has a Samichlaus-themed Märlitram, which makes a loop around the city. On the evening of December 5th, children place their shoes by the front door. If they behaved well, they will find a Samichlaus bag placed in their shoes in the morning, otherwise, they may find a lump of coal or sticks delivered by Schmutzli.

Tomten (Scandinavian)

The Swedish Tomte is a gnome-like figure with a woolly beard and a conical cap that's part of Scandinavian folklore. Originally believed to be the ancestral spirit of the first farmer to have worked a given plot of land, the Tomte is a dutiful worker who cares for the animals, children, and property at the homestead. However, he can be mischievous and fiery-tempered. Despite their shared name, the homestead Tomte and the American Santa Claus don't have much in common.

the Lutzelfrau (German)

Lutzelfrau is a witch in German folklore who gives gifts — particularly apples, nuts and dried plums — to children on Saint Lucy's Day. Lutzelfrau customs are also common in Slovenia and Croatia, where a "dark Luz" was contrasted to the Christian saint.

Knecht Ruprecht (German)

Knecht Ruprecht is a beloved companion of Saint Nicholas in German folklore. He is known as the most popular gift-bringer in Germany, although he remains largely unknown outside the country. In written sources from the 17th century, Knecht Ruprecht appears as a figure in a Nuremberg Christmas procession.

The companions of Saint Nicholas, closely associated figures in territories influenced by the Holy Roman Empire, play a contrasting role to the benevolent gift-bringer. They serve as a reminder to disobedient children, threatening punishment. Jacob Grimm associated Knecht Ruprecht with the pre-Christian house spirit, which possessed both benevolent and mischievous qualities, with a focus on mischief after Christianization.

Various traditions:
Knecht Ruprecht is widely recognized as Saint Nicholas' attendant in Germany. In different regions, he is referred to as Hans Ruprecht, Rumpknecht, or De hêle Christ ("The Holy Christ"). Alternate names such as Rû Clås (Rough Nicholas), Bûr, and Bullerclås are used in specific areas. Samuel Taylor Coleridge encountered a Knecht Ruprecht character during a visit to Ratzeburg in northern Germany in 1798, describing him as wearing high buskins, a white robe, a mask, and an enormous flax wig. Other depictions show him wearing a black or brown robe with a pointed hood, sometimes accompanied by a limp from a childhood injury. He may carry a long staff and a bag of ashes or wear little bells on his clothes. Knecht Ruprecht is occasionally seen riding a white horse or accompanied by men with blackened faces dressed as old women or fairies.

According to Alexander Tille, Knecht Ruprecht originally symbolized an archetypal manservant, with a defined social rank but limited personal individuality, similar to other character archetypes like Junker Hanns and Bauer Michel.

Characters of Christmas

Belsnickel is a Christmas gift-bringer figure in the folklore of southwestern Germany, the Palatinate region, and Pennsylvania Dutch communities. He wears furs and carries a switch to beat naughty children, but also gives cakes, candies, and nuts to good children. Belsnickel is related to other companions of Saint Nicholas in German-speaking Europe, and may have been based on an older German myth, Knecht Ruprecht. The tradition fell into decline toward the end of the nineteenth century but has seen a revival in recent years.

Santa Claus is a popular Christmas character dressed in a red coat, white fur collar, cuffs, black leather belt, and boots. He carries a magical bag filled with gifts and is commonly depicted as a jolly, plump man with a white beard and glasses. The character gained popularity in the US during the 19th century thanks to the poem "A Visit from St. Nicholas."

Santa Claus rides in a miniature sleigh pulled by tiny reindeer, including Dasher, Dancer, Prancer, Vixen, Comet, Cupid, Donner, and Blitzen. He was also known as "Kris Kringle" in some regions of the US.

In Austria and Catholic regions of Germany, a man dressed as St. Nicholas visits houses on December 5 carrying a staff and small gifts for children. Accompanying him are Krampusse, ragged, devil-like creatures that playfully frighten children. This tradition adds a touch of magic to the festive season.

The Yule Lads

Icelandic Christmas folklore, like our food, language, and landscapes, is a bit extreme. Instead of getting a visit from Santa Claus on Christmas Eve, Iceland has the 13 Yule Lads (Jólasveinar), who, in mid-December, start descending one by one from their mountain home to wreak mischief in the nights leading up to Christmas. The Yule Lads are the sons of the hideous trolls Grýla and her husband, Leppalúði. Grýla is incredibly horrible as she has an appetite for the flesh of naughty children, whom she likes to put into a large pot and make into stew.

While the original Yule Lads were pranksters who went about stealing food and causing havoc, in modern times, they have become the Icelandic version of Santa Claus, leaving children with daily gifts.

Every night, starting on December 12th, one Yule Lad will visit every child's home, placing a toy or a piece of candy into shoes that children leave on their window sills... that is, as long as you are well-behaved that day! If you misbehave that day, the Yule Lads are not subtly expressing their disapproval, and they'll fill your shoe with rotting potatoes.

December 12th - Stekkjastaur – Sheep Cote Clod
The first Yule Lad, Sheep-Cote Clod, comes to town on December 12th. He used to try to suckle the yews in the farmers' sheep sheds, which was hard for him since his legs were stiff as wood.

December 13th - Giljagaur – Gully Gawk
Next in line is Gully Gawk. He gets his name because he likes to hide in gullies to sneak into the barn to slurp the foam off the fresh milk when the farmer looks away.

December 14th - Stúfur – Stubby
Stubby is the smallest of his brothers and uses his vertically challenged stature to hide and snatch bits of food left over from the frying pan. That's why he's also sometimes known as Pan Scraper.

December 15th - Þvörusleikir – Spoon Licker
Spoon Licker likes to sneak into houses and lick the wooden spoon used to scrape the pots and pans. Unfortunately, this poor diet has led to malnutrition and his gaunt appearance.

December 16th - Pottaskefill – Pot Scraper
Pot Scraper likes to sneak into houses (much like his brothers) and snatch away pots that have not been washed yet so he can lick the food remains from the insides of the pots. Doesn't exactly sound very appetizing or hygienic, for that matter.

December 17th - Askasleikir – Bowl Licker

In the past, Icelanders ate from wooden bowls with a hinged lid that was sometimes kept under the bed after a night snack. Bowl Licker likes to hide under the bed, and when someone puts their bowl on the floor, he'll grab it and lick it clean.

December 18th - Hurðaskellir – Door Slammer

On December 18th, there's no more peace since that's when Door Slammer arrives. He likes to make much noise, and his favorite activity is slamming doors, making sure no one in the household gets a solid night's sleep.

December 19th - Skyrgámur – Skyr Gobbler

Skyr Gobbler makes his way down from the mountains on the 19th. He is obsessed with skyr, an Icelandic dairy product similar to yogurt. He likes it so much that he'll sneak into the pantry and eat all the skyr until he howls with indigestion.

December 20th - Bjúgnakrækir – Sausage Swiper

December 20th marks the appearance of Sausage Swiper. As you might have guessed from his name, he's a big fan of sausages and will sit up in the rafters waiting for the perfect opportunity to snatch a few.

December 21st - Gluggagægir – Window Peeper

December 21st is when Window Peeper visits. While not as greedy as some of his brothers, Window Peeper can still frighten you. He likes to peep through the windows in search of something to steal.

December 22nd - Gáttaþefur – Doorway Sniffer

Door Sniffer comes to town on December 22nd. You can spot him from miles away due to his huge nose. The smell of Christmas cookies and traditional Icelandic' leaf bread' attracts him to your doorway, and while you're not looking, he'll attempt to steal some.

December 23rd - Ketkrókur – Meat Hook

Second to last is Meat Hook; he arrives on December 23rd. Meat Hook is crazy about meat. He'll climb up to your roof and lower a long hook through the chimney to try and snag a smoked leg of lamb hanging from the rafters or a piece of smoked lamb from the pot.

December 24th - Kertasníkir – Candle Beggar

The last of the brothers is Candle Beggar, who arrives on Christmas Eve. In the old days, candles were the brightest lights available to people in Iceland and were made of tallow. While Icelandic children longed to have their own candle for Christmas, Candle Beggar just wanted a candle to take a bite out of.

After Christmas, the Yule Lads return to their mountain home, one by one, in the same order as they arrived in town until the last one, Kertasníkir, leaves on the last day of Christmas, January 6th.

Yule Cat

The Yule Cat, a peculiar Christmas spirit, is known for its appetite for children who don't receive new clothing during the holiday season. While the origins of the Yule Cat remain mysterious, it differs from other Christmas creatures like the Yule Lads and their mother. While the Yule Lads have evolved into friendly gifts-givers, the Yule Cat has remained unchanged in its menacing nature.

The earliest records of the Yule Cat date back to the 19th century, but its roots are believed to be much older. It is closely associated with the Scandinavian belief in the Yule Goat, which can be traced back to pagan and pre-historic times. Some speculate that the Yule Cat may be a local variation of the goat, possibly influenced by the worship of Thor. The decline of the Yule Goat in Iceland may have been due to the influence of the Medieval Church or the dwindling goat population.

According to Icelandic folklore, children are warned that the Yule Cat will devour those who don't receive new clothing for Christmas. The Cat is said to appear on Christmas morning or the night after. This myth serves as a reminder that any gift, even a simple sweater from a grandparent, is valuable and should be appreciated.

The origins of this myth can be linked to the rural economy of pre-industrial agrarian Iceland. It is believed to be connected to the tradition of farm hands receiving a piece of clothing as a Christmas bonus. The Yule Cat served as a threat to motivate people to complete their weaving and knitting before the holidays. Failure to finish these tasks would result in the terrifying fate of being devoured by the monstrous Cat!

Yule Goat

Among them is the Julbock, a charming goat that joins the Jultomte in delivering presents on Christmas night. Uncover the ancient origins of this beloved tradition, rooted in the spiritual practices of pre-Christian Scandinavia.

According to folklore scholars, Julbock's origins can be traced back to the mighty Nordic god Thor and his faithful goats, Tanngrisnir (Gap-Tooth) and Tanngnjóstr (Tooth-Grinder). These two goats pulled Thor's chariot and miraculously provided sustenance each day. They were slain in the evening, only to rise again the next morning. One fascinating Swedish practice that emerged from this myth is the Juleoffer or Yule sacrifice. In this ritual, a person dressed in goatskins would symbolically be sacrificed and then resurrected at dawn, carrying an effigy of a goat. Though actual sacrifices were likely practiced in the past, as the Norse people were known for their animal and human sacrifices, this custom was abandoned with the arrival of Christianity, and the Julbock was vilified as a demonic figure.

Historical records from the 1600s shed light on the belief in the Julbock among the people of Sweden. It was believed that the Julbock would roam the country on Christmas night, demanding offerings and sparking fear among Christians. Over time, Julbock's image transformed into that of a benevolent being who brought gifts during the Christmas season, accompanied by the Jultomte.

"After the festive dance around the Christmas tree, the Julbock, often symbolized by Father Christmas, enters with presents. Bock means goat, and the bringer of gifts was said to ride on a Yule goat. You may recall the association between the goat and Thor. The Julbock playfully throws parcels into the room. Sometimes, as a playful joke, a small gift may be wrapped in multiple layers with different inscriptions and verses, each intended for different people before reaching its rightful owner." (Cyriax)

In modern-day Sweden, the Julbock is most famous for the Gävle Goat, a colossal straw sculpture erected annually in Gävle since 1966. Unfortunately, this remarkable structure has gained notoriety for being set aflame each year, having been burned down 37 times in its 51-year history. While efforts have been made to prevent these incidents, perhaps the burning is a symbolic offering to the ancient gods. And let's not forget, the ongoing news coverage of the burning goat will surely bring a smile to your face.

Christmas Spider

There are three versions of the story of the Christmas Spider and you can choose your favorite.

Version One: Once upon a time, a poor but hardworking widow lived in a small hut with her children. One summer day, a pine cone fell on the earthen floor of the hut and took root. The widow's children cared for the tree and were excited about having a Christmas tree by winter. The tree grew, but when Christmas Eve arrived, they could not afford to decorate it. The children sadly went to bed and fell asleep. Early the following day, they woke up and saw the tree covered with cobwebs. When they opened the windows, the first rays of sunlight touched the webs, turning them gold and silver. The widow and her children were overjoyed; from then on, they never lived in poverty again.

Version Two: A mother was cleaning for Christmas a long time ago. Spiders fled up to the attic to escape the broom. The spiders slowly came down for a peek on a quiet Christmas Eve. "Oh, what a beautiful tree!" In excitement, they scurried up and out along each branch. They were filled with happiness as they climbed amongst the glittering beauty. But alas! When they were done, the tree was shrouded in its dusty, grey web. When Santa came with gifts for the children and saw the tree covered with spider webs, he smiled because he saw how happy the spiders were, but he knew how heartbroken the mother would be if she saw it covered in dusty webs. So he turned the webs into strands of silver, and the tree was even more beautiful than before. That's the story of tinsel on trees and why every tree should have a Christmas spider in its branches.

Version Three: The story is about two mothers - a peasant woman and a mama spider - struggling to provide for their young children. On Christmas Eve, the woman went into the forest and returned with a small fir tree to serve as a Christmas tree. She discovered that a spider had made a home for her babies among the fir's branches, but the woman didn't have the heart to sweep them away. The spider discovered that the woman was too poor to decorate the tree, let alone place presents beneath it, and hatched a plan out of gratitude and kindness. Later that night, the spider spun sparkling webs throughout the fir tree's branches when the woman and her children went to bed. In the morning, the children woke to the thrilling sight of a Christmas tree draped in the most exquisite, shimmering gossamer!

Do you have a spider ornament on your tree? You can bet I will have one this year as I tell my granddaughter the story of the Christmas Spider.

Tomte Spirits of Yule

The tomte spirits are renowned figures in Swedish folklore tied to the Yule and Christmas festive season. Also known as "homestead men," these magical beings resemble garden gnomes, standing approximately two feet tall. With their long beards, worn-out clothing in shades of grey, blue, or red, and signature red caps, tomtes exude an air of wisdom and agelessness.

Traditionally, tomtes were responsible for the overall well-being of a homestead, tending to animals, clearing forests, and nurturing livestock. Despite their small stature, they possessed incredible strength and endurance. Some experts believe that tomtes may be remnants of ancient reverence practices, possibly connected to ancestral spirits.

Notably, tomtes harbored a special fondness for horses, often braiding their manes and tails. Believed to bring good fortune, the horse that the tomte favored was believed to be the healthiest. This charming and hardworking spirit became a cherished helper around the house and farm, asking for very little in return. Respecting the tomte, displaying teamwork, being considerate of animals, and offering a simple meal of porridge with butter on the Winter Solstice or Christmas Night were the only expectations.

However, be warned—displeasing a tomte had dire consequences. Offending the spirit, neglecting farm responsibilities, mistreating animals, failing to follow traditions, or neglecting to leave porridge with butter on Yule would unleash the tomte's wrath. From mischievous pranks to terrifying acts, the tomte would wreak havoc on homes. Livestock and pets could fall victim to its poisonous bite or be subjected to ruthless attacks. Even unbraiding the horse's mane and tail, a tomte's handiwork was believed to bring ill fortune.

With the arrival of Christianity, tomtes, like many folklore entities, were demonized. Considered idolatrous and associated with witchcraft, the belief in tomtes during the 14th century prompted accusations of practicing heathen rituals or even selling one's soul. Over time, as Christmas became commercialized, the image of the tomte softened. Often paired with the Yule Goat, tomtes evolved into the origins of Christmas Elves or Santa's Helpers, traveling from house to house bearing gifts. Still, it may be wise to remember the tomte's preferences and leave out porridge with butter on top during Yule or Christmas Eve.

The Christmas Scarecrow

The origins of Santa Claus, also known as Saint Nicholas, date back to a fascinating tale from the third to fourth century. Bishop Nicholas, a Greek bishop in the Roman town of Myrna (present-day Turkey), performed remarkable acts, including reviving three murdered children. These extraordinary deeds and Nicholas' charitable endeavors solidified his status as a saint, a protector of children, and a generous gift-giver.

Alongside this benevolence, a terrifying figure emerges Hans Trapp, the dreaded Christmas scarecrow. There has always been someone or something to punish naughty children. This includes the infamous horned Krampus and shape-shifting Christmas witch Perchta. However, Hans Trapp takes the title of the most terrifying. According to one chilling story, he not only harmed a child but also dismembered and consumed their flesh!

The legend of the Christmas scarecrow primarily originates from the French regions of Alsace and Lorraine. Hans Trapp, a powerful and merciless man from the 1400s, struck fear into the people's hearts. Seeking more power, he made a pact with the Devil, resulting in excommunication, banishment, and the loss of his wealth and lands. Forced to seek refuge in the mountains of Germany, Trapp embraced his dark desires. Draped in straw as a disguise, he lurked on desolate roads, waiting for unsuspecting victims.

Inspired by a real person, Hans von Trotha, the legend of Hans Trapp takes a chilling turn. Hans von Trotha was a knight who lived from 1450 to 1503. Engaged in a property dispute with the church, he resorted to extreme measures. Though there is no evidence of cannibalism or hunting children, von Trotha's life was filled with extraordinary events, including excommunication by the Pope.

While the true story of Hans von Trotha is fascinating, local legends also referred to him as the Black Knight, a terrifying specter sometimes associated with Santa Claus to punish unworthy children.

Frau Holle

Meet Frau Holle, the enchanting spirit of the woods and plants, revered as the sacred embodiment of the earth itself. She symbolizes fertility and rebirth, associated with the lush foliage
of the Yule season, particularly mistletoe and holly. Celebrated on December 25, Frau Holle is commonly revered as the goddess of hearth and home but holds various roles across different regions.

Did you know? Frau Holle traces her origins back to the ancient deity Hulda that predates the Norse pantheon. Embracing fertility and rebirth, she is celebrated as the goddess of hearth and home on December 25. Additionally, she is closely linked to women's crafts like weaving and spinning.

Discover Frau Holle in fairy tales, appearing in stories such as Goldmary and Pitchmary from the renowned Grimm brothers' collection. In these tales, resembling a Germanic Cinderella figure, she bestows rewards upon diligent girls and offers appropriate compensation to their lazy counterparts. Legends in certain German regions portray her as a toothless hag, akin to Scotland's Cailleach, appearing in the winter. Conversely, alternative stories depict her as a youthful, beautiful, and fertile being.

In Norse mythology, she goes by the name Hlodyn and presents gifts to women during the Winter Solstice, also known as Jul. Additionally, Frau Holle is associated with winter snowfall; as the story goes, fluffy white feathers descend upon the earth when she shakes her mattresses. Many Germanic communities hold feasts in her honor each winter.

Scholars have noted that Frau Holle derived from the ancient pre-Christian deity Hulda, predating even the Norse pantheon. Representing an older woman connected to the darkness of winter, she watches over children during the coldest months. Archaeologist Marija Gimbutas describes her as a figure who governs death, the wintry dark caves, graves, and tombs within the earth. However, she also receives the fertile seed, the light of midwinter, and the fertilized egg, transforming tombs into wombs for new life to gestate.

In essence, Frau Holle encompasses the cycle of death and eventual rebirth, symbolizing the emergence of new life. Like many deities, her character is multi-faceted and has evolved throughout the centuries, making it impossible to confine her to a single theme.

Hulda, the Goddess of Women

Hulda, a goddess associated with women and household matters, was particularly connected to women's crafts, such as weaving and spinning. This connection to crafts has also tied her to magic and witchcraft, as mentioned in the Canon Episcopi, written in the fourth century. Those who honored her were required to do penance as faithful Catholics.

The Canon Episcopi states: "Have you believed in the existence of a female deity named Holda, whom the ignorant and common people associate with certain supernatural abilities? These abilities require individuals deceived by the devil to participate in the company of a group of demons disguised as women, riding on certain beasts on specific nights. If you have taken part in this belief, you must do penance for one year on designated fast days."

According to Rosemary Ellen Guiley in the Encyclopedia of Witches and Witchcraft, Hulda's nocturnal rides with the souls of the unbaptized dead led to the Christian association of her with the demonic aspects of the wild hunt. She was said to be accompanied by witches and the souls of the dead, riding uncontrollably through the night sky. It was believed that the land they passed would produce a bountiful harvest.

To honor Frau Holle, the spirit of winter, you can focus on domestic crafts as part of a ritual. This can include spinning, weaving, knitting, or sewing. Shirl Sazynski has written a heathen spindle ritual in Witches & Pagans that is worth exploring, or you can incorporate other domestic tasks into a ritual context. As Frau Holle is associated with snowfall, incorporating snow magic into your celebration would also be appropriate.

Krampus

The origins of the Krampus legend, a frightening figure that lurks alongside Santa Claus. Uncover the ancient roots of this tradition, which is believed to have originated from an early horned god and was later assimilated into the Christian devil figure. Krampus, meaning "claw," is known for his terrifying appearance, featuring sheepskin, horns, and a switch used to discipline misbehaving children and unsuspecting young ladies.

While the legend of Krampus has experienced a resurgence in recent years, it is believed to date back centuries. Despite the exact origins remaining a mystery, anthropologists suggest that Krampus emerged from a pre-Christian tradition and was eventually suppressed by the Catholic Church for its rowdy celebrations. Even during World War II, fascists frowned upon Krampus due to its association with the Social Democrats.

One notable event in the Krampus calendar is Krampusnacht, which is celebrated on December 5 in parts of Germany and Bavaria. During this night, men dress up as creepy demons, while women don masks to embody the Nordic figure of Frau Perchta, possibly an aspect of the fertility and war goddess, Freyja. Interestingly, a similar character called Pelsnickel or Belznickel exists within the Pennsylvania Dutch community in America, suggesting the tradition migrated across the Atlantic when Germans settled in the United States.

According to Krampus.com, the official home of "Krampus, the holiday devil," Krampus is considered the dark counterpart of Saint Nicholas. While Saint Nicholas rewards good children with gifts and treats, Krampus takes on the role of punishing the naughty ones, a task delegated to him by St. Nicholas. This unique dynamic sets Krampus apart from the typical jolly Santa Claus figure.

Today, Krampus has gained renewed popularity in various locations, including the United States, where he has become an iconic figure. Annual Krampus celebrations occur in Columbus, Ohio, Philadelphia, and Seattle. These parades celebrate the European tradition and capture the spirit of this captivating, albeit terrifying, holiday character.

Christmas Witches

Christmas as we know it today is celebrated worldwide, but the oldest customs associated with the holiday have been forgotten or adapted to fit modern society. Before jolly old Saint Nick and other mythical beings were linked to Christmas, including witches, who were either nice or naughty. Unfortunately, most children are unfamiliar with these Christmas witches, such as Berchta, La Befana, Cailleach, and the Baker's Dozen witch.

The origin of Christmas witches can be traced back to pre-Christian times when people believed in multiple gods. Many of these gods were demonized by Christianity, and some of the former folk's religious beliefs and customs have survived in the form of fairies, witches, and mythological creatures. The Church turned some goddesses into ugly hags to discourage people from worshipping them. The Christmas witches were once goddesses, and their visits on Christmas are part of an old pagan tradition celebrating the Winter Solstice.

The holiday season has a darker side to it as well. The long, dark night and cold temperatures make us realize how thin the line is between light and dark, warm and cold. Legends of mischievous goblins and demons exist alongside the tales of Santa Claus and gifts under the tree. One such figure is the Krampus, a ghastly, goat-like creature from the Alps that punishes naughty kids by hitting them with birch branches, stuffing them in a sack, and taking them back to Hell.

The Krampus is not the only one who works during the holiday season. There are many other holiday-themed ghouls, including Christmas witches. These female figures come in different forms, from friendly grandmas who give blunt advice to ogresses who descend from the mountains to gobble up whiny children. These witches have as much to say about Christmas as any jolly old elf, and their legends have a message for us - watch yourself and mind the dark.

Many Christmas traditions have roots linked to older pagan practices that existed for centuries before Christian monks arrived. Scholars link the figures of Christmas witches, such as Iceland's Grýla or Italy's Befana, to the same history, especially considering the female spirits and deities that appear in the old beliefs. According to the journal Folklore, the modern traditions of Christmas witches can be traced back to older, more ferocious goddesses like Perchta and Holda. These goddesses ruled over the cold winter months that descended upon Europe. People used to leave out offerings of food and frantically clean their homes. Frau Holle, a later version of Holda, was believed to have control over the weather. Whenever she shook out her feather pillows, it was said that she caused the snow to fall.

Christmas Witches cont.

Monks throughout the continent used to complain about these pagan goddesses, which was a sign that belief in them was real. For instance, Martin Luther, the former monk who initiated the Protestant Reformation, ranted about the people's belief in Holda, going so far as to criticize her depiction as an ugly old woman to emphasize that she was bad news. In the meantime, Bede, a medieval English monk, spoke more generally about a heathen "mother's Night" celebrated on December 25th in The Reckoning of Time.

Gryla

The Dark Legends of GRYLA - the Fearsome Ogress Who Punishes Naughty Children
Get ready to delve into the chilling tales of Grýla, the terrifying ogress residing in Iceland's desolate mountains. According to Smithsonian Magazine, she swoops down from her mountain home to snatch up misbehaving children, throwing them into a sack and returning them to her lair. There, these naughty children meet a gruesome fate, either transformed into a stew or having their stomachs carved out. While some modern versions have softened her edges, Grýla still maintains her eerie place in Icelandic folklore.

But Grýla isn't alone in her reign of terror. As all high-achieving monsters do, she has a family to assist her. Icelandic Folktales and Legends reveal that her husband, Leppa-Ludi, is also a cannibal eagerly awaiting her child-filled meals. Other legends suggest that Grýla disposes of her inconvenient husbands, possibly due to their insatiable appetite for human flesh. It seems Leppa-Ludi should tread carefully in their monstrous union.

Not only does Grýla have a husband, but she also has mischievous offspring known as the Yule Lads. Originally separate entities, the 13 Yule Lads became entwined with Grýla's family in the 19th century, as per Smithsonian Magazine. However, this merging also introduced another horrifying figure into the Icelandic holiday pantheon – the Yule Cat. This feline abductor targets those who haven't received new clothes for Christmas, adding to the terror of the season.

While the Yule Lads have become somewhat less menacing in recent times, their origins reveal a dark side. According to Smithsonian Magazine, they engage in a range of mischief, from disturbing livestock to raiding pantries, slamming doors, and even licking spoons. These creepy tales became so disturbing that in 1746, Icelandic parents were officially prohibited from frightening their children with these legends of the Yule Lads, Grýla, and the rest of her eerie kin.

Frau Perchta

Frau Perchta is a Christmas witch from Austria who holds grudges. Alongside other deities and spirits like Befana and Gryla, she is known for punishing bad children. Additionally, she can bring down snow and cold at her will.

Frau Perchta is generally believed to be most active during the 12 Days of Christmas, from December 25 to January 5. During this time, she roams her lands, seeking out people who have been lazy or negligent during the season. Any homes that were dirty or disorganized might then be subject to a visit from this terrifying figure.

In the darkest versions of her legend, Frau Perchta is ruthless. She punishes lazy housekeepers and sassy children by cutting open their stomachs and filling them with garbage. However, good kids and hardworking people might be rewarded with small treats hidden in their homes instead of facing the sharp knife of the Christmas witch. Other legends say that mountain shepherds have seen her wandering the slopes, holding a spindle and spinning fiber, which suggests that she practices the kind of industriousness she preaches.

Perchta is linked to the legend of the Wild Hunt. According to the legend, the Wild Hunt is a ghostly group that roams the countryside, led by famous or notorious figures. These figures could include local heroes, dead kings, the old Norse god Odin, or the Devil in less subtle retellings. Anyone who encounters the Wild Hunt is in serious trouble. They might be swept up in the horde, which could be as purgatorial as it is potentially fun. No one has ever witnessed the Wild Hunt taking a break.

In Germany, the leader of the Wild Hunt was sometimes identified as Perchta or another witchy figure called Holda. Some Alpine towns still celebrate a tradition known as Perchtenlauf, in which masked figures connected to the legends of Perchta and the Wild Hunt tramp through town, generally making noise and enacting mischief. Their wild ramblings are said to be connected to this older legend of the much more destructive, scary troop led by Perchta in her more spiritual, divine incarnation. Like other ancient goddesses, Perchta and Holda demanded respect and often elicited quite a bit of fear.

In Slovenia, similar groups could be led by Baba, whom the Institute for Slovenian Studies of Victoria says is a hag-like goddess of death. Folklore also notes that Frau Holle, a more domestic version of Holda, has also been spotted at the fore of the Wild Hunt.

Holda

Holda, one of the oldest winter witches, is associated with ancient Germanic goddesses with a mysterious connection to the spirit world. She is often depicted as Mother Holda and is accompanied by a group of ghosts. According to Norse Goddess Magic, she was originally a sky goddess with control over the weather. This led to her household tasks being influenced by the weather, such as using fluffy white clouds to hang linens or causing rain when she washed. Legend also credits her with introducing flax to humanity and teaching peasants to spin plant fibers into linen thread.

In a more compassionate aspect, Holda is said to care for the spirits of the deceased, particularly young or unborn children. Some tales claim she is involved in bringing new lives into the world, suggesting a connection to beliefs about rebirth.

Despite her earlier pagan origins, Indogermanische Forschungen asserts that Holda is associated with the winter holidays. One source describes how the people would set a place at the table for the queen of heaven, Mistress Holda, on the night of Christ's nativity. They believed this would bring good luck and ensure the household's well-being for the upcoming year.

The Ugliness of Christmas Witches and its Significance

Many Christmas witches are depicted as ugly old women, with Befana's hunchback and Perchta's demonic appearance being notable examples. Several theories have been proposed to explain this portrayal. It may symbolize the passage of time, with their physical appearance reflecting the year's aging. Alternatively, Norse Goddess Magic suggests that the crone figure is associated with the wild nature of these Christmas witches, particularly in their older, more pagan forms.

Another explanation is that Christmas witches became ugly in legends to ward off the harshness of winter. Vice suggests that an equally powerful and frightening witch would effectively keep the bitter cold at bay. It is worth noting that many of these witches are connected to holidays around the winter solstice, which brings the return of the sun and warmth.

However, not all Christmas witches are unattractive. Some versions of Perchta are depicted as beautiful, especially in her more divine incarnations. Folklore describes figures like Frau Holle and Perchta as regal and inspiring, dressed in magnificent white garments and bringing both good fortune and misfortune.

La Befana (Italian)

Don't be fooled by her seemingly cuddly appearance; In Italian folklore, La Befana is an iconic figure associated with Epiphany Eve, celebrated on January 5th. Legends intertwine her origins with ancient pagan practices and Christian narratives, creating a multifaceted character with a mysterious lineage. Believed to possibly descend from the Roman goddess Strenia, La Befana symbolizes the beginning of a new year and is revered as a mythical ancestor figure who returns annually during the same period. Often depicted as an old woman or witch, she rides a broomstick through the night sky, clad in a black shawl and covered in soot as she enters homes through chimneys. According to tradition, La Befana visits children throughout Italy, bestowing gifts upon the well-behaved and warnings to the naughty. Good children receive candy, fruit, or toys, while misbehaving ones might find coal or dark candy in their stockings. Yet, her character holds contrasting facets; some stories portray her as a kind and compassionate figure linked to Christian beliefs. One legend involves her encounter with the Three Wise Men seeking the infant Jesus. Initially declining their invitation to join their quest due to her housework, she later regrets her decision and embarks on her own search, forever seeking the Christ child. Another version depicts her as a grieving mother who mistakes Jesus for her lost child. Moved by her offerings, Jesus appoints her as the loving protector of all Italian children.
Apart from her gift-giving, La Befana is renowned for her helpful nature. It's said that before departing, she sweeps the floors of the homes she visits, symbolizing the sweeping away of troubles from the past year. Families often leave her offerings of wine and regional foods, a gesture of hospitality and appreciation. This beloved figure's evolution through folklore mirrors the evolving values and cultural sentiments, blending ancient traditions with Christian themes, creating an enduring symbol of generosity, compassion, and the spirit of giving during the holiday season.

Cailleach Bheur (Celtic)

In Scotland, she is also called Beira, the Queen of Winter. She is the hag aspect of the Triple Goddess and rules the dark days between Samhain and Beltaine. She appears in the late fall, as the earth is dying, and is known as a bringer of storms. She is typically portrayed as a one-eyed old woman with bad teeth and matted hair. Mythologist Joseph Campbell says that in Scotland, she is known as Cailleach Bheur, while along the Irish coast, she appears as Cailleach Beare.

Cailleach Bheur (Celtic)

In Scotland, she is also called Beira, the Queen of Winter. She is the hag aspect of the Triple Goddess and rules the dark days between Samhain and Beltaine. She appears in the late fall, as the earth is dying, and is known as a bringer of storms. She is typically portrayed as a one-eyed old woman with bad teeth and matted hair. Mythologist Joseph Campbell says that in Scotland, she is known as Cailleach Bheur, while along the Irish coast, she appears as Cailleach Beare.

The ancient Celts had many beliefs and legends regarding the Winter season. Winter started after Samhain, which is approximately on November 1st, and lasted until Beltane, which is on May 1st. During the entire winter season, feminine divine forces rule. Therefore, it was considered a woman's time. Unsurprisingly, there is an ancient deity turned hag named Cailleach, who watches over the winter season. Cailleach, also known as the Old Woman of Winter, is responsible for the cold, snow, and the increasing darkness. In Scotland, it is a modern tradition to carve the face of the Cailleach on a log and burn it to banish the Winter and potential hardships.

Cailleach Nollaig, an ancient goddess in Ireland, Scotland, and the British Isles, shares similar traditions with the Italian Christmas Witch, La Befana. Cailleach Nollaig's name means "The Old Woman of Christmas," and her legend covers the landscape in Ireland and Scotland in place names like Glen Cailleach, Hag's Head at the Cliff's of Moher, and the Labbacallee Wedge Tomb in Cork. Like La Befana, Cailleach Nollaig is a complex figure. Although La Befana's worship was once as widespread and prominent as the Cailleach's, the church's long presence in Rome washed out the traces.

Both Cailleach and La Befana are associated with the Winter holidays, and both have a tradition of carving their images into wood and burning them for good luck in the New Year. In Scotland, Cailleach is carved into a log, which is burned for good luck and prosperity in the coming year. This tradition is believed to be the Yule log tradition or a symbolic "burning of the witch."The ancient Celts had many beliefs and legends regarding the Winter season. Winter started after Samhain, which is approximately on November 1st, and lasted until Beltane, which is on May 1st. During the entire winter season, feminine divine forces rule. Therefore, it was considered a woman's time. Unsurprisingly, there is an ancient deity turned hag named Cailleach, who watches over the winter season. Cailleach, also known as the Old Woman of Winter, is responsible for the cold, snow, and increasing darkness. In Scotland, it is a modern tradition to carve the face of the Cailleach on a log and burn it to banish the Winter and potential hardships.be a nod tobe

Cailleach Nollaig, an ancient goddess in Ireland, Scotland, and the British Isles, shares similar traditions with the Italian Christmas Witch, La Befana. Cailleach Nollaig's name means "The Old Woman of Christmas," and her legend covers the landscape in Ireland and Scotland in place names like Glen Cailleach, Hag's Head at the Cliff's of Moher, and the Labbacallee Wedge Tomb in Cork. Like La Befana, Cailleach Nollaig is a complex figure. Although La Befana's worship was once as widespread and prominent as the Cailleach's, the church's long presence in Rome washed out the traces.

Both Cailleach and La Befana are associated with the Winter holidays, and both have a tradition of carving their images into wood and burning them for good luck in the New Year. In Scotland, Cailleach is carved into a log, which is burned for good luck and prosperity in the coming year. This tradition is believed to be a nod to the Yule log tradition or a symbolic "burning of the witch."

The Baker's Dozen and the Christmas Witch! In this captivating story, a baker's dozen equals thirteen, breaking the traditional twelve count. This charming tradition originated in the early nineteenth century, brought to the U.S. by Dutch immigrants.

Legend has it that a beggar-woman approached a baker, asking for a dozen cookies. The twist? She insisted that her dozen consisted of thirteen cookies. Initially turning her away, the baker's greed and lack of compassion lead to many misfortunes. Cookies refuse to rise, and other baking mishaps plague his business. Desperate for a solution, the baker turns to Saint Nicholas for help and, miraculously, bakes a batch of delicious cookies.

Fast forward to The Christmas Witch Returns - the baker now recognizes the beggar-woman as a witch possessing magical powers. She requests a dozen cookies again, and the baker happily gives her thirteen. In exchange, the witch proclaims that the curse has been lifted. As a result, the baker's business thrives once more. This peculiar witch, deeply connected with Saint Nicholas, has rightfully earned the title of the Christmas Witch.

Unfortunately, this delightful tale has fallen into obscurity. So, the next time someone mentions a baker's dozen, share the heartwarming story of the baker and the Christmas Witch, captivating young and old alike!

The Origins of Santa Claus

The Influence of St. Nicholas - Santa Claus finds its roots in St. Nicholas, a 4th-century Christian bishop known for generosity towards children, the poor, and prostitutes. Legend has it that St. Nicholas bestowed dowries upon three impoverished daughters, saving them from hardship. This act of kindness solidified his place as a beloved patron saint, celebrated throughout Europe with his depiction as a bearded bishop in clerical robes.

Odin's Mighty Horse and Santa's Reindeer - Delve into the connection between Odin, the Norse deity, and Santa Claus. Odin, the ruler of Asgard, was often portrayed riding his magical horse, Sleipnir. Sleipnir's ability to leap great distances bears a striking resemblance to the legends of Santa's reindeer. This intriguing parallel draws a fascinating link between ancient Germanic tribes and the modern image of Santa Claus.

From Boots to Stockings - Explore the evolution of gift-giving traditions. Discover how children in Germanic countries would leave boots filled with treats for Sleipnir during winter, receiving gifts in return from Odin. Even as Christianity spread, this practice endured, eventually becoming associated with St. Nicholas. Today, stockings are hung by the chimney instead of boots, continuing the timeless tradition.

The Dutch Influence - Uncover how Dutch settlers brought their customs to the New World, including leaving shoes out for St. Nicholas to fill with gifts. The name "Santa Claus" emerged from these Dutch roots, evolving into the beloved figure we know today.

Embark on a journey through history and mythology to understand the rich tapestry that created the beloved figure of Santa Claus. Uncover the origins and traditions that have captivated generations.

Gift Bringers from Around the World

Santa Claus / Father Christmas in Different Countries
Although Santa Claus/Father Christmas is the best-known Christmas gift-bringer, many different present-givers exist worldwide. Therefore, Santa is also called different things in different countries! Here are some of them! Kinda cool that they all somewhat sound the same.

Afghanistan: Baba Chaghaloo
Albania: Babadimri
Argentina: Papá Noel (Father Christmas), El Niño Diós (the baby Jesus), Reyes Magos (The Three Kings)
Armenia: Gaghant Baba / Kaghand Papa (Father Christmas or Father New Year) and Dzmer Pap[ik] / (Winter Father/Grandfather)
Austria: Christkind (a little angel-like person)
Azerbaijan: Saxta baba (Grandfather Frost)
Belarus: Sviaty Mikalaj / Mikanañ (St. Nicholas) & Dzied Maroz (or Ded Moroz) / Mapo3 (Father Frost)
Belgium: Sinterklaas/St. Niklaas (Flemish) or Saint Nicholas (Walloon) & Père Noël (Father Christmas)
Bosnia and Herzegovina: Djeda Mraz (Grandfather Frost)
Brazil: Papai Noel (Father Christmas) & Bom Velhinho (Good Old Man)
Bulgaria: / Dyado Koleda (Grandfather Christmas)
Chile: Viejito Pascuero (Christmas old man)
China: Shengdan laoren (Traditional: means Old Christmas Man)
Colombia: Niño Dios (Baby Jesus)
Costa Rica: Niño Dios (Child God, meaning Jesus) & Colacho (another name for St. Nicholas)
Croatia: Djed Bozicnjak (Grandfather Christmas)
Czechia / Czech Republic: Svaty Mikulás (St. Nicholas) and Jezisek (the Christ child)
Denmark: Julemanden (Christmas Man)
Ecuador: Papa Noel
Egypt: Baba Noël
Estonia: Jõuluvana (Yule Elder)
Ethiopia: Amharic: Yágena Abät (Christmas Father)
Finland: Joulupukki (Santa Claus) - well, he does live in Lapland in Finland!
France: Père Noël (Father Christmas)
Georgia: / Tovlis Baba, Tovlis Papa (Snow Grandfather)
Germany: Weihnachtsmann (Christmas Man) and Christkind (a little angel-like person)
Greece: Aghios Vassilis / (Saint Basil)
Haiti: Tonton Nwèl
Hungary: Mikulás (Nicholas) / Télapó (Old Man Winter) & Jézuska (the Christ child)
Iceland: Jólasveinn (Yule Man) & Jólasveinarnir (The Yule Lads)

India: Hindi: Christmas Baba, Urdu: Baba Christmas (Father Christmas), Telugu: Thatha (Christmas old man)
Tamil: Christmas Thaathaa, Marathi: Natal Bua (Christmas Elder Man)
Indonesia: Sinterklas
Iran: Baba Noel
Iraq: Baba Noel / Vader Kersfees
Ireland: San Nioclás' (Saint Nicholas) & Daidí na Nollag (Father Christmas)
Italy: Babbo Natale (Santa Claus) or La Befana (an old woman) or The Three Kings (parts of northern Italy)
Japan: Santa-san (Mr Santa) and Hoteiosho (A Japanese god of good fortune - not related to Christmas)
Kazakhstan: Ayaz Ata (Snow Father/Father Frost/Grandfather Frost)
Latvia: Ziemassvetku vecitis (Christmas old man)
Lithuania: Senis Saltis (Old Man Frost) & Kaledy Senelis (Christmas Grandfather)
Lebanon: Baba Noël
Malta: San Niklaw (St. Nicholas)
Mexico: El Niñito Dios (baby Jesus), Los Reyes Magos (The Three Wise Men) & Santo Clós (Santa Claus)
Mongolia: Uvliin Uvuu or Uvliin Uvgun (Winter Grandpa or Winter Old Man)
The Netherlands: Sinterklaas (St. Nicholas) & Kerstman (Christmas Man)
New Zealand: Hana Kökö (Santa Claus in Mãori)
North Macedonia: Aero Mpa3 / Dedo Mraz
Norway: Julenissen (Santa Claus) or 'Nisse' (Small Gnomes)
Pakistan: Christmas Baba
Peru: Papá Noel
Philippines: Santa Klaus
Poland: Swiety Mikolaj (St. Nicholas), Dziadek Mróz (Ded Moroz/Grandfather Frost), Gwiazdor (the Starman),
Dzieciatko (the Baby Jesus), Aniotek (Little Angel), Gwiazdka (Little Star)
Portugal: Pai Natal (Father Christmas)
Puerto Rico: The Three Kings / Magi
Romania: Sfantul Nicolae (St Nicholas), Mos Nicolae (Old Man Nicholas), Mos Cràciun (Old Man Christmas), Mos
Gerilà (Old Man Frost)
Russia: / Ded Morez (Grandfather Frost) / Dedoushka (Grandfather in Russian) or Babushka (an old woman - although this is 'Western' than actually Russian!)
Serbia: / Deda Mraz (Grandfather Frost), / Bozié Bata (Christmas Brother)
Slovakia: Sväty Mikulás (Saint Nicholas) / Jezisko (the Christ child)
Slovenia: Sveti Miklavz or Sveti Nikolaj (Saint Nicholas) / Bozicek or Dedek Mraz (Grandfather Winter); Bozicek on December 24 and Dedek Mraz on December 31!
South Africa: Sinterklaas (St Nicholas) / Kersvader (Father Christmas)
South Korea: (Santa Kullosu), (Santa Grandfather)

Spain: Los tres Reyes Mages (The Three Magic King / Magi) & Papá Noel (Father Christmas); in Catalonia, the gift bringer is Tió de Nadal, a Christmas log with a face on it!; In the Basque country, the gift bringer is Olentzero, a man who wears a beret and smokes a pipe.
Sri Lanka: Naththal Seeya
Sweden: Jultomten (Santa) & Nissar / Tomte (Christmas Gnomes/Elves)
Switzerland: Samichlaus (St. Nicholas) or the baby Jesus or Befana (South Switzerland) or the Three Kings
Syria: Baba Noël & The Smallest Camel
Tajikistan: / Bobo Barfi (Grandpa Snow)
Turkey: Noel Baba (Santa Claus)
Ukraine: Svyatyy Mykolay (St. Nicholas) & Did Moroz / (Grandfather Frost)
United Kingdom: Father Christmas (inter-changeable with Santa Claus), Wales: Siôn Corn (Chimney John)
USA: Santa Claus, Hawaii: Kanakaloka
Uzbekistan: Qor bobo (Grandfather Snow - more related to New Year's Eve than Christmas)
Venezuela: San Nicolás (St. Nicholas) & Niño Jesús (Baby Jesus)
Vietnam: Öng già Noel (Christmas old man)

You Don't Need to Believe

You don't need to believe in
Yule, the Scandinavian fertility god, to enjoy the tradition of Yuletide carols and greetings.

You don't need to be a
Wiccan to enjoy the tradition of wreaths
or decking the halls with holly.

You don't need to be a
Druid to enjoy the tradition of hoping for a kiss under the mistletoe.
You don't need to believe in the god
Saturn to enjoy the tradition of decorating
a Saturnalia tree in your home.

You don't need to believe in
Thor, Odin, or St. Nicholas to enjoy the tradition of a visitor bringing gifts at night.
You don't need to believe in
Sleipnir, Odin's flying 8-legged horse, to enjoy the tradition of listening for the sound of hooves on your
rooftop

You don't need to believe in
Mithras to enjoy the tradition of celebrating the sun's rebirth on December 25th.

And you don't need to believe in
Jesus Christ to enjoy the tradition of renaming
this ancient holiday to Christ's Mass.

Happy Holidays!

When someone says "Happy Holidays" instead of "Merry Christmas," remember they're not doing it to be politically correct. They're doing it out of respect because from November 20th to January 24th, there are at least 14 different holidays. So when someone says "Happy Holidays," just thank them. They don't know what you believe in, it's called respect. Not a war on Christmas.

Winter Solstice

The Winter Solstice, also known as midwinter, is the day filled with the least daylight and the longest night of the year. Following the night of the Winter Solstice, the sun grows stronger in the sky – so it's actually a key turning point and a time of rebirth. Its old traditions and symbolism have influenced many winter traditions today. As an example, the Scandinavian Christian winter solstice festival of lights (St. Lucia's Day) probably stemmed from earlier Norse solstice customs like lighting fires to ward off spirits in the longest night.

Christmas Customs With Pagan Roots
Let's take a look!

Christmas carols – wassailing
Kissing under the mistletoe – fertility rituals
Santa Claus – Joulupukki and La Befana
Greenery indoors – Saturnalia
Christmas elves – Tomte
Christmas ornaments – trees decorated with food and lights for Odin during the solstice

There are so many more correlations between Christmas present and pagan past than one might expect...

Celebrating Yule Today

Here are some ways to celebrate Yule in the modern era:

Family and the Yule Log - Celebrate Yule by attending festivals, feasting, singing, dancing, and spending time with your loved ones. Lighting the Yule log together is a significant and fun-filled activity. You can hold a ceremony where you and your family can light it together. Nothing says warm and cozy like bonfires with your nearest and dearest while keeping evil spirits at bay.

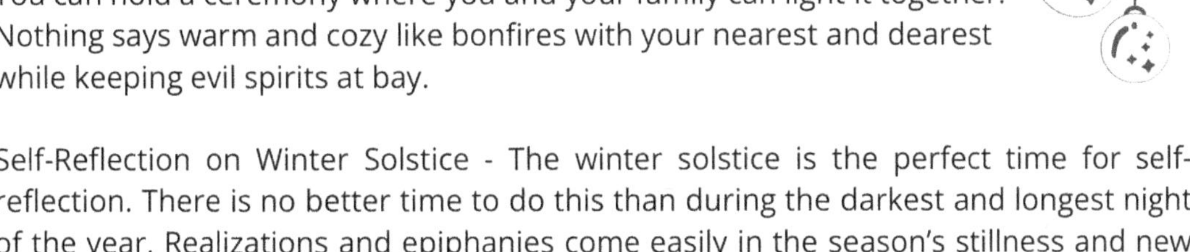

Self-Reflection on Winter Solstice - The winter solstice is the perfect time for self-reflection. There is no better time to do this than during the darkest and longest night of the year. Realizations and epiphanies come easily in the season's stillness and new beginnings if you grapple with an issue. This is also an excellent time for shadow work.

Yule Prayers - Offering a Yule prayer is one of the easiest things you can do. It will make you realize that as the days go by, the cycle turns, and the areas of your life that seem stagnant will no longer be as evident as Spring. By offering a prayer, you can welcome the coming of Spring and the new beginnings it brings.

Sunrise, Sunset, and Snow Prayers - You can also offer a Yule Sunrise prayer, welcoming the Sun as it first rises on the 21st. If you want to venerate all the astronomical occurrences during this season, offer a Sunrise prayer, a Sunset prayer, and a Snow prayer. You can also honor your gods by offering Yule prayers to the Winter Goddess, the Sun Gods, and the Old Gods. You can either search for the prayers that resonate with you or craft your own. You can even combine both if you want.

Twelve Days of Yule Devotionals - If you are tired of praying, you can try a different devotional for 12 days or until the Yule celebrations end. This is as easy as lighting a candle once a day for 12 days of Yuletide. Each day can be dedicated to a specific god, goddess, ancestor, faery, spirit, etc.

Cleansing Ritual - Clean your space of physical and vibrational dirt before decorating your home with Yuletide decorations. You can perform a cleansing ritual to clear out the stagnant energy and negativity from your home before the festive season.

Yule Altar and Winter Solstice Tree - Don't forget to set up your Yule altar and holiday tree. As most people use a tree, don't forget to bless it before cutting it and give thanks before throwing it away after the season. Use whatever calls to you the most. Make it your unique holiday. This is how traditions are born.

Wassailing - This is an ancient Anglo-Saxon tradition where people sing blessings for a household or the trees in an orchard. You can also make and share a spiced cider called wassail, traditionally drunk during Yuletide. You can celebrate this old tradition by caroling and making your batch of wassail.

Ancestral and Divine Feasting - Sacrifices to the gods were customary on Yule, and we can carry on this tradition by eating a Christmas ham or pork roast instead of the wild boar sacrificed to the gods. Set aside a plate for the gods and the ancestors or have two feasts: one for the gods and one for the ancestors.

Mothers' Night (Modraniht) - Celebrate this night in honor of our ancestors' goddesses and the Disir. In Norse mythology, a dís is a female deity, ghost, or spirit associated with Fate who can be benevolent or antagonistic toward mortals. Disir may act as protective spirits of Norse clans. The Disir are potent spirits and require offerings of gratitude on Modraniht. Celebrate your Disir and goddesses on the Winter Solstice or the night before the Winter Solstice.

Yule Goat (Bock) - This is a Scandinavian Christmas tradition where a decorative goat made out of straw or wood is hung on the Yule tree or placed elsewhere around the home. The goat can either represent Thor's sacred animals or be a nod to the calendar moving into the sign of Capricorn. Either way, the Yule goat brings prosperity and luck in the coming year.

Ghost Stories at Yule - Yuletide is a season of ghosts, ghouls, and gods. Telling ghost stories near a roaring fire is a well-known and beloved Christmas custom that has fizzled out. So, let's bring it back and celebrate the season of ghosts and spirits.

Goodbye, Long Night - Incorporate new or old traditions that resonate with you into your Yule rituals. You can do this as a solitary practitioner or with your loved ones. Say goodbye to the old and welcome in the new. Celebrate the New Year with ancient and modern traditions. Celebrate as the sun returns to the Earth and life blossoms once more.

Winter Solstice

During the winter solstice season, people practice various traditions such as eating candy canes and giving presents. However, many don't know that the roots of many Christmas customs can be traced back to pagan origins.

The winter solstice usually falls on December 21 in the northern hemisphere and June 21 in the southern hemisphere. It marks the day of the Pagan holiday called Yule. On this day, the Earth's axis tilts away from the Sun, and the Sun reaches its farthest distance from the equatorial plane in the Northern Hemisphere. As a result, the day has reduced daylight, making it the longest night of the year. Almost every ancient culture acknowledged or celebrated the winter solstice in some way, and many of our Christmas traditions today stem from much older pagan traditions of Germanic, Greek, Roman, and Celtic people.

Depending on where you are, you likely have your traditions and beliefs about the Yuletide season. Yule is an ancient Germanic holiday season believed to derive from a name for Odin himself - JOLFADR, which means Yule Father. Some say Yule lasted for 12 days from the winter solstice forward, while others say the festivities lasted an entire two months, from December through January, according to the modern calendar. Other names for Yule include Jol, Jólablót, Jul, Yule time, and Yuletide.

Yule is a time of great symbolism and power. It reminds us that the sun's return is imminent after a season of long, cold nights and short days. Our ancient Germanic ancestors believed that Yule was a liminal time when faeries, spirits, and gods could visit and walk among us. It was not a time to take things lightly, as the threads of fate called wyrd could be bound or rewoven at Yuletide. People offered sacrifices to the old gods, typically a boar or pig. The gods honored at Yule included Odin, Thor, Freyr, Frigg, and Freya. People were afraid of the Wild Hunt, a procession of gods led by Odin, Freya, and Berchta, who traveled through the wintery night skies. Some believed they gathered recently lost souls, while others thought it was simply Odin passing through on one of his travels to Midgard, also known as Earth.

Apart from feasting, partying, and processions, a few other sacred winter holidays during Yuletime are Modraniht (Mothers' Night) and Alfablöt (Elven Sacrifice). Mothers' Night is an Anglo-Saxon Heathen holiday in which pagans honor their tribal goddesses and the Disir (ancestral mothers and matriarchs). During Alfablöt, the pagan people in Sweden provided ritual offerings to the elves. However, the elves referred to here are not the ones we usually imagine from modern-day Christmas stories. These elves were more god-like.

Customs, Tradition, History and Lore

Eating Fruitcake - Fruitcake has its origins in ancient Egypt. There's a tale in the culinary world that the Egyptians placed cakes made of fermented fruit and honey on the tombs of their deceased loved ones—and presumably, these cakes would last as long as the pyramids themselves. In later centuries, Roman soldiers carried these cakes, made with mashed pomegranates and barley, into battle. In addition, there are records of soldiers on crusades taking honey-laden fruitcakes into the Holy Land.

Giving Presents - Today, Christmas is a substantial gift-giving bonanza that is a relatively new practice developed within the last two to three hundred years. Most people who celebrate Christmas associate the tradition of gift-giving with the Biblical tale of the three wise men who gave gifts of gold, frankincense, and myrrh to the newborn baby Jesus. However, the tradition can also be traced back to other cultures. For example, the Romans gave gifts between Saturnalia and the Kalends (the first day of the month), and during the Middle Ages, French nuns gave gifts of food and clothing to the poor on St. Nicholas' Eve. Interestingly, up until around the early 1800s, most people exchanged gifts on New Year's Day.

Christmas Holly - For those who celebrate the spiritual aspects of Christmas, there is a significant symbolism in the holly bush. For Christians, the red berries represent the blood of Jesus Christ as he died upon the cross, and the sharp-edged green leaves are associated with his crown of thorns. However, in pre-Christian pagan cultures, the Holly was associated with the god of winter—the Holly King, doing his annual battle with the Oak King.

Yule Log - When we hear about the Yule log, most people think of a deliciously rich chocolate dessert. But the Yule log originates in the cold winters of Norway, on the night of the winter solstice, where it was common to hoist a giant log onto the hearth to celebrate the sun's return each year.

Yuletide Prayer

This is the season of cold and white. May your spirits shine bright this very night with intuitive vision and the beauty of sights. May your heart embrace the return of the light and the beauty of sights. May your heart welcome the return of the light.

Rituals

Monthly Rituals: What to Do on the First Day of the Month
The first day of the month is an excellent opportunity to set the tone for the upcoming weeks. Make sure to follow these simple yet effective rituals to attract good luck, prosperity, and positive energy into your home:

Blow cinnamon through your front door to welcome luck and abundance.
Repeat an affirmation such as:
"When this cinnamon blows, prosperity here will enter."
Blow the cinnamon through the doorway into the home.
Leave it on the floor after blowing until the first day of the month is over.

Sprinkle salt or cascarilla at your doorways for protection.

Set a new monthly goal or affirmation to keep yourself motivated.

Pick a room to clean to invite new energy into your home.
Burn incense or smoke, and cleanse your home to start the month fresh and renewed.

Sprinkle salt on your doorstep on the first Friday of the month for good luck and extra home protection.

Wash down your front door with warm water and peppermint essential oil or peppermint tea. This refreshes the vibrations and welcomes luck, wealth, and abundance.

Before bed each night, take a moment to give thanks for the best part of your day, even if that's just eating a meal or drinking some water. the more you are thankful for, the more you will receive.

CHAPTER 5

The Phases of the Moon

New

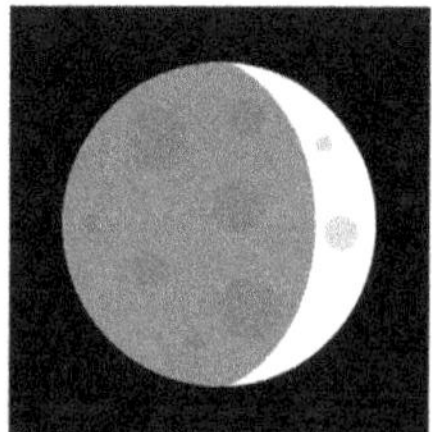

Sometimes called the Crescent Moon, when you can see the very first sliver of light in the sky. This phase promotes new beginnings, new endeavors, and new relationships. It is the time to make positive changes and plant seeds of ideas that will be harvested later.

Waxing

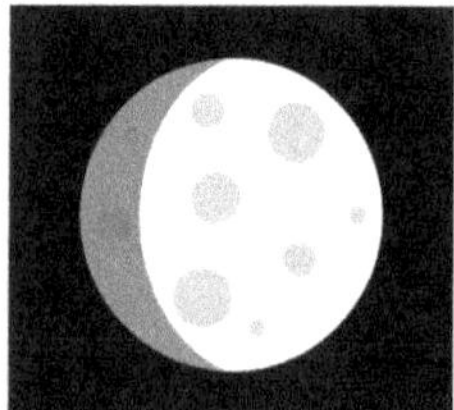

In this phase, the Moon appears to be growing in size, shifting from new to full as though it's gaining strength. It makes sense, then, that this is an excellent time to focus on increasing your knowledge, bank accounts, and relationships. This phase promotes healing.

Full

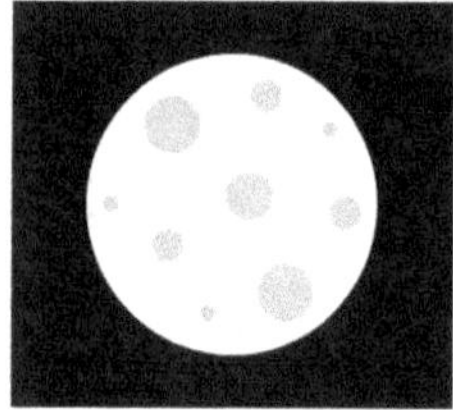

The Moon's most potent phase is when we see her entire illuminated face. This is a time of fulfillment, activity, and increased psychic ability for perfecting ideas, in other words, "getting your act together," celebrations, or renewing commitments to people or projects—the best time for spells of any kind.

Waning

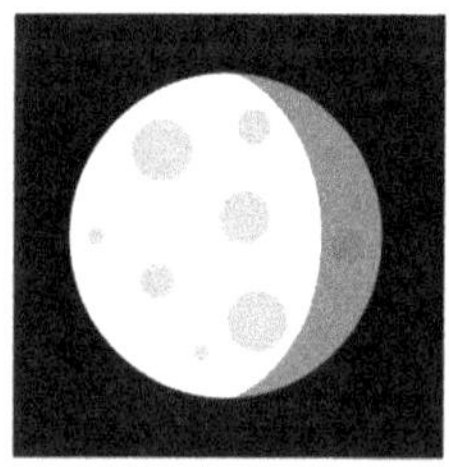

The Moon is decreasing in size as it journeys from full to dark. The waning Moon is a time of decrease, release, letting go, and completion. It is an excellent time to begin dieting, breaking bad habits, breaking off relationships, or dealing with legal matters.

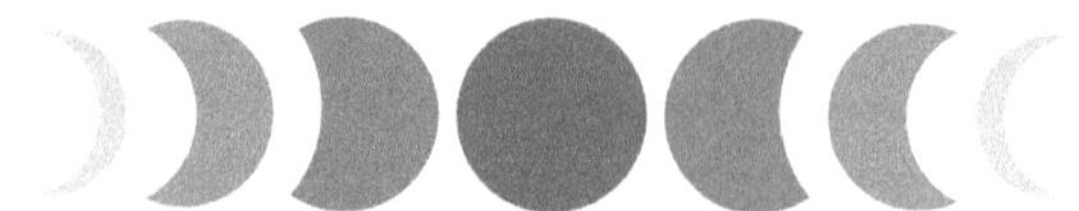

Oh Crap, a Full Moon!

Is it true that the Moon can affect our behavior or emotions? While there is no conclusive evidence, recent studies suggest that the Moon can impact our sleep patterns, regardless of whether we live in the city or the countryside.

The Luna-Lunacy Connection

Ancient scholars such as Aristotle, Paracelsus, and Pliny the Elder believed that the full Moon drove some people mad. The Latin word for Moon, "luna," is the root of modern words like "lunacy," "lunatic," and "loon." Today, many healthcare professionals, including doctors, nurses, EMTs, police officers, and elementary school teachers, believe full Moons can trigger strange behavior. While 43 percent of healthcare professionals and 81 percent of mental healthcare providers believe in this idea, there is no scientific proof of a lunar connection to abnormal behavior.

The Moon and Sleep

A recent study conducted in 2021 found that people tend to go to bed later and sleep for shorter periods in the days leading up to a full Moon. Specifically, people went to bed an average of 30 minutes later and slept almost an hour less per night. This can be attributed to the brighter light from the Moon after sunset in the days leading up to the full Moon. However, what's surprising is that this phenomenon occurs regardless of whether people live in the city or the countryside, where there is more light pollution.

One theory suggests that our ancestors relied on the Moon's light for hunting, fishing, and other social activities. People paid attention to the Moon and its cycles. For example, the "Harvest Moon" in the autumn provided several nights of light for farmers to gather their crops. Every month, the nights leading up to the full Moon bring more light to the evening, which may have influenced our circadian rhythms.

Our circadian rhythms control our sleep-wake cycles and are driven by Earth's rotation around the Sun. However, there are also circalunar rhythms, which are tied to lunar cycles. The Moon influences the behaviors of some animal species. For instance, birds use the Moon for migration and even time their reproduction to coincide with lunar cycle phases. While there is no proof that the Moon causes lunacy, lack of sleep for several nights in a row may result in irritability and mood swings.

Moon and Lunacy

It is peculiar that there have been numerous studies conducted on the connection between the Moon and its effect on human behavior, but the few studies that suggest a link have been repeatedly disproven or contradicted by others.

For instance, one study found that more animal bites, like those from cats, rats, dogs, and horses, occur during a full Moon, while another study found no increase in dog bites. Similarly, one study shows an increase in crime during a full Moon, while others have found no evidence of an increase in arrests, calls for police assistance, prison assaults, batteries, or homicides.

Interestingly, admissions for psychosis are lowest during the full Moon, and psychiatric emergency room visits decline. On the other hand, calls to suicide prevention hotlines peak at the new Moon, not the full Moon.

It is unclear how one could prove the connection between the Moon and lunacy, but some psychologists suggest that the phenomenon could be explained by "confirmation bias." In other words, people tend to notice things that confirm their preexisting beliefs.

In certain professions, such as emergency rooms, it is common for colleagues to attribute strange happenings to a full Moon, which psychologists refer to as "communal reinforcement." However, if something unusual occurs during a different lunar cycle phase, nobody makes a connection. And when nothing out of the ordinary happens during a full Moon, nobody comments.

Folklore is a term used to describe widespread beliefs that lack factual evidence. Erika Brady, a folklore teacher at Western Kentucky University, suggests that such beliefs help people impose order on situations that feel out of control.

The belief that strange things happen during a full Moon may provide a sense of safety, as a full Moon only occurs once every 29.5 days, implying that the other four weeks of the lunar month are less hazardous and unpredictable. Therefore, this folk belief suggests that our fears about everything from increased bleeding to werewolves may be limited to only 12 or 13 days per year, which could explain why the number 13 is considered unlucky.

What do you think about the Moon? Do you believe it influences behavior or emotions, or do you think it is all in our imagination and dreams?

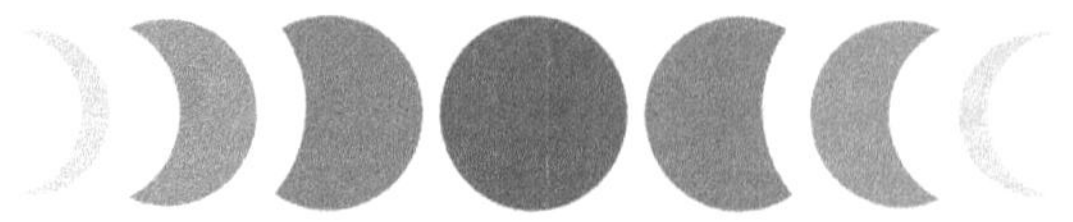

Moons of the Year

A rare second Full Moon in a single month is called a "Blue Moon." A rare second New Moon in a month is called a "Black Moon."

Different cultures gave the Moon different titles to express what the Moon means to them in a given month. As a result, some of the moon names make sense, while others may not make any sense.

Full Moon – January
Native American Tribes: Old Moon, Wolf Moon, Ice Moon, Moon after Yule, and Winter Moon
Siouan (Assiniboines) Tribe: Hard Time Moon
Inuit People of Northern Canada: Dwarf Seal Moon
Celtic: Wolf Moon, Stay Home Moon, Moon after Yule
Chinese: Holiday Moon
Fairy: Icicle Moon

Full Moon – February
Native American Tribes: Hunger or Starvation Moon, Storm Moon, Trapper's Moon, Moon of Ice, and Tree Moon
Siouan (Assiniboines) Tribe: Long Day Moon
Inuit People of Northern Canada: Seal Pup Moon
Celtic: Storm Moon, Ice Moon, and Snow moon
Chinese: Budding Moon
Fairy: Snowdrop Moon

Full Moon – March
Native American Tribes: Worm Moon, Crow Moon, Moon of Winds, Sap Moon, Fish Moon, Chaste Moon, and Death Moon
Siouan (Assiniboines) Tribe: Sore Eye Moon
Inuit People of Northern Canada: Snow Bird Moon
Celtic: Plough Moon, Wind Moon, Lenten (lengthening) Moon
Chinese: Sleeping Moon
Fairy: Waking Wood Moon

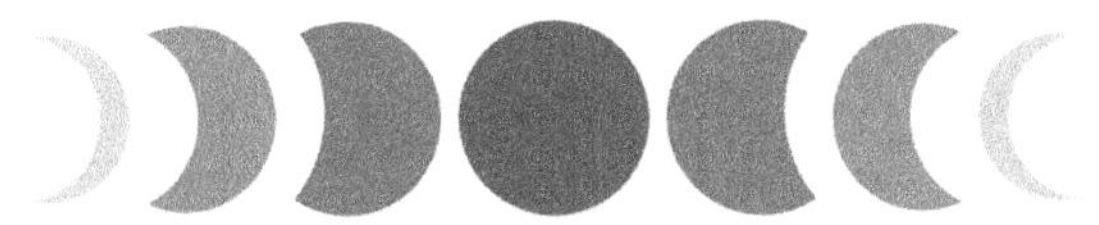

Moons of the Year

Full Moon – April
Native American Tribes: Pink Moon, Seed Moon, Frog Moon, Egg Moon, and Awakening Moon
Siouan (Assiniboines) Tribe: Frog's Moon
Inuit People of Northern Canada: Snow Melt Moon
Celtic: Budding Moon, New Shoots Moon, and Seed Moon
Chinese: Peony Moon
Fairy: Birthing Moon

Full Moon – May
Native American Tribes: Flower Moon, Hare Moon, Milk Moon, and Grass Moon
Siouan (Assiniboines) Tribe: Idle Moon
Inuit People of Northern Canada: Goose Moon
Celtic: Mother's Moon and Bright Moon
Chinese: Dragon Moon
Fairy: Moon of White Petals

Full Moon – June
Native American Tribes: Strawberry Moon, Planting Moon, and Green Corn Moon
Siouan (Assiniboines) Tribe: Full Leaf Moon
Inuit People of Northern Canada: Hunting Moon
Celtic: Mead Moon, Horse Moon, Dyan Moon, and Rose Moon
Chinese: Lotus Moon
Fairy: Wild Cherry Moon

Full Moon – July
Native American Tribes: Hay Moon, Summer Moon, Thunder Moon, and Buck Moon
Siouan (Assiniboines) Tribe: Red Berries Moon
Inuit People of Northern Canada: Dry Moon
Celtic: Claiming Moon, Wyrt or Herb Moon, and Mead Moon
Chinese: Hungry Ghost Moon
Fairy: Dancing Delight Moon

Full Moon – August
Native American Tribes: Sturgeon Moon, Corn Moon, Green Corn Moon, Dog Days Moon, and Lightening Moon
Siouan (Assiniboines) Tribe: Black Cherries Moon
Inuit People of Northern Canada: Swan Flight Moon
Celtic: Dispute Moon, Lynx Moon, and Grain Moon
Chinese: Harvest Moon
Fairy: Blackberry Harvest Moon

Moons of the Year

Full Moon – September
Native American Tribes: Singing Moon and Barley Moon
Siouan (Assiniboines) Tribe: Yellow Leaf Moon
Inuit People of Northern Canada: Harpoon Moon
Celtic: Wine Moon, Song Moon, Harvest Moon, and Barley Moon
Chinese: Chrysanthemum Moon
Fairy: Chestnut Moon

Full Moon – October
Native American Tribes: Traveller's Moon and Blackberry Moon
Siouan (Assiniboines) Tribe: Gophur Looks Back Moon
Inuit People of Northern Canada: Ice Moon
Celtic: Hunter's Moon, Blood Moon, and Seed Fall Moon
Chinese: Kindly Moon
Fairy: Moon of the Wild Hunt

Full Moon - November
Native American Tribes: Frosty Moon, Beaver Moon, Dark Moon, Tree Moon, Snow Moon, Freezing Moon, Ice Moon, and Migrating Moon
Siouan (Assiniboines) Tribe: Frost Moon
Inuit People of Northern Canada: Freezing Mist Moon
Celtic: Mourning Moon and Darkest Depths Moon
Chinese: White Moon
Fairy: Moon of the Wild Hunt

Full Moon – December
Native American Tribes: Cold Moon, Long Night Moon,
Siouan (Assiniboines) Tribe: Younger Hard Time Moon
Inuit People of Northern Canada: Dark Night Moon
Celtic: Oak Moon, Full Cold Moon
Chinese: Bitter Moon
Fairy: Mistletoe Moon

CHAPTER 6

Days of the Week for Spells and Rituals

Monday
Best for psychic endeavors, invoking power, creative ideas, divine/inspirational messages, and healing.

Tuesday
Best for protection and building the strength of mind, body, and confidence.

Wednesday
Best for career/job issues, intellectual pursuits, travel planning and research.

Thursday
Best for finances, legal matters, spirituality, and development.

Friday
Best for romantic attraction, all relationships, reconciliation, physical makeovers, and beautifying your environment.

Saturday
Best for home-related issues, brainstorming future projects, committing to personal goals, weight loss, releasing bad habits, ending relationships, etc.

Sunday
Best for healing (body, mind, soul), management/decision-making, insights into problem-solving, divine intervention/miracles, and unique friendships.

Do what makes you comfortable waiting for the "right" day to perform rituals or divination is unnecessary. So you do you, Boo!

Monday

Zodiac: Cancer
Solar System: Moon
Rune: Lagu
Numbers: 2, 9
Colors: Blue (pale), Gray, Silver, White
Tarot: High Priestess, Moon
Trees: Birch, Elder, Myrtle, Willow
Misc. Plants: Moonwort, Wormwood
Herb and Garden: Bluebell, Chamomile, Gardenia, Jasmine, Poppy, Rose (white), Violet
Gemstones and Minerals: Emerald, Moonstone, Quartz (clear, white), Sapphire
Metal: Silver
From the Sea: Pearl
Goddesses: Hecate, Selene
Gods: Aegir, Thoth
Angel or Magical Beings: Gabriel
Issues, Intentions, and Powers: astral realm, clairvoyance, creativity, dream work, emotions, family, fertility, healing, the home, illumination, inspiration, intuition, love, magic (general, moon), prophecy, protection, psychic ability, travel, truth

Tuesday

Zodiac: Aries, Scorpio
Solar System: Mars
Rune: Tyr
Number: 5
Colors: Black, Orange, Red, Scarlet
Tarot: Strength, Wands (5, 6)
Trees: Cedar, Elm, Holly, Palm (dragon's blood)
Misc. Plants: Allspice, Ginger, Patchouli, Thistle
Herb and Garden: Basil, Garlic, Snapdragon
Gemstones and Minerals: Bloodstone, Emerald, Garnet, Ruby, Sapphire (star), Topaz
Metal: Iron
From the Sea:
Goddess:
God: Mars
Angel or Magical Beings: Elves
Issues, Intentions, and Powers: action, aggression, assertiveness, battle/war, challenges, courage, discipline, energy, healing, honor, integrity, justice, passion, purification, strength, truth

Wednesday

Zodiac: Gemini
Solar System: Mercury
Rune: Odal
Number: 3
Colors: Orange, Purple, Silver, Violet, Yellow
Tarot: The Magician, Wheel of Fortune, Pentacles (8)
Trees: Aspen, Hazel, Rowan
Misc. Plant: Fern
Herb and Garden: Dill, Jasmine, Lavender, Lily of the Valley
Gemstones and Minerals: Agate, Amethyst, Aventurine, Lodestone, Opal, Ruby (star), Turquoise
Metal: Mercury
From the Sea:
Goddess: Athena
Gods: Hermes, Mercury, Odin
Angel or Magical Beings: Raphael
Issues, Intentions, and Powers: business, cleverness, communication, creativity, crossroads, divination, fear, improvement (self), insight, intelligence, introspection, knowledge, loss, money, problems, skills, travel, wisdom

Thursday

Zodiac: Capricorn, Pisces
Solar System: Jupiter
Rune: Thorn
Numbers: 4, 8
Colors: Blue (royal), Green, Indigo, Purple
Tarot: Pentacles (ace, 9, 10)
Trees: Laurel, Maple, Oak, Pine
Misc. Plants: Cinnamon, Cinquefoil, Grain (wheat), Nutmeg
Herb and Garden: Honeysuckle, Sage
Gems and Minerals: Amethyst, Carnelian, Cat's Eye, Chrysoberyl, Sapphire, Turquoise
Metal: Tin
From the Sea:
Goddess: Juno
Gods: Jupiter, Thor, Zeus
Angel or Magical Beings:
Issues, Intentions, and Powers: abundance, business, desire, endurance, fidelity, honor, justice (legal matters), leadership, loyalty, luck, money, prosperity, relationships, success, well-being

Friday

Zodiac: Taurus
Solar System: Venus
Rune: Peorth
Numbers: 6, 9
Colors: Aqua, Blue, Green, Indigo, Pink
Tarot: Empress, Lovers, Cups (2)
Trees: Apple, Birch, Myrtle
Misc. Plants: Saffron, Sandalwood
Herb and Garden: Feverfew, Raspberry, Rose, Strawberry, Thyme, Violet
Gemstones and Minerals: Alexandrite, Amber, Cat's Eye, Chrysoberyl, Emerald, Rose Quartz, Ruby
Metal: Copper
From the Sea:
Goddesses: Aphrodite, Freya, Frigg, Lakshmi, Venus
God: Eros
Angel or Magical Beings: Auriel
Issues, Intentions, and Powers: beauty, emotions, fertility, friend/ ship, happiness, love, magic, passion, pleasure, romance, sex/uality, wisdom

Saturday

Zodiac: Aquarius
Solar System: Saturn
Rune: Dag
Number: 7
Colors: Black, Gray (dark), Indigo, Purple (dark)
Tarot: Temperance, Swords (knight, 2)
Trees: Alder, Cypress, Hawthorn, Pomegranate
Misc. Plants: Mullein, Myrrh
Herb and Garden: Morning Glory, Thyme
Gems and Minerals: Amethyst, Apache Tears, Diamond, Hematite, Jet, Labradorite, Turquoise
From the Sea:
Goddess: Hecate
God: Saturn
Angel or Magical Beings: Fairies
Issues, Intentions, and Powers: banish, bind, business, death, discipline (self), freedom, justice, karma, life, limitations/ boundaries, money, motivation, negativity, obstacles, peace, problems, protection, willpower, wisdom

Sunday

Zodiac: Leo
Solar System: Sun
Rune: Sigel
Number: 1
Colors: Gold, Gray, Orange, Pink, White, Yellow
Tarot: Chariot, Sun, Wands (ace)
Trees: Ash, Birch, Laurel
Misc. Plants: Cinnamon, Frankincense
Herb and Garden: Carnation, Marigold, St. John's Wort, Sunflower
Gemstones and Minerals: Amber, Carnelian, Diamond, Quartz (clear), Sunstone, Tiger's Eye, Topaz
Metal: Gold
From the Sea: Pearl
Goddess: Brigid
God: Helios
Angel or Magical Beings: Elves
Issues, Intentions, and Powers: accomplishment, action, ambition, attraction, authority, beauty, confidence, creativity, energy (solar), fame, freedom, friend/ship, goals, growth (personal), healing, hope, illumination, justice, leadership, light, money power (personal), pride, prosperity, protection, spirituality, strength, success, visions, warmth, well-being

Time of the Day for Spells and Rituals

Dawn

At dawn, the sun's fragile rays spread like a blanket of hope over an awakening world. At this time, choices are made, and paths unfold before us, full of life-giving potentiality.

Midday/Noon

Midday is when sunlight shines the strongest - a reminder of our strength and courage to tackle whatever lies ahead. It provides the motivation we need to persevere, no matter what obstacle stands in our way.

Dusk/Twilight

As dusk approaches, the sun bids a wistful farewell to the sky. Its goodbye is made of change and final goodbyes, an invitation to new beginnings if we're brave enough to open our hearts.

Midnight

At midnight, we come to the precipice of a journey into uncertainty; here is where paths diverge, and endings have no choice but to be accepted. It's an inevitable transition from one day to another, filled with promise yet also cloaked in sadness.

Do what makes you feel comfortable. There's no need to wait for the "right" time to perform rituals or divination. You do you, Boo!

Dawn

Zodiac:
Solar System: Venus
Runes: Beorc, Hagal, Thorn
Number:
Color:
Tarot: Swords
Trees:
Misc. Plants:
Herb and Garden:
Gemstones and Minerals:
Metal:
From the Sea:
Goddess: Brigid
Gods: Byelobog, Janus, Njord, Surya
Angel or Magical Beings: Raphael
Issues, Intentions, and Powers: activate/awaken, beginnings, crossroads, fertility, hope, life (vitality), light, nurture, purpose, romance, youth

Midday/Noon

Zodiac: Leo
Solar System: Sun
Runes: Dag, Rad, Sigel
Number:
Color:
Tarot: Wands
Trees:
Misc. Plants:
Herb and Garden:
Gemstones and Minerals:
Metal:
From the Sea:
Goddess:
God: Byelobog
Angel or Magical Beings: Michael
Issues, Intentions, and Powers: determination, obstacles, strength, willpower

Dusk/Twilight

Zodiac: Cancer
Solar System: Venus
Runes: Feoh, Jer, Peorth
Numbers:
Colors:
Tarot: Cups
Trees:
Misc. Plants:
Herb and Garden:
Gemstones and Minerals:
Metal:
From the Sea:
Goddess:
God: Gabriel
Issues, Intentions, and Powers: banish, change/s, endings, the otherworld/underworld, sorrow

Midnight

Zodiac: Taurus
Solar System: Earth, Venus
Runes: Is, Tyr, Ur
Number:
Color:
Tarot: Pentacles
Trees:
Misc. Plants:
Herb and Garden:
Gemstones and Minerals:
Metal:
From the Sea:
Goddess:
God:
Angel or Magical Beings: Auriel
Issues, Intentions, and Powers: crossroads, endings, release

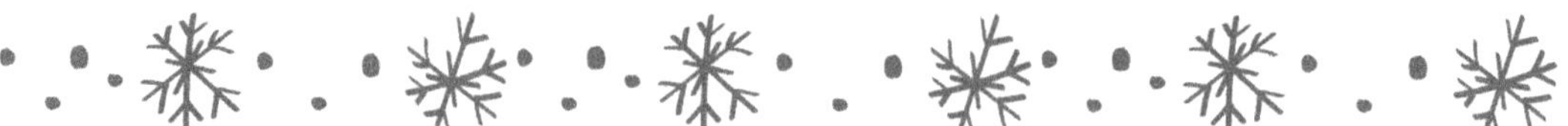

CHAPTER 7

Planetary Retrogrades

Planetary retrograde is an astrological occurrence that happens when a planet seems to move backward in its orbit from the perspective of Earth. This happens due to differences in the orbital speed of the planets relative to Earth's position. It's important to note that planets don't actually change their direction, but the apparent retrograde motion occurs due to how the Earth orbits around the Sun.

Astrologers believe that planetary retrogrades can influence the energy and vibration of the planet in question, which can affect us. During a retrograde, the planetary energy is said to turn inward, and its impact can be felt more strongly in our lives. Different planets are believed to affect us in different ways, and their retrogrades may also have other effects.

Mercury Retrograde: It occurs three to four times a year for around three weeks. It is known for causing communication issues, technology malfunction, and travel delays. It's essential to take extra care when making important decisions or signing contracts during this time.

Venus Retrograde: This happens every eighteen months for about 40-43 days. It's a time for re-evaluating relationships, romantic connections, and money matters. It's a good time for reflection and introspection on handling these areas.

Mars Retrograde: This happens every two years for two months
It brings up feelings of frustration, anger, and aggression. It is important to be patient and avoid impulsive actions during this time.

Jupiter Retrograde: This happens every thirteen months for around four months. It can be a time for introspection and personal growth, but it can also cause setbacks in areas of expansion and growth.

Saturn Retrograde: This occurs every year for around four months. It is time to take stock of responsibilities and make necessary changes. obstacles and lead to personal growth and development.ItCanBringChallengesAnd

Uranus Retrograde: This happens every year for around five months. It can bring unexpected changes and upheavals, but it can also bring innovation and new ideas.

Neptune Retrograde: This occurs every year for around five months; it's time for spiritual growth and reflection but can also cause confusion and delusion.

Pluto Retrograde: This happens every year for around six months. It's a time for transformation and personal growth, but it can also bring power struggles and intense emotional experiences.

Birth Chart Meanings

Your **Sun** is about yourself.

Your **Moon** is your heart.

Your **Rising** is how you look.

Your **Mercury** is the way you think.

Your **Venus** is how you love.

Your **Mars** is how you deal with life.

Your **Jupiter** is your luck.

Your **Saturn** is how you discipline yourself and your responsibilities.

Your **Uranus** is how unique you are.

Your **Neptune** is your imagination.

Your **Pluto** is your transformation.

Your **Chiron** is how you heal.

Your **Ceres** is how you take care of yourself.

Your **Pallas** is your relationship.

Your **Juno** is beauty and influence.

Your **Vesta** is your potential and your organization.

Your **North Node** is how you develop in your current life.

Your **South Node** is how you developed in your past life.

Your **Midheaven** is your career; how others view you.

Your **Lilith** is your hidden emotions.

Astrological Signs

Aries
March 21 - April 19
for those born under the sign of
The Ram

Taurus
April 20 - May 20
for those born under the sign of
The Bull

Gemini
May 21 - June 20
for those born under the sign of
The Twins

Cancer
June 21 - July 22
for those born under the sign of
The Crab

Leo
July 23 - August 22
for those born under the sign of
The Lion

Virgo
August 23 - September 22
for those born under the sign of
The Virgin

Libra
September 23 - October 22
for those born under the sign of
The Scales

Scorpio
October 23 - November 21
for those born under the sign of
The Scorpion

Sagittarius
November 22 - December 21
for those born under the sign of
The Archer

Capricorn
December 22 - January 19
for those born under the sign of
The Goat

Aquarius
January 20 - February 18
for those born under the sign of
The Water Bearer

Pisces
February 19 - March 20
for those born under the sign of
The Fishes

Pisces
Aries
Aquarius
Taurus
Capricorn
Gemini
Sagittarius
Cancer
Scorpio
Leo
Libra
Virgo

PISCES
ARIES
AQUARIUS
TAURUS
CAPRICORN
GEMINI
SAGITTARIUS
CANCER
SCORPIO
LEO
LIBRA
VIRGO

Solar System

The boundless expanse of the universe holds a captivating realm known as the solar system, a complex web of celestial bodies that has fascinated humanity for generations. At the heart of this cosmic spectacle is the radiant and mighty Sun, a colossal star that provides the life-giving energy that fuels our world. Orbiting Earth, our loyal companion, the Moon, enchants us with its shimmering phases and mysterious allure. Together, these elements paint a mesmerizing portrait of the grandeur and diversity present in our cosmic neighborhood. In this journey of exploration, we'll delve into the wondrous dynamics that define the solar system, bask in the brilliance of the Sun, and unravel the enigma of the Moon's influence on our planet.

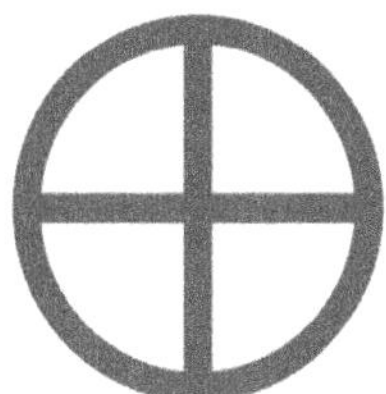

Solar System: Earth
Zodiac: Capricorn, Taurus, and Virgo
Chakra: Root
Celebrations: Earth Day and Walpurgis
Season: Winter
Day:
Time of Day: Midnight
Rune:
Number: 4
Colors: Black, Brown, Green, and White
Tarot:
Trees: Acacia and Oak
Misc. Plant: Grain
Herb and Garden:
Gemstones and Minerals: Agate (brown), Ametrine, Andalusite, Bloodstone, Carnelian, Chrysoprase, Citrine, Diopside, and Moss Agate
Metal:
From the Sea:
Goddesses: Anat, Ceres, Coatlicue, Cybele, Demeter, Gaia, Inanna, Isis, Maia, and Nanna
Gods: Adonis, Attis, Dionysus, Dumuzi, Ea, Enki, Faunus, Geb, and Vertimnus
Angel: Auriel
Issues, Intentions, and Powers: agriculture, creativity, grounding, healing, the home, magic (animal), nurture, peace, protection, purpose, revenge, and spirits

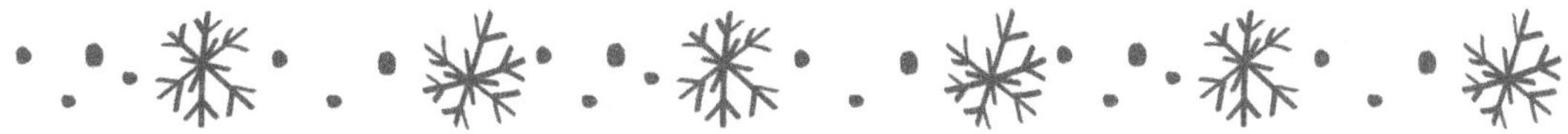

Solar System: Jupiter
Zodiac: Pisces and Sagittarius
Chakras: 3rd Eye, Heart, and Solar Plexus
Celebrations:
Season:
Day: Thursday
Time of Day:
Rune: Man
Numbers: 3, 4, and 5
Colors: Blue, Green (light, sea), Indigo, Purple, Turquoise, and Violet
Tarot: Wheel of Fortune
Trees: Birch, Cedar, Chestnut, Fir, Horse Chestnut, Linden, Magnolia, Maple, Oak, Olive, Palm (coconut), Pine, Sycamore, Walnut, and Yew
Misc. Plant: Aloe, Anise, Betony, Cinquefoil, Meadowsweet, Myrrh, Nutmeg, and Star Anise
Herb and Garden: Agrimony, Borage, Clove, Dandelion, Honeysuckle, Lemon Balm, and Sage
Gemstones and Minerals: Amethyst, Ametrine, Diopside, Emerald, Lepidolite, Sapphire,
Sugilite, Turquoise, and Zircon (red)
Metal: Tin
From the Sea:
Goddesses: Devi, Hera, Justitia, and Nut
Gods: Baal, Indra, Jupiter, Marduk, and Zeus
Mythical Being: Unicorn
Issues, Intentions, and Powers: abundance, astral realm, authority, business, control, dignity, discipline, favors, generosity, honor, influence, intuition, justice, kindness, leadership, luck, the mind, money, opportunities, optimism, power, pride, problems, prosperity, responsibility, spirituality, success, wealth, well-being, and wisdom

Solar System: Mars
Zodiac: Aries and Scorpio
Chakras: Root, Sacral, Solar Plexus, and Throat
Celebrations:
Season:
Day: Tuesday
Time of Day:
Rune: Man
Numbers: 2, 3, 5, and 9
Colors: Crimson, Maroon, Orange, Pink, and Red
Tarot: Devil, Emperor, and Tower
Trees: Alder, Blackthorn, Fir, Hawthorn, Holly, Juniper, Palm (dragon's blood), Pine, and Yew
Misc. Plant: Allspice, Anise, Asafoetida, Black Cohosh, Blessed Thistle, Bloodroot, Coriander, Cumin, Deer's Tongue, Galangal, Ginger, High John, Mustard, Nettle, Pepper, Reed, Thistle, and Wormwood
Herb and Garden: Anemone, Basil, Broom, Garlic, Gorse, Honeysuckle, Pennyroyal, Rue, Snapdragon, and Sweet Woodruff
Gemstones and Minerals: Beryl, Bloodstone, Citrine, Diamond, Garnet, Hematite, Jasper (red), Onyx, Pyrite, Rhodochrosite, Rhodonite, Ruby, Sard, Sardonyx, Tourmaline (red, watermelon), Tsavorite, and Zircon (red)
Metals: Iron and Steel
From the Sea: Coral (red)
Goddesses: Anat, Astarte, Badb, Durga, Macha, Maeve, Minerva, and Nanna
Gods: Ares, Indra, Mars, Nergal, Odin, Set, and Thor
Mythical Being: Unicorn
Issues, Intentions, and Powers: action, aggression, anger, assertiveness, battle/war, beginnings, courage, death, defense, desire, determination, emotions, endurance, energy (sexual), enmity, growth, justice, life, lust, magic (general, defensive, dragon, sex), passion, power, sexuality (male), skills, strength, and willpower

Solar System: Mercury
Zodiac: Gemini and Virgo
Chakras: 3rd Eye, Root, Sacral, Solar Plexus, and Throat
Celebrations:
Season:
Day: Wednesday
Time of Day:
Rune:
Numbers: 1, 4, 5, and 8
Colors: Blue (navy), Gray, Green, Orange, Purple, Silver, Violet, and Yellow
Tarot: Hermit, Lovers, and Magician
Trees: Ash, Aspen, Cedar, Cherry, Elder, Hazel, Juniper, Linden, Olive, Pomegranate, and Acacia
Misc. Plants: Anise, Betony, Bittersweet, Cinquefoil, Flax, Horehound, Mandrake, Mistletoe, and Sandalwood
Herb and Garden: Agrimony, Bergamot, Clover, Dandelion, Dill, Fennel, Fern, Honeysuckle, Jasmine, Lavender, Lilac, Lily of the Valley, Marjoram, Peppermint, Periwinkle, Rosemary, Sage, and Valerian
Gemstones and Minerals: Agate (fire, green, red, snakeskin, tree), Amber, Aventurine, Blue Lace Agate, Carnelian, Cat's Eye, Citrine, Fluorite, Hematite, Jasper, Moss Agate, Onyx, Opal, Peridot, Rhodochrosite, Sardonyx, Sodalite, Sphene, and Topaz
Metals: Aluminum and Mercury
From the Sea: Coral (red)
Goddesses: Athena, Maat, Maia, Minerva, and Seshat
Gods: Anubis, Arawn, Coyote, Hermes, Loki, Lugh, Mercury, Odin, Ogma, Thor, and Thoth
Angels: Michael and Raphael
Issues, Intentions, and Powers: adaptability, balance, business, change(s), cleverness, communication, creativity, crossroads, deceit, divination, fear, improvement, inspiration, intelligence, justice, learning, love, magic, memory/memories, messages/ omens, the mind, money, moods, power, rebirth, renewal, skills, travel, wealth, and wisdom

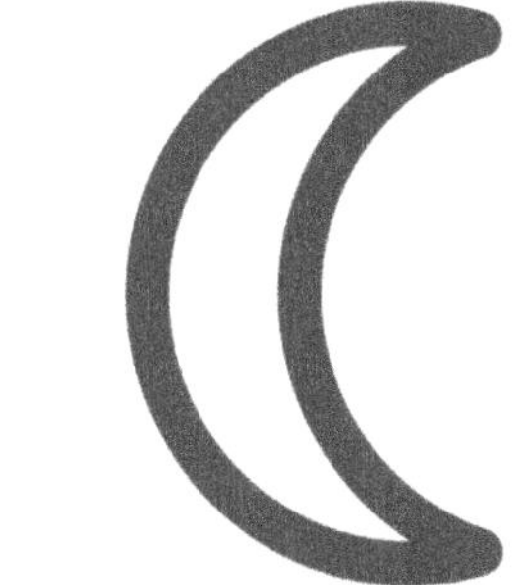

Solar System: Moon
Zodiac: Cancer
Chakra: Sacral
Celebrations: Beltane, Imbolc, Lughnasadh, and Samhain
Season:
Day: Monday
Time of Day:
Runes: Is and Lagu
Numbers: 2, 3, 0, and 13
Colors: Blue, Gray Green (sea), Orange, Silver, and White
Tarot: Chariot, High Priestess, and Moon
Trees: Birch, Mesquite, Olive, Palm, Rowan, and Willow
Misc. Plants: Aloe, Lotus, Moonwort, Myrrh, Nutmeg, Saffron, and Sandalwood
Herb and Garden: Bergamot, Blackberry/Bramble, Gardenia, Grape, Iris, Jasmine, Lemon Balm Lily, Poppy, and Rosemary
Gemstones and Minerals: Agate, Angelite, Aquamarine, Beryl, Calcite (clear), Herkimer Diamond, Moonstone, Morganite, Opal, Quartz, Sapphire, Selenite, and Turquoise
Metal: Silver
From the Sea: Coral (white), Moon Snail, Mother-of-Pearl, Mussel, and Pearl
Goddesses: Aine, Aphrodite, Ariadne, Arianrhod, Artemis, Cerridwen, Diana, Freya, Hecate, Ishtar, Isis, Juno, Luna, Nanna, Persephone, Rhiannon, Sedna, Selene, and Spiderwoman
Gods: Aegir, Hermes, Horus, Janus, Jupiter, Khensu, Shiva, and Thoth
Angel: Gabriel
Magical Beings: Fairies, Mermaids and Dragons
Issues, Intentions, and Powers: action, agriculture, animals, balance (inner), beginnings, change(s), consciousness (and subconscious), creativity, cycles, darkness, death, divination, dream work, emotions, enchantment, endings, energy (general, receptive), family, fertility, growth, guidance, healing, hexes, the home, illumination, imagination, inspiration, intuition, jealousy, life (rhythms), light, loneliness, love, magic (general, crone, moon, night), manifestation, moods, negativity, night-mares, obstacles, peace, power, pregnancy/childbirth, protection, psychic ability, rebirth/renewal, secrets, self-work, sensitivity, sorrow, spirits, transformation, wisdom, and witches/ witchcraft

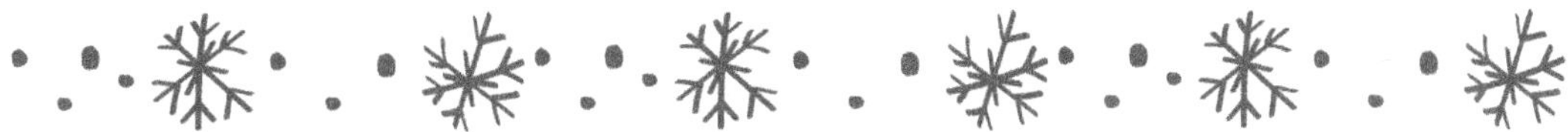

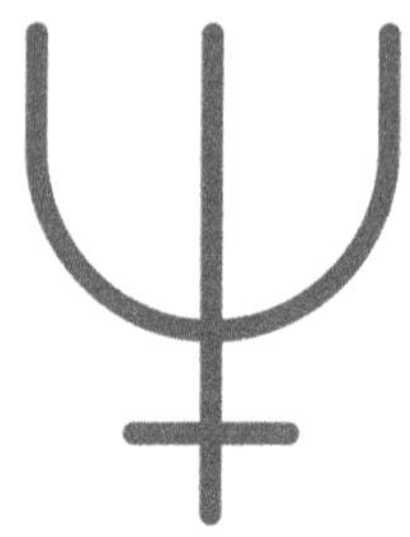

Solar System: Neptune
Zodiac: Aquarius and Pisces
Chakras: 3rd Eye and Crown
Celebrations:
Season:
Day:
Time of Day:
Rune:
Number: 7
Colors: Blue, Green (light, sea), Indigo, Lavender, Purple, and Turquoise
Tarot: Hanged Man
Trees: Ash
Misc. Plants:
Herb and Garden:
Gemstones and Minerals: Amethyst, Angelite, Aquamarine, Beryl, Celestite, Fluorite, Jade, Labradorite, Lapis Lazuli, Lepidolite, Sapphire, and Turquoise
Metal:
From the Sea: Coral and Mother-of-Pearl
Goddesses: Amphitrite, Brigid, Ran, Sedna and Tiamat
Gods: Aegir, Manannan, Neptune, and Poseidon
Angel:
Magical Beings: Fairies and Mermaids
Issues, Intentions, and Powers: awareness (expand), clairvoyance, community, consciousness (subconscious), creativity, dream work, enchantment, energy (psychic), guardian, guidance, inspiration, intuition, life, the otherworld/ underworld, power, protection, psychic ability, sensitivity, visions

Solar System: Pluto
Zodiac: Cancer and Scorpio
Chakra: Sacral
Celebrations:
Season:
Day:
Time of Day:
Rune:
Number:
Colors: Blue, Green (light, sea), Indigo, Lavender, Purple, and Turquoise
Tarot: Hanged Man
Tree: Cypress
Misc. Plants: Belladonna, Bittersweet, Nettle, and Reed
Herb and Garden: Basil and Fern (bear paw)
Gemstones and Minerals: Amethyst, Garnet, Jet, Kunzite, Labradorite, Obsidian, Quartz (tourmalated), Spinel, Tourmaline, and Tsavorite
Metal:
From the Sea:
Goddesses: Ereshkigal, Hathor, Hecate, Hel, Hera, Kali, the Morrigan, and Persephone
Gods: Pluto and Osiris
Angel:
Magical Beings:
Issues, Intentions, and Powers: the afterlife, changes, danger, darkness (inner), death, dream work, justice, karma, memory/memories, the otherworld/underworld, rebirth/renewal, secrets, sexuality, spirituality, transformation, and wealth

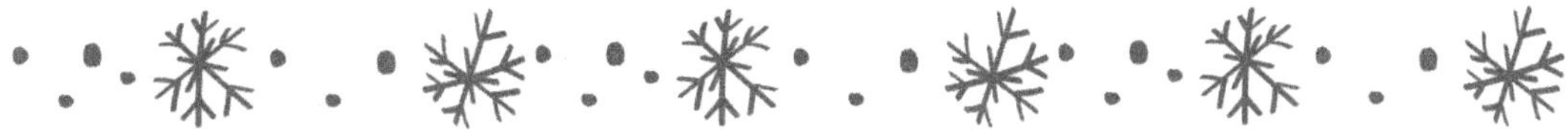

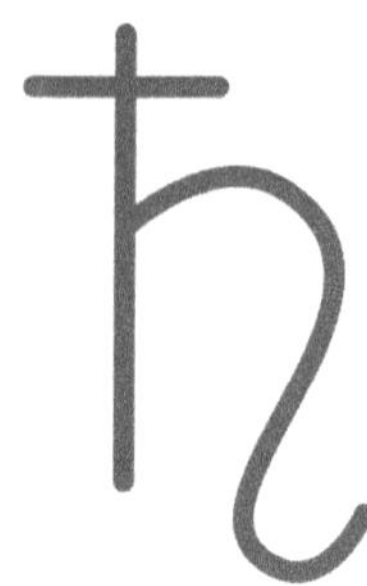

Solar System: Saturn
Zodiac: Aquarius, Capricorn, and Libra
Chakra: Crown, Heart, Root, and Throat
Celebrations:
Season:
Day: Saturday
Time of Day:
Rune: Peorth
Numbers: 3, 7, and 8
Colors: Black, Blue (navy), Brown, Gray (dark), Green (dark), Indigo, and Yellow (light)
Tarot: Death, Hanged Man, and World
Tree: Aspen, Beech, Blackthorn, Cypress, Elm, Fir, Holly, Magnolia, Mesquite, Mimosa, Pine, Poplar, Rowan, Witch Hazel, and Yew
Misc. Plants: Cinnamon, Clove, Bamboo, Eyebright, Frankincense, Galangal, Ginseng, Grain
Herb and Garden: Amaranth, Carnation, Comfrey, Ivy, Monkshood, Morning Glory, Rue, and Solomon's Seal
Gemstones and Minerals: Apache Tears, Azurite, Carnelian, Hematite, Jasper (brown), Jet, Obsidian, Onyx, Sapphire, Sardonyx, Serpentine, and Tourmaline (black)
Metal: Lead
From the Sea: Coral (black)
Goddesses: Ariadne, Ceres, Demeter, Dôn, Durga, Hecate, Hera, Juno, Kali, and Rhea
Gods: Amun, Khensu Saturn
Angel:
Magical Beings:
Issues, Intentions, and Powers: agriculture, ambition, astral realm, authority, banish, bind, business, concentration/ focus, darkness, death, discipline, endings, endurance, freedom, goals, grounding, justice, karma, knowledge, limitations/ boundaries, longevity, loyalty, lust, the mind, obstacles, peace, purification, relationships, stability, strength.

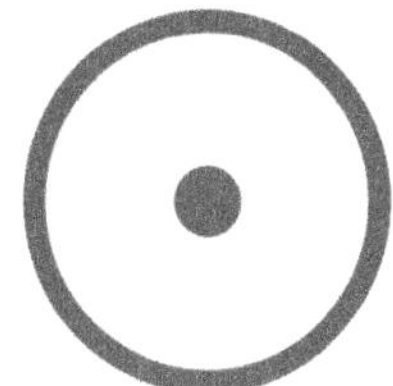

Solar System: Sun
Zodiac: Aries, Cancer, and Leo
Chakra: Solar Plexus
Celebrations: Litha, Mabon, Ostara, Walpurgis, and Yule
Season:
Day: Sunday
Time of Day: Noon
Rune: Jera and Sigel
Numbers: 1 and 6
Colors: Gold, Orange, and Yellow
Tarot: Death, Hanged Man, and World
Tree: Acacia, Ash, Birch, Cedar, Chestnut, Hazel, Horse Chestnut, Juniper, Laurel, Linden, Oak, Olive, Palm, Rowan, Walnut, and Witch Hazel
Misc. Plants: Belladonna, Bittersweet, Henbane, Lady's Slipper, Mandrake, Mullein, Patchouli, Skullcap, and Thornapple
Herb and Garden: Angelica, Broom, Carnation, Chamomile, Chrysanthemum, Daffodil, Daisy, Goldenseal, Gorse, Heliotrope, Lovage, Marigold, Peony, Rosemary, St. John's Wort, and Sunflower (com), Lotus, Mistletoe, and Saffron
Gemstones and Minerals: Amber, Ametrine, Beryl (golden), Calcite (orange, red), Carnelian, Chrysoberyl, Citrine, Diamond, Herkimer Diamond, Peridot, Quartz, Ruby, Sunstone, Tiger's Eye, Topaz, Tourmaline (black), and Zircon
From the Sea: Coral (black)
Goddesses: Aine, Amaterasu, Bast, Brigid, Hathor, Phoebe, Sekhmet, and Spider Woman
Gods: Adonis, Agni, Amun, Apollo, Baal, Belenus, Helios, Horus, Jupiter, Lugh, Marduk, Mithras, Ogma, Osiris, Pushan, Ra, Shiva, Surya, and Vishnu
Angel: Raphael
Magical Beings: Dragon, Griffin, Phoenix, Sphinx, Unicorn, Dragon, Griffin, Phoenix, Sphinx, and Unicorn
Issues, Intentions, and Powers:

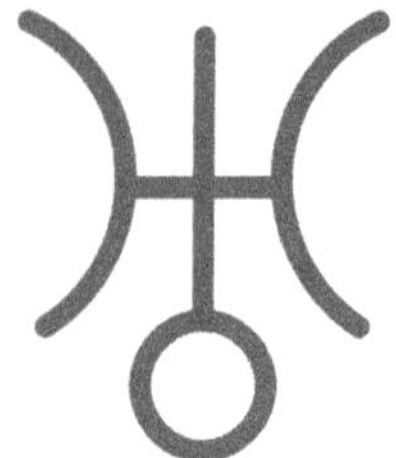

Solar System: Uranus
Zodiac: Aquarius and Gemini
Chakras: Brow, Crown, and Throat
Celebrations:
Season:
Day: Sunday
Time of Day:
Rune:
Number: 4
Colors: Indigo and Yellow (light)
Tarot: Fool, Star, and Tower
Tree: Ash and Rowan
Misc. Plants: Belladonna, Bittersweet, Henbane, Lady's Slipper, Mandrake, Mullein, Patchouli, Skullcap, and Thornapple
Herb and Garden: Angelica, Broom, Carnation, Chamomile, Chrysanthemum, Daffodil, Daisy, Goldenseal, Gorse, Heliotrope, Lovage, Marigold, Peony, Rosemary, St. John's Wort, and Sunflower (com), Lotus, Mistletoe, and Saffron
Gemstones and Minerals: Amazonite, Aventurine, Herkimer Diamond, Labradorite, and Quartz
From the Sea: Coral (black)
Goddesses: Anat, Aphrodite, Danu, Inanna, Ishtar, and Isis
Gods:
Angel:
Magical Beings:
Issues, Intentions, and Powers: ambition, anger, change(s), community, cooperation, freedom, goals, hope, illumination, improvement, intuition, motivation, power, and relationships

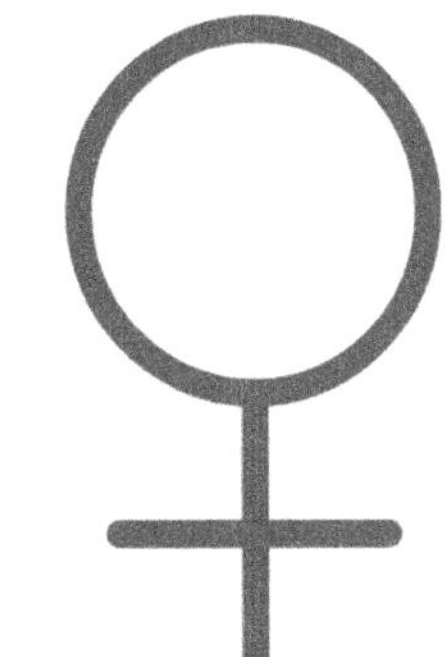

Solar System: Venus, Also known as the Morning and Evening Star
Zodiac: 3rd Eye, Heart, Sacral, and Throat
Chakras: Brow, Crown, and Throat
Celebrations:
Season:
Day: Friday
Time of Day: Dawn, Dusk, and Midnight
Rune: As and Ken
Numbers: 5, 6, and 7
Colors: Aqua, Blue (light), Green, Indigo, Lavender, Mauve, Pink, Rose, White, and Yellow (light)
Tarot: Empress, Justice, and Star
Tree: Alder, Apple, Aspen, Birch, Cherry, Elder, Magnolia, Myrtle, Sycamore, and Willow
Misc. Plants: loe, Burdock, Cardamom, Coltsfoot, Cowslip, Dittany, Orris Root, and Sandalwood
Gemstones and Minerals: Alexandrite, Aventurine, Azurite, Calcite, Carnelian, Cat's Eye, Celeste Chrysoberyl, Chrysocolla, Chrysoprase, Desert Rose, Diamond, Dioptase, Emerald, Jade, Jasper (green), Kunzite, Lapis Lazuli, Lodestone, Malachite, Peridot, Rhodochrosite, Rose Quart, Sapphire, Sodalite, Tourmaline (blue, green, pink, watermelon), Tsavorite, Turquoise
Metal: Copper
From the Sea:
Goddesses: Astarte, Ishtar, and Venus
Gods: Quetzalcoatl
Angel:
Magical Beings:
Issues, Intentions, and Powers: affection, agriculture, astral realm, attraction, beauty, beginnings, connections, creativity, desire, emotions, energy (receptive, sexual), fertility, friendship, gentleness, happiness, harmony: kindness, love, lust, magic (sex), needs, passion, pleasure rebirth/renewal, relationships, reversal, romance, sensuality, sexuality, stress, and unity

CHAPTER 8

Elemental Magic

The elements are another essential aspect of Witchcraft; we often call on them during spells and rituals. There are four primary elements, each of which has particular associations. Each element represents a different type of energy that you can harness.

Earth Magic - The element of Earth is the foundation of all life. The color green and the northern quarter align with the element of Earth. It is potent in spells that require wisdom and spells for fertility, prosperity, strength, and wealth.

Air Magic - The element of air is light fuel for all living things. It is represented by the color yellow and the eastern quarter when casting a circle. Spells for renewal, change, intuition, and knowledge call upon the air.

Fire Magic - The element of fire is a source of creation and destruction of life. It is represented by the color red and the southern quarter when casting a circle. Spells for passion, inspiration, intuition, creativity, and protection use fire.

Water Magic - Water represents the flow of life. It is represented by the color blue and the western quarter when casting a circle. It is powerful in spells for healing, peace, and compassion.

Earth

Symbol: ▽
Numbers: 4, 6, 8
Solar System: Earth, Saturn, and Venus
Zodiac: Capricorn, Taurus, and Virgo
Celebrations: Earth Day, Hunting of the Wren, and Yule
Season: Winter
Time of Day: Midnight
Runes: Is, Tyr, and Ur
Ogham: Ioho
Tarot: Pentacles
Direction: North
Sense: Touch
Energy: Yin
Chakra: Root
Colors: Black, Brown, Green, and White
Trees: Ash, Blackthorn, Cedar, Cypress, Elder, Elm, Holly, Juniper, Locust, Magnolia, Maple, Oak, Olive, Pine, Pomegranate, Rowan, Spruce, and Witch Hazel
Herbs and Flowers: Comfrey, Fern, Honeysuckle, Ivy, Jasmine, Mugwort, Primrose, Sage, and Vervain
Misc. Plants: Cinquefoil, Clove, Grains, Henbane, High John, Horehound, Mandrake, Patchouli, and Reed
Gemstones and Minerals: Agate, Alexandrite, Amazonite, Amber, Andalusite, Apophyllite, Calcite (green), Cat's Eye, Cerussite, Chrysocolla, Chrysoprase, Diopside, Emerald, Fluorite, Hematite, Jade, Jasper, Jet, Kunzite, Malachite, Moss Agate, Peridot, Petrified Wood, Quartz (rutilated), Salt, Smoky Quartz, Staurolite, Sugilite, Tourmaline (black, brown, green, watermelon), Turquoise, and Unakite
Metals: Lead and Mercury
From the Sea: Coral (black)

Earth

Angels: Gabriel and Auriel

Goddesses: Anat, Ariadne, Artemis, Asherah, Bertha, Ceres, Demeter, Gaia, Kore, Nephthys, Persephone, Rhea, and Rhiannon

Gods: Adonis, Arawn, Cernunnos, Dionysus, Geb, the Green Man, Khnum, Marduk, Mimir, Pan, Prometheus and Vishnu

Magical Beings: Brownies, Dryads, Elves, Fairies, Gnomes, Pixies

Animals: Antelope, Armadillo, Badger, Bear, Boar, Buffalo / Bison, Cattle, Deer (stag), Dog, Elephant, Goat, Groundhog, Hippopotamus, Jaguar, Mole, Otter, Pig, Prairie Dog, and Wolverine.

Birds: Blue Jay, Chicken, Crow, Goose, Sparrow, Swan, Turkey, and Woodpecker

Reptiles: Crocodile, Snake, Toad, Tortoise, and Turtle

Insect/Misc: Dragonfly

Mythical: Dragon and Selkies

Ritual Tool: Pentacle

Principle: To Be Silent

Issues, Intentions, and Powers: abundance, acceptance, agriculture, anxiety, balance, beginnings, business, comfort, communication, consecrate/bless, consciousness, creativity, cycles, death, endurance, energy (general, receptive), family, fertility, gentleness, grounding, growth, healing, hexes, the home, justice, life, magic (dragon), manifestation, money, nurture, the otherworld/underworld, patience, peace, pregnancy/childbirth, prosperity, protection, purpose, rebirth/renewal, relationships, the senses (smell, touch), sensuality, sexuality, spirits (nature spirits), stability, strength, success, support, travel, warmth, wealth, weather, well-being, willpower, and wisdom

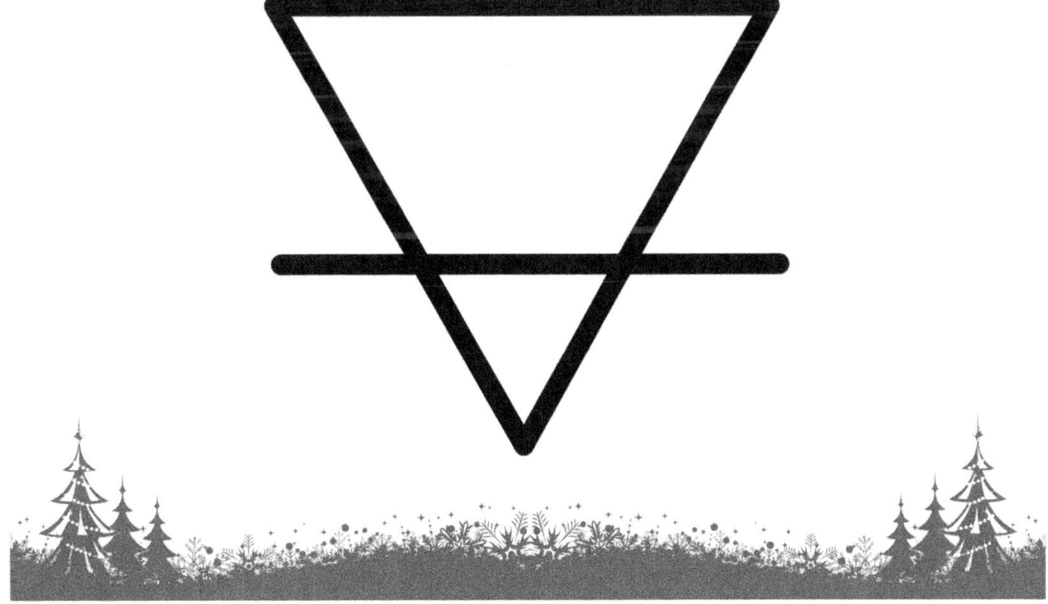

Air

Symbol: △
Number: 5
Solar System: Jupiter, Mercury, and Uranus
Zodiac: Aquarius, Gemini, and Libra
Celebration: Ostara
Season: Spring
Time of Day: Dawn
Runes: Beorc, Hagal, and Thorn
Ogham: Onn
Tarot: Fool, Swords, and Wands
Direction: East
Sense: Smell
Energy: Yang
Chakras: Crown, Heart, and Throat
Colors: Blue (light), Gray, Lavender, Pink, Red, Silver, White, and Yellow (bright, light)
Trees: Acacia, Alder, Apple, Ash, Aspen, Cedar, Chestnut, Elder, Elm Fir, Hawthorn, Hazel, Holly, Horse Chestnut, Laurel, Linden, Maple, Mesquite, Oak, Olive, Palm, Pine, Sycamore, Walnut, and Yew
Herbs and Flowers: Agrimony, Anemone, Bergamot, Borage, Broom, Clover, Comfrey, Dandelion, Fern, Ivy, Lavender, Lily of the Valley, Marjoram, Marigold, Mugwort, Peppermint, Primrose, Sage, Spearmint, Thyme, Vervain, Violet, and Yarrow
Misc. Plants: Anise, Bamboo, Bittersweet, Eyebright, Frankincense, Goldenrod, Horehound, Meadowsweet, Mistletoe, Myrrh, Nutmeg, Reed, Sandalwood, Star Anise, and Wormwood
Gemstones and Minerals: Agate (tree), Ametrine, Angelite, Aragonite, Aventurine, Blue Lace Agate, Celestite, Chrysoberyl, Desert Rose, Moldavite, Opal, Quartz (clear), Sodalite, Sphene, Staurolite, Topaz (blue), and Tourmaline (blue)
Metals: Aluminum, Mercury, and Tin
From the Sea: Angel Wing and Jingle

Air

Angels: Michael and Raphael
Goddesses: Amaterasu, Athena, Arianrhod, Hera, Nut, and Phoebe
Gods: Hermes, Khnum, Mimir, Mercury, Quetzalcoatl, Thoth, and Zeus
Magical Beings: Elves, Fairies, Pixies
Animal: Gazelle
Birds: Albatross, Condor, Eagle, Falcon, Hawk, and Seagull
Reptile:
Insect/Misc.: Firefly
Mythical: Dragon, Sphinx, and Thunderbird
Ritual Tools: Athame, Incense, and Sword
Principle: To Know
Issues, Intentions, and Powers: acceptance, action, Astral Realm, beginnings, business, clairvoyance, clarity, communication, concentration/ focus, consecrate/bless, creativity, divination, enchantment, energy, enlightenment, fairness, freedom, harmony, healing, imagination, inspiration, intelligence, intuition, justice, knowledge, learning, life, light, loss, magic (animal, dragon), memory/memories, the mind, money, motivation, order/ organize, power, protection, psychic ability, purification, relationships, release, the senses (hearing, smell, touch), shamanic work, spirits, spirituality, travel, visions, weather (general, lightning, storms), willpower, and wisdom

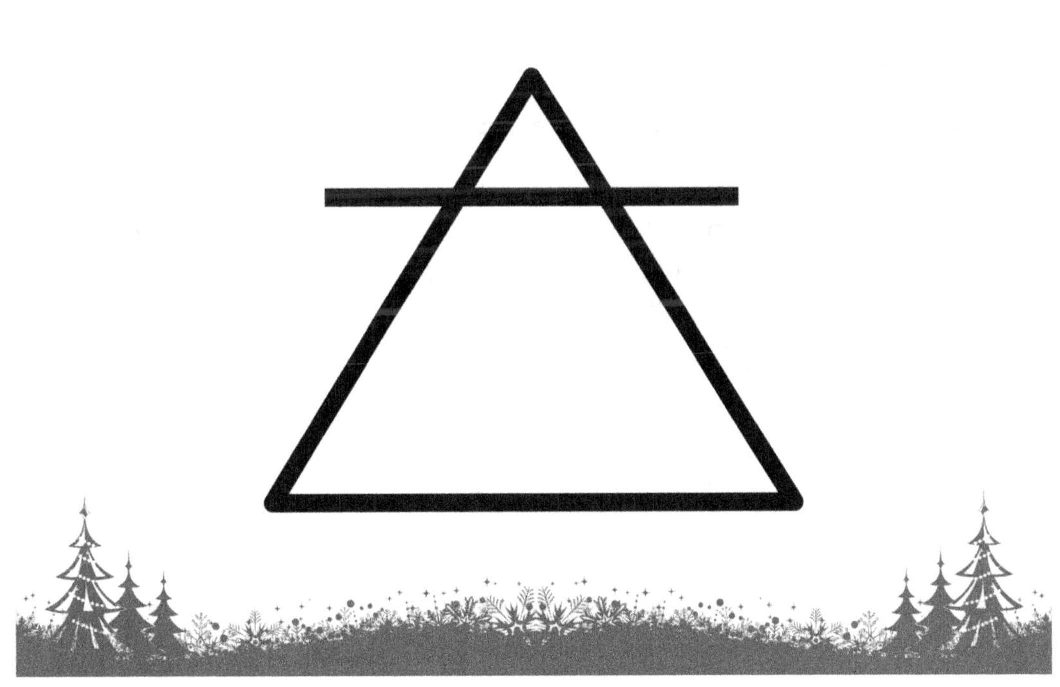

Fire

Symbol:
Numbers: 1, 3, 9
Solar System: Jupiter, Mars, and Sun
Zodiac: Aries, Leo, and Sagittarius
Celebrations: Beltane, Imbolc, and Litha
Season: Summer
Time of Day: Midday
Runes: Dag, Ken, Rad, and Sigel
Ogham: Ur
Tarot: Judgement, Swords, and Wands
Direction: South
Sense: Sight
Energy: Yang
Chakra: Solar Plexus
Colors: Crimson, Gold, Orange, Pink, Red, White, and Yellow
Trees: Alder, Ash, Beech, Blackthorn, Cedar, Cherry, Chestnut, Elder, Hawthorn, Holly, Horse Chestnut, Juniper, Laurel, Mesquite, Oak, Olive, Palm (dragon's blood), Pine, Pomegranate, Rowan, Walnut, Willow, Witch Hazel, and Yew
Herbs & Flowers: Amaranth, Anemone, Angelica, Basil, Carnation, Chrysanthemum, Dill, Fennel, Garlic, Goldenseal, Gorse, Heliotrope, Hibiscus, Holy Basil, Lovage, Marigold, Pennyroyal, Peony, Peppermint, Poppy, Primrose, Rosemary, Rue, St. John's Wort, Snapdragon, Sunflower, Sweet Woodruff, and Vervain
Misc. Plants: Allspice, Asafetida, Betony, Black Cohosh, Blessed Thistle, Bloodroot, Cinnamon, Cinquefoil, Clove, Coriander, Cumin, Deer's Tongue, Flax, Frankincense, Galangal, Ginger, Ginseng, High John, Mandrake, Mullein, Mustard, Nettle, Nutmeg, Pepper, Thistle, and Wormwood
Gemstones & Minerals: Agate (banded, black, brown, fire, red, red-banded, snakeskin), Amber, Amet-rine, Apache Tears, Beryl (golden), Bloodstone, Calcite (orange, red), Carnelian, Citrine, Diamond, Garnet, Hematite, Herkimer Diamond, Jasper (red), Obsidian, Onyx, Opal (fire), Peridot, Pyrite, Quartz, Rhodochrosite, Rhodonite, Ruby, Sard, Sardonyx, Serpentine, Smoky Quartz, Spinel, Staurolite, Sunstone, Tiger's Eye, Topaz, Tourmaline (red), Tsavorite, and Zircon (red)
Metals: Antimony, Brass, Gold, Iron, and Steel
From the Sea: Coral (red)

Fire

Angel: Michael

Goddesses: Aine, Amaterasu, Bertha, Brigid, Danu, Durga, Freya, Hestia, Kupala, Pele, Phoebe, Sekhmet, Spider-Woman, and Vesta

Gods: Agni, Belenus, Brahma, Dionysus, Hephaestus, Horus, Inari, Indra, Khnum, Mimir, Nergal, Nord, Perun, Prometheus, and Vulcan

Magical Beings: Mermaids and Salamanders

Animals: Goat, Hedgehog, Horse, Lion, Porcupine, Sheep (ram), and Tiger

Birds: Crane, Eagle, Falcon, Heron, Macaw, Peacock, Quail, Robin, Swallow, Woodpecker, and Wren

Reptiles: Lizard, Salamander, and Snake

Insects/Misc.: Bee, Cicada, Firefly, Ladybug, Praying Mantis, and Scorpion

Mythical: Dragon and Phoenix

Ritual Tools: Censer and Wand

Principle: To Will

Issues, Intentions, and Powers: action, activate/awaken, ambition, anger, authority, battle/war, cheerfulness, communication, concentration/ focus, confidence, consecrate/bless, courage, creativity, defense, desire, destruction, divination, energy, faith, freedom, healing, honor, illumination, influence, inspiration, intelligence, intuition, justice, leadership, life, light, love, lust, magic (general, defensive, dragon, sex), the mind, motivation, passion, power, protection, psychic ability, purification, purity, purpose, release, revenge, sexuality, stimulation, transformation, truth, warmth, weather (general, lightning), and willpower

Water

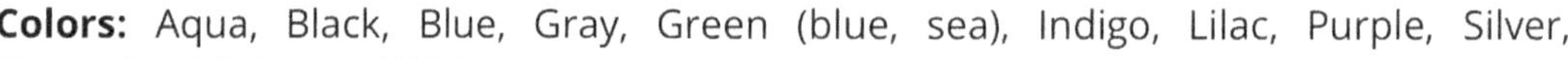

Symbol:
Numbers: 2, 7
Solar System: Mercury, Moon, Neptune, Pluto, and Saturn
Zodiac: Cancer, Pisces, and Scorpio
Celebrations: Mabon and Neptunalia
Season: Autumn
Time of Day: Dusk
Runes: Feoh, Jera, Lagu, and Peorth
Ogham: Eadha, and Eamhancholl
Tarot: Cups, Hanged Man, and Moon
Direction: West
Sense: Taste
Energy: Yin
Chakra: Sacral
Colors: Aqua, Black, Blue, Gray, Green (blue, sea), Indigo, Lilac, Purple, Silver, Turquoise, Violet, and White
Trees: Alder, Apple, Ash, Aspen, Beech, Birch, Cedar, Cherry, Chestnut, Cypress, Elder, Elm, Hazel, Horse Chestnut, Locust, Magnolia, Mesquite, Mimosa, Myrtle, Olive, Poplar, Spindle-tree, Spruce, Sycamore, Willow, Witch Hazel, and Yew
Herbs & Flowers: Aster, Blackberry / Bramble, Catnip, Chamomile, Columbine, Comfrey, Daffodil, Daisy, Feverfew, Foxglove, Gardenia, Geranium, Grape, Heather, Hibiscus, Hyacinth, Iris, Ivy, Jasmine, Lady's Mantle, Lemon Balm, Lilac, Lily, Monkshood, Morning Glory, Passionflower, Periwinkle, Poppy, Raspberry, Rose, Solomon's Seal, Spearmint, Strawberry, Thyme, Valerian, Violet, and Yarrow
Misc. Plants: Aloe, Belladonna, Burdock, Cardamom, Coltsfoot, Cowslip, Dittany, Henbane, Lady's Slipper, Lotus, Meadowsweet, Moonwort, Myrrh, Orris Root, Reed, Sandalwood, Skullcap, Spikenard, Star Anise, Thornapple, Vanilla, and Water Lily
Gemstones & Minerals: Alexandrite, Amethyst, Ametrine, Angelite, Aquamarine, Aragonite, Azurite, Beryl, Blue Lace Agate, Calcite, Charoite, Chrysocolla, Dioptase, Fluorite, Jade, Jasper (ocean), Jet, Kyanite, Labradorite, Lapis Lazuli, Larimar, Lepidolite, Lodestone, Moonstone, Morganite, Obsidian (gold sheen), Opal, Quartz, Rose Quartz, Sapphire, Selenite, Sodalite, Staurolite, Sugilite Topaz (blue), Tourmaline (black, blue, pink, watermelon), Tsavorite, Turquoise, and Zircon (blue)
Metals: Copper, Mercury, and Silver
From the Sea: Coral, Mother-of-Pearl, and Pearl

Water

Angels: Raphael

Goddesses: Amphitrite, Aphrodite, Bad, Boann, Brigantia, Chalchiuhtlicue, Coventina, Isis, Kupala, Ran, Sarasvati, Sedna, and Tiamat

Gods: Aegir, Belenus, Ea, Khnum, Mabon, Manannan, Mimir, Neptune, Njord, Osiris, Poseidon, and Prometheus

Magical Beings: Mermaids, Norns, and Undines

Animals: Bat, Beaver, Cattle (cow), Dog, Hare, Hippopotamus, Horse, Moose, Otter, Polar Bear, and Raccoon

Birds: Albatross, Blackbird, Cormorant, Crane, Dove, Duck, Heron, Kingfisher, Seagull, Stork, Swan, Swift, and Vulture

Reptiles: Crocodile, Frog, Salamander, Snake, and Toad

Insect/Misc.: Dragonfly

Mythical: Dragon and Selkies

Ritual Tools: Cauldron, Chalice, and Cup

Principle: To Dare

Issues, Intentions and Powers: adaptability, agriculture, balance, beginnings, change/s, clairvoyance, compassion, consecrate/bless, consciousness (subconscious), creativity, desire, divination, dream work, emotions, empathy, energy (general, psychic, receptive), fertility, friendship, grace, growth, healing, heartbreak, influence, introspection, intuition, life, magic (animal, dragon, moon), memory /memories, nurture, patience, power, pregnancy/childbirth, protection, psychic ability, purification, purity, rebirth/ renewal, reconciliation, reversal, secrets, sensitivity, sensuality, shamanic work, sleep, sorrow, spirituality, strength (inner), stress, transformation, weather (general, storms), well-being, and wisdom

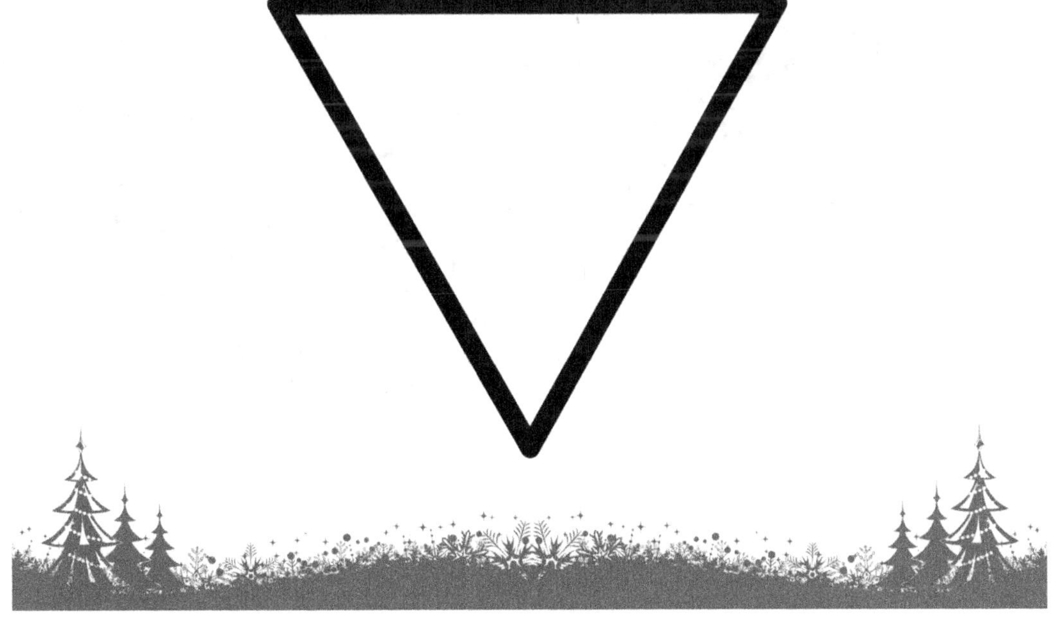

CHAPTER 9

Auras

Are in constant motion with every breath.

They are not always the same color.

Are a physical representation of the energy surrounding your physical body

May have one or more colors per layer.

Are not a perfectly rounded shape.

They are multidimensional (above, below, and all around you).

Are composed of layers that may blend into each other.

Surround every living thing (human, plant, animal).

Need regular cleansing.

Can rip and tear due to physical injury.

Need maintenance to repair rips, holes, and tears.

Can expand up to 30 feet outside your physical body.

Help you to feel external energies.

Are a natural part of your body.

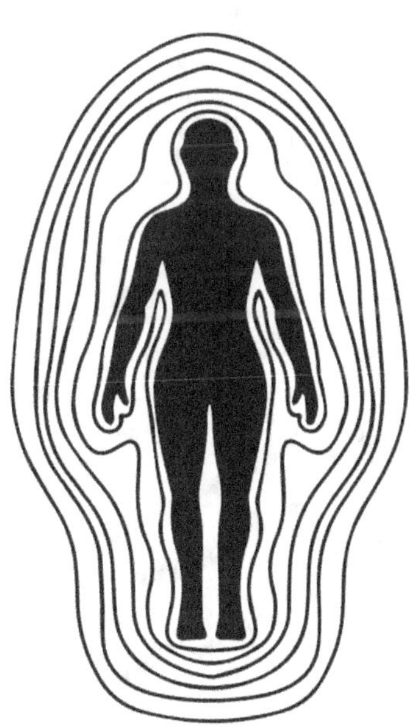

Aura Layers

Aura layers, starting on the outside and moving inward:

1 Ketheric Template
2 Celestial/Divine
3 Etheric Template
4 Astral
5 Mental
6 Emotional
7 Etheric

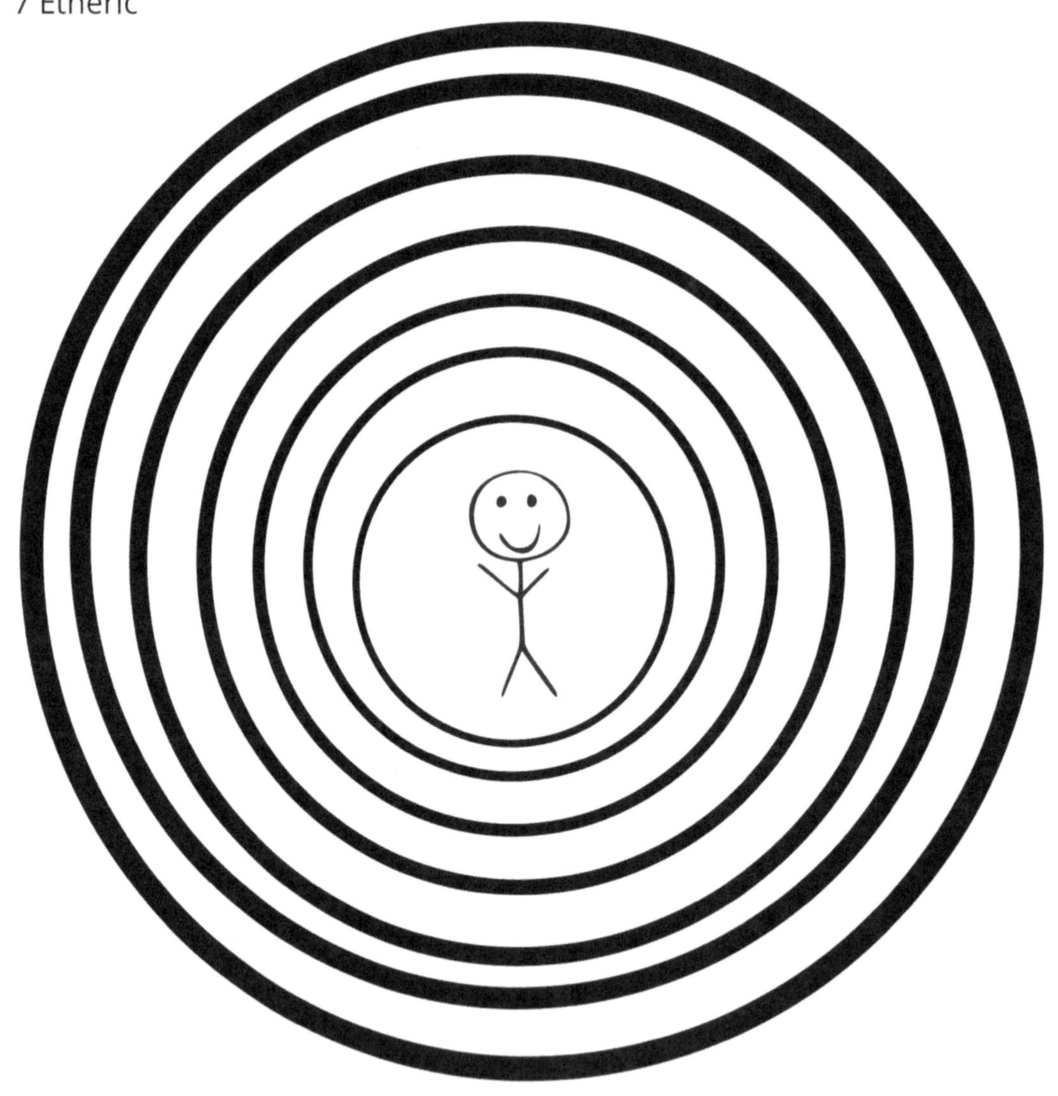

Aura Colors

Yellow
Energetic, optimistic, confident, childlike, fun-loving, sensitive, happy, free-spirited, creative, generous, and connects with nature and animals.

Orange
Creative, independent, adventurous, risk-taker, resourceful, strategic, loves to test physical limits, mentally focused, and overcomes challenges.

Blue
Loving, nurturing, compassionate, sensitive, forgiving, loyal, spiritual, emotional depth, teaching, caretaker of people and the planet.

Red
Intense, passionate, hard-working, grounded, literal, raw courage, sensual, honest, self-confident, experiences the world through touch.

Green
Healing, teaching, organized, entrepreneurial, highly intelligent, driven, successful, perfectionist, empowers others, ability to accomplish goals.

Magenta
Non-conformist, creative, intelligent, free-spirited, eccentric, original, likes to be the center of attention, strong-willed, unique, and innovative.

Tan
Detail-oriented, practical, cautious, private, calm, clean, logical, intuitive, committed, values love, gentle, analytical, controlled.

Violet
Artistic/creative, visionary, loves to take chances, enjoys travel, charismatic leader, humanitarian, inspirational to others, has big ideas.

Lavender
Enchanting, daydreamer, fragile, sensitive, imaginative, creative, intelligent, gentle, intuitive, love to change directions.

Indigo
Wise, intuitive, believe in higher ideals + principles, peaceful, creative, non-judgemental, spiritually gifted, sensitive, enlightened consciousness.

White
Gifted healer, highly spiritual, quiet, sensitive, one with nature, adaptable, highly intuitive, loves simplicity, meditative, calming.

Cleanse Your Aura

Smudging: Burning sage or other herbs like palo santo to release smoke and cleanse the energy around you.

Crystal Cleansing: Placing crystals like clear quartz or selenite in sunlight or moonlight to recharge and purify their energies.

Salt Bath: Take a bath with your physical body and your physical body, and Epsom salt or sea salt to cleanse both your physical body and your aura.

Meditation: Using focused breathing and visualization techniques to release negative energy and restore balance.

Sound Healing: Listening to or creating SHAZDI sounds, such as singing bowls, bells, or chanting to clear stagnant energy.

Nature Connection: Spending time outdoors, in nature, to absorb fresh energies and reconnect with the natural world.

CHAPTER 10

Energy: Yin

Zodiac: Cancer, Pisces, Scorpio, Taurus, Virgo
Solar System: Moon, Neptune, Venus
Rune:
Numbers: 1, 2, 4, 6, 7, 8, 10, 12
Color: Black
Tarot:
Trees: Apple, Beech, Birch, Cherry, Cypress, Elder, Elm, Horse Chestnut, Laurel, Magnolia, Mesquite, Mimosa, Myrtle, Palm, Poplar, Spindletree, Spruce, Sycamore, Willow, Yew
Misc. Plants: Aloe, Belladonna, Black Cohosh, Burdock, Cardamom, Coltsfoot, Cowslip, Dittany, Goldenrod, Henbane, Lady's Slipper, Lotus, Meadowsweet, Moonwort, Mullein, Myrrh, Orris Root, Patchouli, Reed, Sandalwood, Skullcap, Spikenard, Thornapple, Vanilla
Herb and Garden: Amaranth, Aster, Blackberry / Bramble, Catnip, Columbine, Comfrey, Daffodil, Daisy, Foxglove, Gardenia, Geranium, Grape, Heather, Hibiscus, Hyacinth, Iris, Ivy, Jasmine, Lady's Mantle, Lemon Balm, Lilac, Lily, Monkshood, Mugwort, Passionflower, Periwinkle, Poppy, Primrose, Raspberry, Rose, Sage, Solomon's Seal, Spearmint, Strawberry, Thyme, Valerian, Vervain Violet, Yarrow
Gemstones and Minerals: Agate (black with white veining, green, snakeskin, tree), Amazonite, Amethyst, Ametrine, Andalusite, Apophyllite, Aquamarine, Azurite, Beryl, Blue Lace Agate, Calcite, Celestite, Cerussite, Chrysocolla, Chrysoprase, Desert Rose, Diopside, Emerald, Iolite, Jade, Jasper (brown, green, ocean, pink), Jet, Kunzite, Labradorite, Lapis Lazuli, Larimar, Lepidolite, Lodestone, Malachite, Moonstone, Morganite, Moss Agate, Opal, Peridot, Petrified Wood, Quartz (blue, clear, green, tourmalated), Rose Quartz, Salt, Sapphire, Selenite, Smoky Quartz, Sodalite, Staurolite, Sugilite, Tourmaline (watermelon), Tsavorite, Turquoise
From the Sea: Coral, Cow, Mother-of-Pearl, Pearl
Metals: Copper, Lead, Mercury, Silver
From the Sea:
Angel and Mythical Being: Dragon, Unicorn

Energy: Yang

Zodiac: Aquarius, Aries, Capricorn, Gemini, Leo, Libra, Sagittarius
Solar System: Mars, Pluto, Sun
Runes:
Numbers: 1, 3, 5, 7, 9, 11, 13
Color: White
Tarot:
Trees: Acacia, Alder, Ash, Aspen, Blackthorn, Cedar, Chestnut, Fir, Hawthorn, Hazel, Holly, Juniper, Linden, Locust, Maple, Oak, Olive, Palm (dragon's blood), Pine, Pomegranate, Rowan Walnut, Witch Hazel, Yew
Misc. Plants: Allspice, Anise, Asafoetida, Bamboo, Betony, Bittersweet, Blessed Thistle, Bloodroot, Cinnamon, Cinquefoil, Clove, Coriander, Cumin, Deer's Tongue, Eyebright, Flax, Frankincense, Galangal, Ginger, Ginseng, High John, Horehound, Mandrake, Mistletoe, Mustard, Nettle, Nut-meg, Pepper, Reed, Star Anise, Thistle, Wormwood
Herb and Garden: Agrimony, Anemone, Angelica, Basil, Bergamot, Borage, Broom, Carnation, Chamomile, Chrysanthemum, Clover, Dandelion, Dill, Fennel, Fern, Feverfew, Garlic, Goldenseal, Gorse, Heliotrope, Holy Basil, Honeysuckle, Lavender, Lily of the Valley, Lovage, Marigold, Marjoram, Morning Glory, Pennyroyal, Peony, Peppermint, Rosemary, Rue, Saffron, St. John's Wort, Snapdragon, Sunflower, Sweet Woodruff
Gemstones and Minerals: Agate (banded, black, brown, fire, red, red-banded, snakeskin), Amber, Amethyst, Ametrine, Andalusite, Apache Tears, Aventurine, Beryl (golden), Bloodstone, Calcite (orange, red), Carnelian, Cat's Eye, Chrysoberyl, Citrine, Diamond, Fluorite, Garnet, Hematite, Herkimer Diamond, Jasper (leopard skin, red, yellow), Lodestone, Obsidian, Onyx, Opal, Pyrite, Quartz (clear, rutilated), Rhodochrosite, Rhodonite, Ruby, Sard, Sardonyx, Serpentine, Sphene, Spinel, Staurolite, Sunstone, Tanzanite, Tiger's Eye, Topaz, Tourmaline (red, watermelon), Zircon
Metals: Aluminum, Antimony, Brass, Gold, Iron, Mercury, Steel, Tin
From the Sea: Coral (red)
Godesss:
God:
Angel and Mythical Being: Dragon, Phoenix, Unicorn
Issue:

CHAPTER 11

Chakra Energy

Each chakra is connected to the central energy channel in the spine, called the Sushumna, and is also connected to the idea and the Pingala, which are the yin and the yang energy channels crisscrossing along the Sushumna. The points where they cross are the locations of the seven major chakras.

The chakras act like transformers, draw in and distribute subtle energy from the Universal supply of ki, and act as exit points for unwanted energy.

The Chakras store the energy of thoughts, feelings, memories, experiences, and actions. They influence and direct our present and future mindset, behavior, emotional health, and activities.

Our energy system governs our energetic and psychic well-being.

The life force in each chakra can be processed, transmuted, and released so that we consciously manifest what we want to call in rather than experience more of the same. Prana informs us and influences our actions and behaviors, determining our health, career opportunities, relationships, etc. The subtle body depicts how our inner reality creates our outer reality.

Balancing Act

Your chakras are responsible for your health and well-being. You'll feel physically and emotionally good when they're balanced and healthy. However, when one or more of your chakras needs to be balanced, it can lead to problems. To keep your chakras balanced, ensure they're all spinning in the same direction and are the same size. Also, check that they're free of obstruction and appear bright.

When one of your chakras is blocked, it's not spinning as quickly or smoothly as the others. This can be due to a buildup of dense energies, making the chakra appear smaller than normal. In some cases, the chakra might spin in the opposite direction. If you have a blocked chakra, addressing the issue as soon as possible is important.

An overactive chakra is often spinning too quickly, appearing out of control. It may also appear larger than normal and begin to dominate the energy of neighboring chakras if left unbalanced. An overactive chakra can also change shape, becoming oval or oblong rather than a perfect circle.

Meditation Frequencies

174 Hz - Removes Pain
285 Hz - Heals Energy Field
396 Hz - Removes Guilt & Fear
417 HZ - Facilitates Change
432 Hz - Miracle Tone of Nature
528 Hz - Repairs DNA
639 Hz - Heals Relationships
741 HZ - Awakens Intuition
852 Hz - Attracts Soul Tribe
963 Hz - Connects With Spirit

Vibration

Nothing rests. Everything moves. Everything vibrates At the most fundamental level, the Universe and everything which comprises it is pure vibratory energy manifesting itself in different ways. The Universe has no "solidity," as such. Matter is merely energy in a state of vibration.

Polarity

Everything is Dual.
Everything has poles.
Everything has its pair of opposites.
Opposites are identical in nature but different in degree.
Extremes meet.
All paradoxes may be reconciled.

At A Glance Chakras

Crown Chakra
Sahasrara
Represents spiritual consciousness and transformation.

Third Eye Chakra
Ajna
Responsible for spiritual communication, awareness, and perception.

Throat Chakra
Visuddha
Governs self-expression, communication, and the ability to speak one's truth.

Heart Chakra
Anahata
Governs people's love for themselves and those around them, supporting empathy.

Solar Plexus Chakra
Manipura
Represents confidence, self-esteem, and personal power.

Sacral Chakra
Svadhisthana
It supports emotional and physical health aspects and governs many of the body's fluids (from the sex organs, the bladder, and the kidneys).

Root Chakra
Muladhara
Good health in the body, a sense of connection to the Earth, and a feeling of support and stability in the physical world.

Chakra Symbols

Crown Chakra:
To Know and Understand

Third Eye:
To See

Throat Chakra:
To Speak and Be Heard

Heart Chakra:
To Love and Be Loved

Solar Plexus Chakra:
To Act

Sacral Chakra:
To Feel and Desire

Root Chakra:
To Be Here and To Have

Chakras

Chakra is a Sanskrit word meaning wheel or vortex. They are an integral part of the body's energy system and transformers of subtle energy. They take the Ki around us and transform it into the various frequencies our subtle energy system needs to keep us healthy.

The Root Chakra (1st) — Reproductive glands (testes in men; ovaries in women); controls sexual development and secretes sex hormones. This chakra is located in the pelvic region at the base of the spine. It is responsible for our physical reality, safety, security, and survival instincts.

The Sacral Chakra (2nd) — Adrenal glands; regulates the immune system and metabolism. This chakra influences our emotions and creativity. It's located just a few inches below the belly button. In addition, this chakra affects our views on intimacy, boundaries, and trust.

The Solar Plexus Chakra (3rd) — Pancreas; regulates metabolism. This chakra is situated in the upper belly, at the diaphragm. It guides our will and mental layers. It is also responsible for our energy, personal power, and issues related to the Ego.

The Heart Chakra (4th) — Thymus gland; regulates the immune system.
The heart chakra is located in the center of the chest and governs our ability to experience unconditional love. This chakra also influences our relationships and how we demonstrate compassion and hope.

The Throat Chakra (5th) — Thyroid gland; regulates body temperature and metabolism. It governs our ability to communicate clearly and effectively. When this chakra is balanced, we can express ourselves truthfully and listen and understand others better.

The Third Eye Chakra (6th) — Pituitary gland; produces hormones and governs the function of the previous five glands; sometimes, the pineal gland is linked to the third eye chakra and the crown chakra. The third eye chakra is a powerful tool for intuition and spiritual insight. It is located behind the middle of the forehead, near the pineal gland. This chakra helps us to open up to greater awareness, psychic senses, and spiritual gifts.

The Crown Chakra (7th) — Pineal gland; regulates biological cycles, including sleep.
This chakra, located at the top of the head, is associated with spirituality and our connection to higher intelligence. It helps us to achieve enlightenment. By opening this chakra, we can access greater knowledge and guidance.

The Transpersonal Chakras

Earth Star Chakra - Vasundhara in Sanskrit, is a sub-personal chakra located below the feet. The energy center is off the body, but the exact distance is unknown, estimated to be between 6 to 18 inches below the soles of your feet. The Earth Star Chakra has a grounding, earthy energy like the root chakra and is described as the "grounding cord" that pulls our Lightbody towards the Earth's center.

The Soul Star Chakra Sutara in Sanskrit is the 8th energy center 6-12 inches above the 7th Chakra. The 8th Chakra, also known as the Halo Chakra, represents a luminous circle of divine light above your head. This Chakra is the primary channel for divine energy to travel to the rest of the chakra system below. As a transpersonal chakra above the body, the 8th Chakra represents the higher planes of the etheric body.

Spirit Star Chakra - The Spirit Star Chakra or Spirit Chakra is located above the soul star and is connected to profound levels of connection with the divine. The Chakra is associated with communicating with angels, light beings, and guides and represents the expansive spiritual realm. While activation of the Soul Star Chakra allows you to connect to your true purpose, Spirit Chakra activation enables you to tap into the full extent of your soul's gifts and abilities. Your ability to manifest and create increases through this direct connection to the divine.

Universal Chakra -The Universal Chakra is the 10th Chakra located directly above the Spirit Chakra and governs all universal aspects of being. Here, we experience merging our masculine and feminine energies, allowing us to tap into the best qualities of both. The Universal Chakra is the portal to the limitless flow of creation. When activated, you align your light being with your physical being, resulting in perfect harmony with the universe.

Galactic Chakra - The 11th Chakra, known as the Galactic Chakra, is related to time travel and carries supernatural powers like teleportation, instant manifestation, and bi-location. This energy center encompasses total cosmic wisdom, and when activated, it is said that a person can travel beyond the limits of time and space.

Divine Gateway - The last of the 12 chakras is the Divine Gateway Chakra, also known as the Stellar Gateway Chakra. This final point on the chakra journey represents full ascension and complete oneness with the divine. Activating this energy century opens the door to the divine world. It is believed that a person who has opened this Chakra has the spiritual knowledge to guide others along their chakra journey to cosmic connection.

How to Use Chakra Affirmations

Meditation: You can connect with one or all of your chakras during a single meditation. For instance, if you're connecting with the root chakra, envision it as a bright red glowing orb at the base of your spine. As you breathe in, see the orb getting bigger. As you breathe out, see it growing brighter. As you do this, recite grounding root chakra affirmations. To connect with each of your chakras in a single meditation, start at the root chakra and repeat one or two affirmations. Then, move to the sacral chakra and work upwards along your spine.

Mirror Work: Stand in front of the mirror and look yourself in the eyes. Take a deep breath and focus on one chakra at a time. You can look at the physical location of the chakra in the mirror but also try to connect to it within. Recite the chakra affirmations that your soul needs most at this moment.

Post-Its: Leave post-it notes in visible places you'll see throughout the day. On each Post-it note, write a chakra affirmation that resonates with you. Then, whenever you see the post-it note, recite the affirmation silently or out loud, feeling the positive words in every cell of your being. For a bonus, you can use post-its that correlate with the color of each chakra.

Color Therapy: Color therapy is the act of immersing yourself in the color associated with that chakra. One way to use color therapy and affirmations in conjunction is to make it a game. For instance, if you're working with your heart chakra, pay attention to the world around you as you go about your day. Then, recite a heart chakra affirmation silently or aloud whenever you see something green in your external world. You can do this with one or multiple chakras at a time.

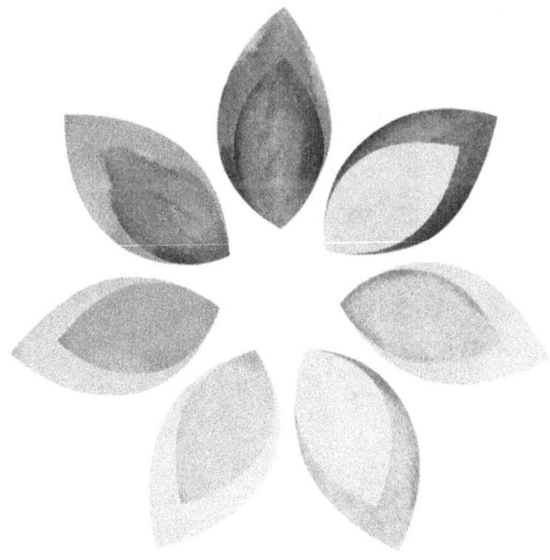

Grounding

Grounding is a straightforward and natural way to connect ourselves back to Earth. We often hear people talking about grounding and telling us to ground ourselves, but why do we need to do it, and how do we do it?

Some of us are more prone than others to live in the clouds, so we do not feel deeply rooted in our bodies. If this happens occasionally is acceptable; however, if this becomes a permanent state of being can lead to some problems.

Ungrounded Symptoms:
High sensitivity to light and noise.
Not finding the keys or other things, constantly dropping stuff, forgetting appointments, etc.
I am constantly daydreaming.
Often feeling dizzy and spaced out.
I cannot meditate and constantly fall asleep during the exercise.
Usually, feeling tired, drained, and lacking energy.
I was feeling grumpy and nervy.
I am losing track of what a person says to me, unable to converse normally.
I was getting lost while driving/walking, even in familiar areas.
Unable to see synchronicities happening in our lives.
Feeling ungrounded can make life difficult, so sometimes we do not belong here.

What To Do?

Fortunately, there are several many simple ways to ground ourselves:

Concentrate on our breathing.
Pay attention to the body.
Walking in a mindful way.
Being in nature.
Eating healthy food.

Anything that brings us back into our body is basically grounding, but it's also smart to know and practice grounding exercises that we can do quickly. At first, you should practice them with care, attention, and intention for a few minutes, but you can instantly ground them after a while.

Grounding Exercise 1

One of the easiest ways to ground is to bring your attention to the breath as it enters and leaves the body, not trying to change it in any way, just observing it. After about 10 breaths, you will probably find that you are more connected to your physical body. Then bring your awareness to the sensations in your body, moving from your head down to your feet, exploring and inquiring as you work your way around the body. Just a few minutes of this can bring you home to your body and to the Earth, and this is what it means to ground ourselves.

Then imagine that you have roots growing out of the soles of your feet, and imagine those roots flowing down into the Earth. The roots flow with us so we can always move, but at the same time, they keep us grounded. Imagine these roots flowing down through all of the layers of the Earth and connecting right down into the magnetic core of the planet (or however you see the center).

Then feeling anchored to the center of the planet, imagine the energy from there flowing up through these roots into the soles of your feet and then up your legs into your pelvic area and into your root chakra. Then feel it continuing to flow up through your chakras: your sacral chakra, the solar plexus, and then the heart chakra. If you want to, then you can ground all the way up to your crown chakra.

We receive powerful energy from the Earth just as we do from the forms of energy we associate with the sky, and our body is a tool that brings these two energies together. When we are grounded, we become a strong container in which our spirits can safely and productively dwell. This is why grounding every day, especially at the beginning of the day, is such a beneficial practice. Fortunately, it's as simple as bringing our conscious awareness to our bodies and the Earth on which we walk.

Grounding simply re-connects your body's energy with the energy of the Earth, and this is a good practice for everybody as it's very refreshing and invigorating.

Grounding Exercise 2

First, ensure you sit comfortably, relaxed, with your eyes closed and your feet flat on the floor. Focus on your breathing. Breathe in with your nose and out through your mouth.

Focus your attention on the bottom of your spine (root chakra)
Imagine that you are sending an anchor from your spine deep into the Earth on a very long rope or chain.

Allow it to drop deeper, maybe feeling that you are being pulled downwards or that your spine is being extended.

Focus on your feet and imagine dropping an anchor, long rope, or chain from each foot.

Again, allow them to drop deeper and deeper, and you may feel like your legs are pulling downwards.

Your legs may feel heavy, and your feet may feel as if they are stuck to the floor.
This feeling is good because it now means you are grounded – your body is heavy and relaxed.

Imagine the Earth's energy flowing into your root chakra and feel that connection to the Earth is both permanent and stable.

There are many grounding exercises. For example, you could imagine yourself as a tree, with roots deep into the Earth below you, with your legs and body as the trunk and arms and head as the branches.

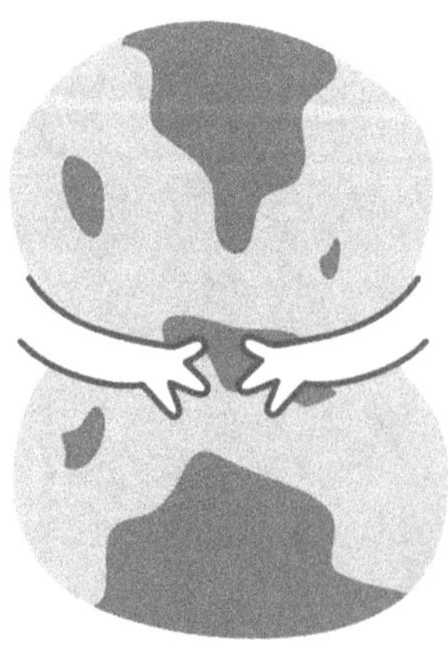

Self-Healing Your Chakras

You can use several tools and techniques to open, heal and balance your chakras.

Yoga Poses: Yoga is an excellent way to get your chakras to open up and help your energy flow freely throughout your body. Yoga helps to move stuck and stagnant energy from your energy field, which can prevent the chakras from functioning correctly. For example, if someone is having trouble opening their heart chakra, I recommend spending ten minutes a day doing back bending poses that help open their chest, heart, shoulders, and upper spine.

Essential Oils: Aromatherapy can be a helpful tool for recalibrating our thoughts, emotions, and energies. Scents containing earthy scents and tree properties can help the root chakra better align and focus a person's energy downward. This can be helpful for individuals who are struggling to keep their energy grounded.

Crystals: Healing crystals can balance, replenish and restore energy levels. People who love crystals also often like to bathe with them, infuse water with their energies, sleep with gemstones, or decorate their homes with rocks. When chakra healing, you can place a healing stone directly on or near the chakra you want to work with while meditating or resting.

Sounds: Singing bowls, tuning forks, and Solfeggio frequencies can be used to open and heal blocked chakras. Listening to certain sounds in nature can also be helpful. For example, listening to water sounds such as rain, waves, or waterfalls can help a person to connect more deeply to their sacral chakra and the watery properties of the womb.

Foods: Certain diets can help to open chakras or clear blocked energies. One example is eating more "yellow foods," such as peppers, lentils, squash, bananas, and/or corn, to assist with the healing of the solar plexus chakra.

Energy Work: You can do several daily things to help clear your energy and raise your vibration. This includes things like clearing your chakras and balancing your energy field. These activities can be beneficial in removing stuck energy and keeping yourself in balance.

Using A Pendulum To Check Your Chakras

Using a pendulum is one way to tell if your chakras are out of balance. This is a quick and easy way to check your chakras, and anyone can do it. To check your chakras with a pendulum, follow these steps:

Hold the pendulum in your dominant hand, and place it a few inches above the palm of your other hand.

Wait for the pendulum to stop moving, or command it to be still by saying "stop" out loud. Then, ensure the pendulum has always stopped moving before asking a new question.

Tell your pendulum: "Show me what a healthy chakra on my body looks like." Wait for the pendulum to respond and begin moving. Note the direction the chakra spins, how fast it spins, and how big of a circle it makes.

Once the pendulum has stopped moving, ask it to show you what each chakra looks like. For example, say: "Now, show me what my root chakra looks like." Then, take note of what the pendulum does. If it spins in the opposite direction, changes size, or barely moves, it could indicate a blockage in that chakra. It could mean an overactive chakra if it starts spinning faster, makes oblong shapes, or spins in a large circle.

Repeat this for each of your 7 main chakras.

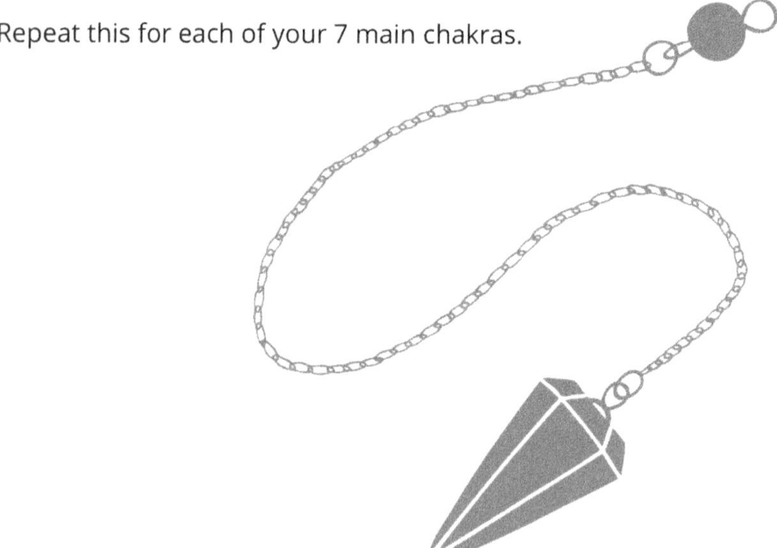

CHAPTER 12

Simplified Psychic Abilities

Clairvoyance - When you see stuff (clear vision)

Clairaudience - When you hear stuff (clear hearing)

Clairsentience - When you feel stuff (clear sensing and feeling)

Clairempathy - When you feel other people's stuff

Claircognizance - When you just know stuff (clear knowing)

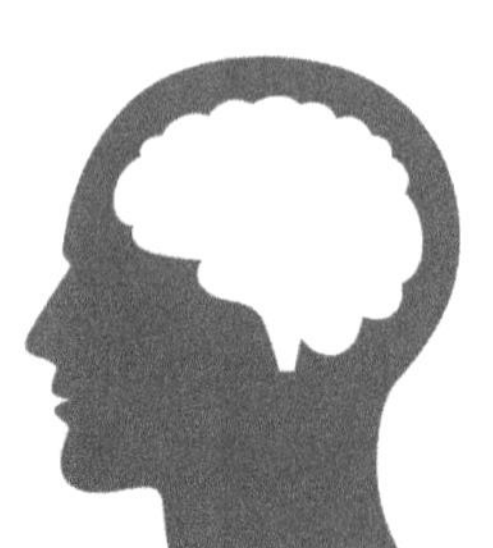

Clairsgustance - When you taste stuff (clear taste)

Clairalience or Clairscent - When you smell stuff (clear smell)

Clairtangency /Pyschometry - When you get touched and stuff (clear touch)

Telepathy - When you can communicate through thoughts and stuff

Telekenisis - When you can move things with your mind and stuff

Types of Empaths

It's extremely rare to be an empath. Research estimates that just 1-2 percent of the population possesses empath traits.

Empaths tend to everyone else's needs before their own, and they tend to experience emotional burnout more than others.

Empaths are considered excellent listeners; people often approach them with their problems. They are also regarded as good problem-solvers and caring and nurturing individuals with unique abilities to feel or read people or situations, depending on their type.

Empaths are also very receptive and perceptive to their environment and the energy surrounding them.

These types of people will take on the world's problems if they can and carry that burden around with them — they are more prone to depression and chronic fatigue due to their heightened emotional nature and inability to let others deal with their emotions on their own, with time.

Claircognizant/Intuitive Empath
Being a claircognizant or intuitive empath, you can know if and what must be done in a situation without any solid evidence or rationale.
Depending on the context and circumstances, this type of empath can know whether or not they should do something. Claircognizant empaths can vibe off of the energy field of others, and, having that ability, they can scan people.

Psychometric Empath
The psychometric empath can receive information and energy from objects, photographs, or locations that are significant to a person.

Psychometric empaths can also form impressions and relate situations or past events with inanimate objects. They can use the energy from a place or inanimate object to receive information and impressions about it.

Types of Empaths

Flora Empath

This type of empath can communicate with plants and receive their signals. A flora empath, also known as a plant empath, can sense what plants need and communicate more intimately with plants. As a result, they can use plants' energy to help plants stay alive, grow and prosper. For example, if plants are in danger, the flora empath can communicate this with the plants.

Fauna Empath

This pertains to the ability to feel and communicate with animals. Fauna empaths, also called animal empaths, can also send messages to animals.

Typically, communication is initiated by the empath and rarely by the animals. Those who hear these messages may realize that animals are requesting a change in the animal's life.

Geomantic Empath

A geomantic empath can read signs and get signals from the soil or earth. This empath is especially sensitive to reading and feeling future natural disasters. Geomantic empaths can detect when natural disasters, such as hurricanes and earthquakes, will be hit by the earth's energy signals and changes in that energy.

Telepathic Empath

This type of empath can read another person's thoughts and feelings, even when they aren't vocalized or expressed by the person. This type of empath can read other people's thoughts, feelings, and beliefs using the five senses.

Telepathic empaths can also take objects and form impressions on feelings associated with the particular object.

Precognitive Empath

The precognitive empath can feel a situation or event occur before it happens. This can be seen through dreams of extreme emotional and physical upheaval.

Precognitive empaths may experience sudden anxiety and nervousness, and their intuition becomes intensified or heightened. This type of empath usually has heightened sensitivity.

CHAPTER 13

Practitioners

Alexandrian	Death	Green	Satanic
American Folk Magic	Desert	Grey	Sea
Ancestral/Hereditary	Dianic	Hedge	Seasonal
Appalachian	Divination	Hellenic	Secular
Art	Druid	Hermit	Shadow
Astronomy	Eclectic	Hoodoo	Shamanic
Augury	Elemental	Kitchen	Sun/Solar
Baby	Elf	Lunar	Storm
Blood	Enchanter	Music	Swamp
Celtic	Energy	Natural	Tech
Ceremonial	Faerie	Nature	Thelma
Chaos	Fire	Nocturnal	Thunder
Christian	Folk	Norse	Traditional
Correllian	Forest	Ozarks	Urban
Cosmic	Garden	Pagan	Voodoo
Cottage/Hearth	Gardnerian	Pow-Wow	Wiccan
Coven	Gothic	Religious	White
Crystal		Santeria	

The Gardnerian Witch follows the traditions of Gardnerian Wicca, which Gerald Garner created in the 1950s. This type of witchcraft has a hierarchical system with a high priest and priestess; these witches often practice in covens. To become a Gardnerian Witch, you must go through a variety of initiations. You must learn the traditions and culture of that branch of witchery and complete initiation into a coven to be considered a true witch.

The Alexandrian Witch is similar to the Gardnerian Witch in that they both follow some of the same traditions and are based on Wicca belief systems. However, Alexandrian witchcraft has its own unique traditions and initiation processes. The Alexandrian Witch also practices more ceremonial magic than the Gardnerian, and many Alexandrians practice Oabalah as well.

Which witch are you? Sorry for the pun. Are you more confused now than you were before? Me too, but what is a name? You know who and what you are,

OK, so, which witch are you? Sorry for the pun. Are you more confused now than you were before? I am, too, but what is a name? You know who and what you are; that is all you need.

"A rose by any other name would smell as sweet" - Williams Shakespeare.

CHAPTER 14

Witch Words

Blessing is a spell or prayer intended to spiritually purify a person, place, or thing while infusing it with the positive energy of the divine and one's own hopes.

Botany - A retail store that sells spiritual goods such as herbs, oils, statues, etc...

Butting - A term used in the magic candle to describe cutting the tip of a candle, turning it upside down, and invading a new tip from the bottom. Symbolically, it is said that this reverses people and conditions as symbolized by the color of the candle or the words engraved on it. Sometimes also referred to as Flipping.

Cold reading is a technique used by psychics, mediums, and unreal fortune tellers that uses general statements to determine a person's details. By measuring the individual's reaction to these general statements, an experienced soothsayer can extrapolate more information on the subject, giving the impression of having a true psychic ability. This technique is also used by mentalists, illusionists, and stage magicians in the entertainment industry. Compare it with Hot Reading.

Condition oil - a term used to describe oils that are designed to address a specific problem or determine a specific condition.

Crossroads is where two roads connect to form an X. Crossroads are places of spiritual power where magical objects are often eliminated, and ritual pacts are formed.

Curse - a type of spell that aims to cause harm to an individual in some form and for various reasons (e.g., punish, teach a lesson, etc.). Other related terms include hex or jinx.

Divination - The ritual process of obtaining information about the past, present, or future using tools such as tarot cards, playing cards, spells, etc. ... or without tools that use their psychic faculties or through observing signs and omens.

Dressing/dressing - A term that refers to rubbing an oil condition on an inanimate object, such as a candle, a mojo bag, or a talisman. It is sometimes used interchangeably with anointing.

Feeding is dressing a mojo bag with oil or limestone with oil/magnetic sand to feed it and keep it strong to work for you.

Hand - another word for a Mojo Bag (see also "Root")

Witch the word comes from the Old English/Germanic word "wicca" (male) and "wicce" (female), which means the Wise One

Saining is a traditional Scottish method of ritually cleansing and blessing. Use dried rosemary tied up in a long bundle and light it. The smoke from the rosemary will remove negative energy image.

Honey Jar - A type of spell that uses sweeteners such as honey, syrup, molasses, etc. ... combined with a candle(s) designed to force an individual to favor your petition in business, love, or lawsuits.

Hoodoo - A form of folk magic originating in Africa that, through syncretism, has absorbed beliefs and practices from other cultures, such as Native American spirituality and European grimoires.

Hot Footing is a spell or ritual designed to drive out a person, such as an enemy or some other problematic person. It is synonymous with banishment in other magical traditions.

Hot Reading - The use of knowledge acquired about an individual in advance while performing a reading for another individual. See also cold reading.

Work - Another term for spell. Also working.

Lady Hearted - A root practitioner or spiritual practitioner who is morally opposed to causing harm to another individual or animal through spells and magic.

Things live in you - A term that refers to the belief that, through magic, living beings such as snakes, scorpions, and spiders have been introduced into the human body.

Loading - A term that refers to excavating a small hole in the bottom of a candle and introducing herbs, personal concerns, oils, dust, etc. ... before closing the hole.

Mojo Bag - A type of talisman that takes the form of a small flannel drawstring bag containing an assortment of animal, plant, and mineral curiosities believed to attract or dissipate specific influences.

Personal Worries - A term used to describe anything associated with a person's physical body or once was part of or has intimate contact with the body. Personal concerns include blood, semen, hair, clothes, signature, photography, etc.

Poisoned through the feet - A term used to describe when a person has walked or passed through pixie dust placed in their path to affect them adversely.

Reader - A root or spiritual practitioner who is psychically endowed.

Root/Root - 1) The part of a plant that attaches it to the ground 2) A spell or work 3) A mojo hand or talisman.

Root-worker - A Hoodoo practitioner.

Executions - A term used by candelabra that refers to the practice of lighting a new candle for the same intention shortly before an old one runs out until it achieves satisfactory results

Establish intentions - Make a firm decision about something you want to be, do, or have and then continue to be, do, or have it. Making your decision is the first step; the second step is to perform a symbolic act like a spell or ritual and then continue to think, speak, and act according to your intentions.

Lighting the Lights - This refers to preparing a candle for an individual's petition and praying on it every day until it runs out.

Throwing - A term that refers to the throwing of powders in which a person will step on or through them. See also Poisoning through the feet.

Two-Headed Doctor - A root-worker, or spiritual practitioner, who is also a reader.

CHAPTER 15

Witchy Tips

Freeze your candles before using them. Not only does this make your candles burn for a lot longer once they're used, but freezing them also help to purify their energy.

As a beginner Pagan or Witch, tools can help direct and amplify your energy. Some practitioners argue that tools have no power and that you already possess all the power. However, as an animist, I believe that herbs, crystals, animals, and other elements have their consciousness. When used in magic or ritual, these elements can channel their power to intensify it. It's worth mentioning that most of these tools can be found in nature (in your backyard, forest, or beach), or you can purchase them inexpensively at the dollar or grocery store.

Here are some items you can use in your witchcraft practice that don't require you to break the bank:
Candles: votives, tapers, bell candles, tealights, etc. White candles can be used as a substitute for any other color.
Chalice: You can use a wine cup or stemmed champagne glass instead of a more expensive chalice.
Jars and bottles: Reuse old spaghetti sauce and pickle jars to store herbs and curios. You can also learn how to do jar spells.
Athame: An old wood-handle kitchen knife can work just fine.
Bowls and baskets: Use these to hold offerings on your altar or when you harvest herbs and other natural items. You can find these at the dollar store or thrift stores or use what you already have at home. Bowls can also hold water and salt to represent the elements of water and earth for Wicca.
Stones and crystals: You don't need to buy expensive crystals and stones. Simply use a river stone, a piece of coral from the beach, or a rock from a place you feel drawn to.
Herbs: Grow your on a sunny windowsill or in your own garden using a bag of soil. You can also buy them from the grocery store. Your spice cabinet may already be full of magical herbs.

It's important to keep a record of your spiritual journey. Use any notebook or journal as your spiritual journal, also known as a grimoire.

Document your magical knowledge, spells, and sabbats. Just jot notes as you go or organize it as you like. Review your notes and have a chronological record of your journey. Use a binder with page protectors for a more organized way to keep records.

Quicky Witch Tips

Write a protective sigil inside your door to prevent bad energies from entering your room.

Making sigils yourself works better because you pour your intention into it and can be a great way to manifest.

White candles can replace any candle when doing candle magic.

Clear quartz can replace any crystal.

I'm sure you have heard of this one, but it bears repeating. When drinking your daily coffee/tea, stir clockwise to manifest something and anti-clockwise to let go of something. Repeat your favorite affirmations as you stir.

Salt baths absorb bad energies, so having a salt bath once in a while helps balance your energies.

Write an affirmation in a bay leaf and burn it to manifest it.
Always keep iron on you for protection.

Work with the moon phases and its phases to make your spells more powerful.

Keep a sigil in your phone case for protection.

After giving an offering to a deity, return it to the Earth.

Drink mugwort tea for lucid dreaming/astral projection (don't drink it if you are pregnant!!)

Before you put a crystal under water or in the sun, research it.

Keep a dream journal. It helps with lucid dreaming. Put an amethyst under your pillow to sleep better and to recall your dreams.

Charge your tarot/oracle cards by putting a crystal on top of them while you are not using them.

Mix moon or sun water with your cosmetics for a quick beauty spell.

Try to do an activity to connect yourself with each element every day. (ex, a bath for water, walking barefoot for earth, lighting a candle for fire, singing for air)

Quicky Magic Tip:

Burn stick incense as a natural timer for meditation. When the incense is finished burning, and the scent dissipates, you will know it is time to slowly bring your practice to an end.

Using an actual alarm or timer for meditation will leave you with anticipation, disrupting your meditation.

Before sweeping away any stagnant or negative energy in your sacred space, bless your Besom by running it through the smoke of White Sage, Rosemary, or Lavender. This will help purify the energy of your besom and call upon the spirits of light for assistance as you sweep between this world and the spirit world.

If you have trouble visualizing energy or feeling it, rub your hands together quickly and then take them apart. Feel that kinetic energy from your body moves between them. Now, try to manipulate it. I do this with almost every spell; it helps me feel the energy move and visualize it.

Place a "Burden Basket" close to your front door. Before entering, leave your troubles there and let the wind carry them away.

Burn your loose incense over a layer of salt. When it's done, stir with your magical intentions and combine salt and ash to make your black protection salt.

Save your altar dust and remnants when you clean and reorganize it. It's excellent for protection.

Make time to journal. Writing your words creates something beyond thought. This helps to manifest. Manifesting starts action and movement!

Never throw your burnt herbs in the bin after a spell or ritual. Bury it in your garden or throw it to the wind.

Hang 3 bells by your door to keep out unwanted spirits. Chant 3 times.. " guard my home, bells on the door. Only let blessings walk on my floor. Block all evil and dark arts, and may only good approach our hearts."

To end bad luck on paper, write out the problem. "From paper to fire, from fire to ash, from ash to ember, this curse must surrender.' then burn the paper.

Doorstep Rice Spell
Fill up a jar with raw white rice without placing a cap on it. Put the jar by the front door for protection. Rice does not repel evil but instead absorbs it. Replace with fresh raw rice weekly or as needed.

Do not bring old rice back into your home or cook it. Dispose of it outside of your home by burning, scattering, or throwing it away.

Altar Tip

Sprinkle cinnamon on your altar space for protection, good luck, money, love, and a boost to your spell work.

Clapping Hands

Provides instant cleansing and raising power. Only a few know that a secondary chakra resides in each center of your palms. Ancient techniques advise us to vigorously clap our hands once or twice right before we cast a spell to let the energy flow from you. Also, we do this every time we feel stagnant, or anytime we ask for divine help. You just clap your hands and then raise them facing the sky, acting as a beacon of energy signaling the divine realms, inviting spirits and angels. Or we could be pulling a Mr. Miyagi (1984 Karate Kid).

Do you feel like your spell jar is losing its effects? If it worked the first time, there is no need to make a new one. Give it a good shake and light a new candle to reignite the workings.

Your computers and cell phones are portals that bring energies from others into your space. Cleanse them well and cleanse them often.

Coffee can be used to speed up spells. Mostly used for love, money, and success spells. It's also a good ingredient to add to motivational spells.

Freeze your candles. It helps them burn longer.

Place a bowl (or small glass) of salt and bay leaves in any room of your home to absorb negative energy! When you feel it has served its purpose, dispose of the ingredients as you see fit.

Sprinkle some basil in your wallet, purse, or backpack to attract prosperity. Add cinnamon to ensure it arrives fast and sweet.

Hidden Home Spell
"Give your house a name that only you will know. It will keep your enemies from targeting and cursing your spaces and protect you from psychic attack while safely inside."

A quick way to attract positive energy while simultaneously deflecting negative energy is to always keep a metal key on you—Magicc keys open doors of opportunity.
Old metal keys are the best. They have unlocked many doors before finding their way to you. They will both guide and protect you. Keys are sacred to Hecate, Goddess of Witchcraft and Crossroads.

Red brick dust is used in spells of protection and cleansing. A line of red bri dust across your doorway is an old way to protect a house from unwanted presence. Add it to mojo bags or amulets for personal protection. Or mix with vinegar or ammonia a cleansing floor wash.

Red Brick Dust is a traditional protective and cleansing powder used to clean your front steps. Window sills or other entrances or doorways. It can be mixed with floor washes or sprinkled directly to ward off evil and curses and keep enemies away.

Place star anise on your altar to increase its power. Burn star anise to increase psychic awareness. Place star anise under your pillow for protection against nightmares. Carry star anise for luck and protection against the evil eye.

Use lemon juice to write sigils everywhere.
Doorposts, doors, walls, cabinets, books, book pages, work desks...
The "ink" is invisible, so the possibilities are endless. Moreover, lemon juice is generally safe on most surfaces (aside from brass-plated items, which it damages) and smells nice.

Bonus points: lemons are associated with cleansing and purification, which can add a little boost to your sigils, wards, etc.

Rowan twigs and strings of red. Deflect all harm, gossip, and dread. String together Rowan twigs using red string. To make crosses for good luck and magickal protection. Twist marjoram and thyme around mistletoe and hang them in the corners of each room to attract luck and good fortune.

Simple Banishing Spell

Write the names) of the person/people or thing you want to banish on paper. Write your name over the top of what you want to banish so your name crosses names/things out.
Dress a black candle with banishing oil and light it
Say this chant 3 times:
'I cover you, I cross you, I command you, I compel you, (name of person) get out of my life! Burn the piece of paper the flame of the candle.   Let the candle burn out. Throw away the remains in the trash as a symbol of banishment.

Use honey to sweeten the outcome of your spells.
Add it to witch jars, potions, or even cooking to sweeten the disposition of others.
And, of course, don't forget to leave out a little as an offering for the faeries, particularly if objects have been going missing around your home!

Pick up the first acorn you find in Autumn and carry it in your purse or pocket all through fall and winter. It will protect you from negativity and bring prosperity and good luck to you all through the dark months. Then, come Spring, return it to nature as a 'thank you' for all its assistance.

CHAPTER 16

Divination

Divination is a practice deeply rooted in human history, spanning cultures and civilizations across time. At its core, divination is the art of seeking insight and guidance from mystical or supernatural sources to gain an understanding of the past, present, or future. It's a fascinating journey involving various methods, such as reading omens in nature, interpreting patterns in celestial bodies, or deciphering symbols through intricate tools like tarot cards, runes, and crystal balls. Divination offers us a unique perspective into the unknown, providing a glimpse into the threads of fate that weave through our lives.

Manifesting with Colored Ink

Blue - clarity, creativity, faith
Pink- love, kindness, harmony
Purple - intuitive, needs, imagination
Black - protection, banishing, releasing
Silver - emotions, reflection, moon energy
Orange - joy, optimism, excitement
Brown - earthly needs, material needs, security
Red - motivation, ambition, passion
Yellow - strength, positive thought, sun energy
Green - healing, wealth, growth

Knot Your Troubles

You can use this one no matter what your problem is. If you choose a color for the yarn to suit your purpose, you can fine-tune the spell to your particular situation.

All you need for this spell is a piece of yarn in the appropriate color, at least 12 inches long.

Now hold the yarn, with one end in each hand, and pull it taut. Think about your problem (just one per spell, please).
Concentrate on your difficult situation and start tying knots in the yarn. Visualize all your troubles getting bound up in the knots and trapped there. Keep tying until you feel it's enough.

Take the knotted yarn outside and bury it to keep your problems away.

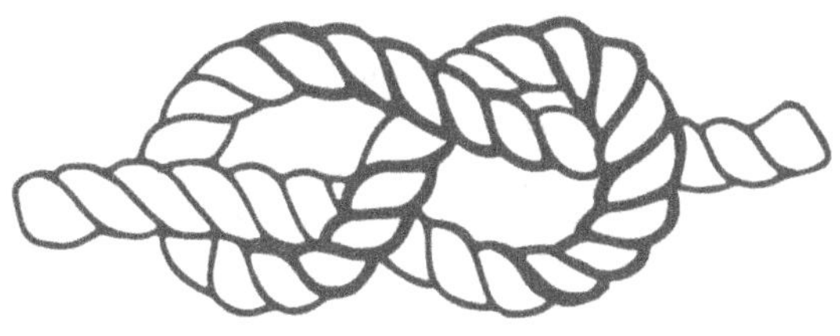

Runes

The Germanic tribes of Northern Europe used runes for religious and secular purposes—the earliest examples of runes phonetically representing language date back to the second century BCE. The development of the rune alphabet was spurred by increased trade activity with Mediterranean cultures that already had a fully developed alphabet.

Before, the runes were primarily used as a magical system of pictographs representing natural forces and objects. People believed that invoking the appropriate rune could contact the corresponding force in nature.

There were several different runic alphabets throughout Northern Europe over the centuries, but the most common is the Germanic alphabet.

Tyr / Thorn
Tyr represents the powerful god of warriors, known for his fierce determination.

Beorc / Berkana / Berkano
Beorc represents the birch tree and new beginnings.

Ehwaz / EH
Ehwaz represents the noble and powerful horse.

Man / Mannaz / Mann
Mannaz represents the concept of humanity.

Lagu / Laguz /Logr / Laf
Laguz represents the raw and untamed energy of water.

Ing / Inguz / Ingwaz
Inguz represents the god Ing and symbolizes the abundance of fertility.

Dag / Dagaz / Daeg
Daeg represents the end of one cycle and start of a new one.

Odal / Othila / Othala / Ethel
Othala represents home and family, symbolizing those around us.

Feoh / Fehu / FE / FA
Fehu, a rune that translates to "cattle," denotes abundance and fertility.

UR / Uruz
Uruz, a rune that translates to "wild ox," represents determination, courage.

Thorn / Thurisaz
Thurisaz is a complex symbol that has a few different translations..

AS / Ansur / Ansuz / OS
Ansuz symbolizes the breath of Odin and can represent the concept of a god.

Runes

 **Rad / Raido / Reidh / Raidho**
Raido represents the concept of a journey, both literally and spiritually.

 **Ken / Kenaz / Kano**
Kenaz represents the concept of a torch, which symbolizes illumination.

 **Gyfu / Gebo**
Gifu represents the gift or exchange.

 **Wyn / Wunjo / Wynn**
Wunjo brings the concept of joy.

 **Hagal / Hagalaz / Haegl / Hagal**
Hagalaz represents hail, symbolizing the destructive power of nature.

 **NYD / Nauthiz / Naudhr**
Nauthiz represents necessity and the struggle that comes with it.

 **IS / Isa / ISS**
Isa symbolizes the concept of ice or being frozen.

 **Jera / Ger**
Jera signifies the idea of reaping the rewards of one's labor.

 **elhaz / Algiz / Eolh**
Eihwaz is a rune that represents the ash or yew tree.

 **Peorth / Perth / Perthro**
Perthro represents the concept of fortune.

 **Eoh / Eihwaz**
Eolh represents the concept of the elk, but in the context of protection.

 **Sigel / Sowelu / Sowilo**
Sigel represents the life-giving energy of the sun and the illumination it brings.

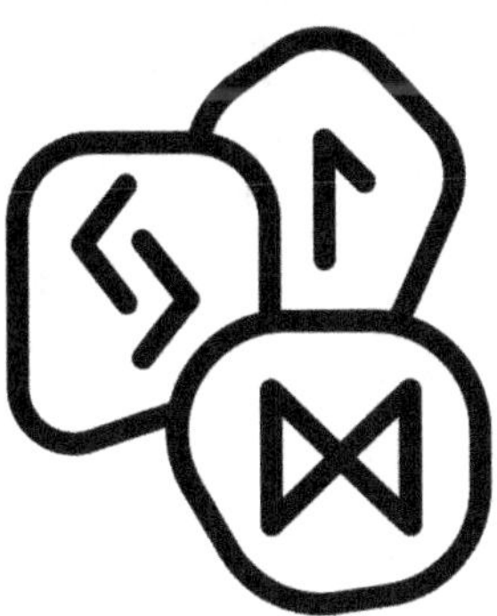

Tarot Cards

Tarot is an intricate divination system consisting of 78 cards divided into major and minor arcana cards. Heavily relying on classical mythology and symbolism, tarot allows one to receive answers to events by interpreting messages based on how the cards are dealt. This can be done utilizing card spreads like the classic Celtic cross or a simple 3 card past, present, and future layout.

Oracle Cards

Less structured than tarot, oracle cards use a combination of artwork and written interpretations, which can sometimes include exercises. Oracle cards can be based on nearly any subject matter and are open to various styles and formats. Perfect for guiding without the intricacies associated with tarot.

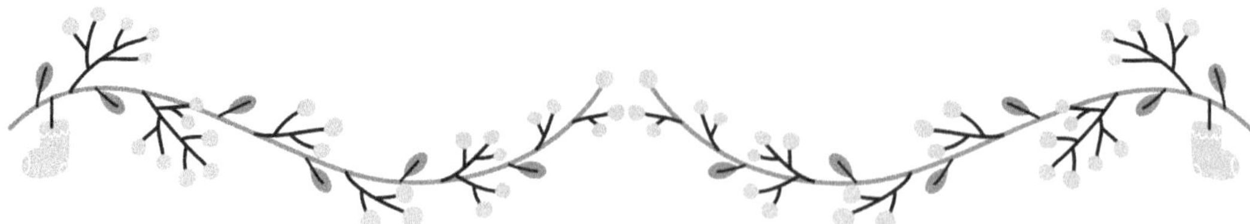

Draw Your Cards

There are multiple ways to select the cards for your reading.
Cutting the deck with one hand and pulling the card on top is a simple, no-nonsense approach. Another way is to hold the deck in one hand and tilt it to reveal a gap; you can take the top card. Next, you can fan the cards out and choose the card your intuition pulls you to. Finally, draw a single card for a simple reading or several cards for what's known as a spread. Tarot spreads can speak more broadly to your situation. The more cards you use in a spread, the more in-depth the reading tends to be, but a big spread can be overwhelming for beginners.

After you choose your card(s), lay them down in your pattern for the spread. Now, you can gaze at them, pay attention to what comes immediately to mind, and then go from there.

Interpret the card(s) you draw.
Stay focused on the cards and the feelings you get, connect the cards to your senses, and write down what comes to mind. After your impressions are completely logged, look in the companion book for the general meaning of the cards you pulled. That's it. Eazy Peezey.

Yule/Winter Solstice

Card 1 - Gifts of the season.
Card 2 - Lessons and blessings to hold.
Card 3 - What needs to die so I can live?
Card 4 - How to bring the Sun back.

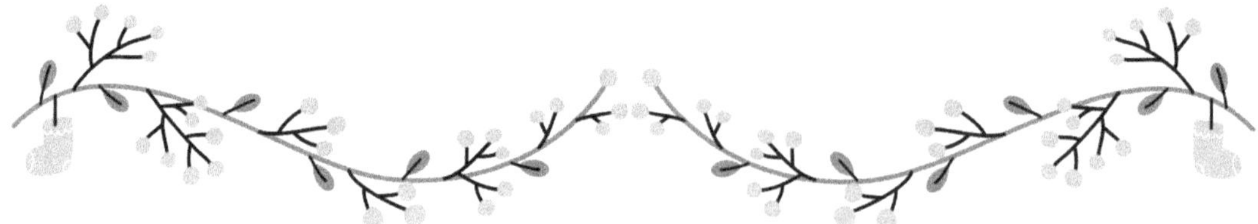

Yule

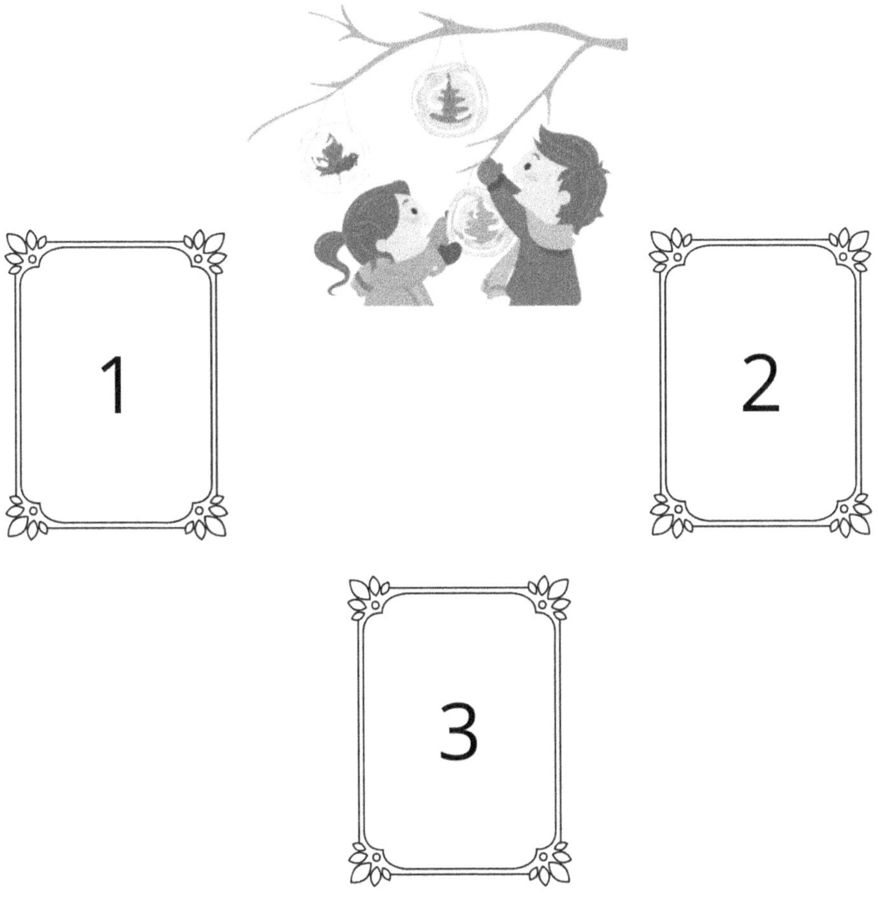

Card 1 - Holly King: What am I leaving behind?
Card 2 - Oak King: What will I be growing in the year to come?
Card 3 - Goodwill: How can I share good cheer with others at this time?

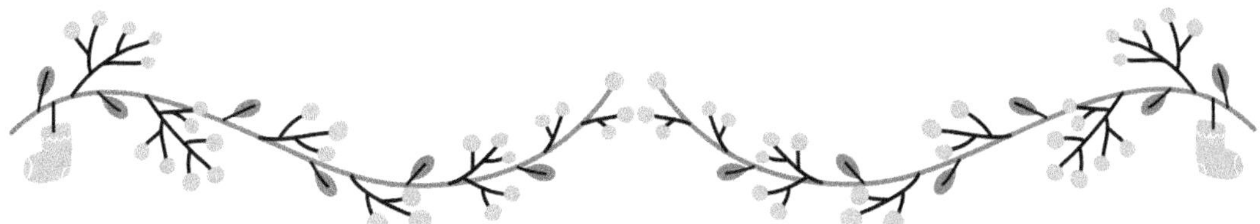

Yule

Card 1 - My Night - Shadow self and spiritual matters.
Card 2 - My Day - Extreme affairs and external self.
Card 3 - My Fire - Creative spark, ambition and motivation.

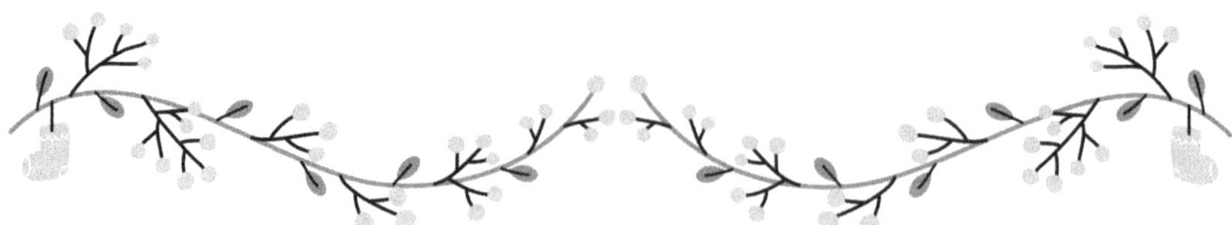

Yule

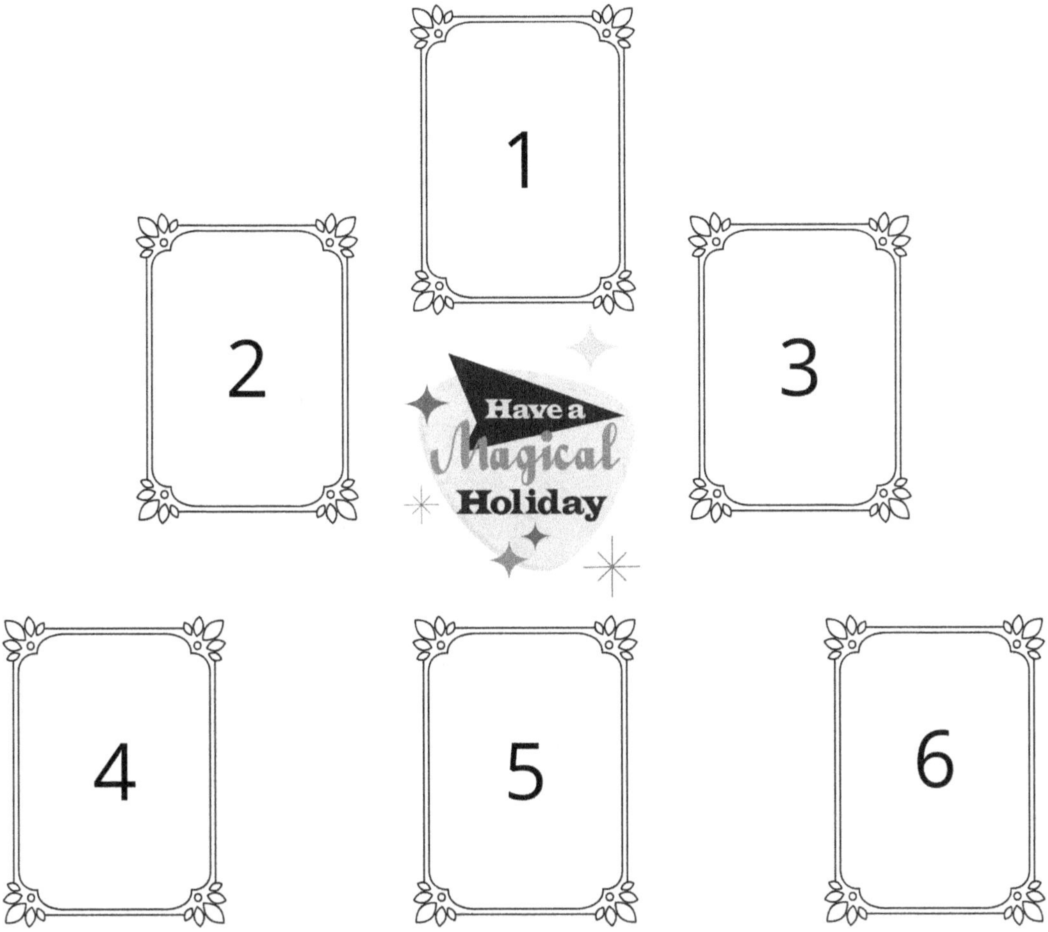

Card 1 - Where have I grown?
Card 2 - What lessons were learned?
Card 3 - What mistakes were made?
Card 5 - What to focus on going into the next year?
Card 6 - Message from the Holly King.

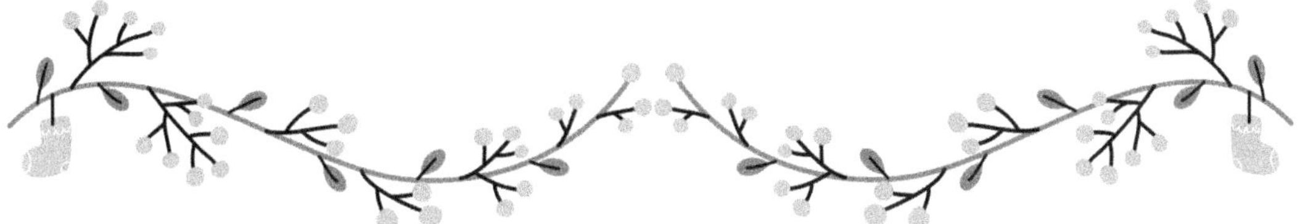

Hello Darkness

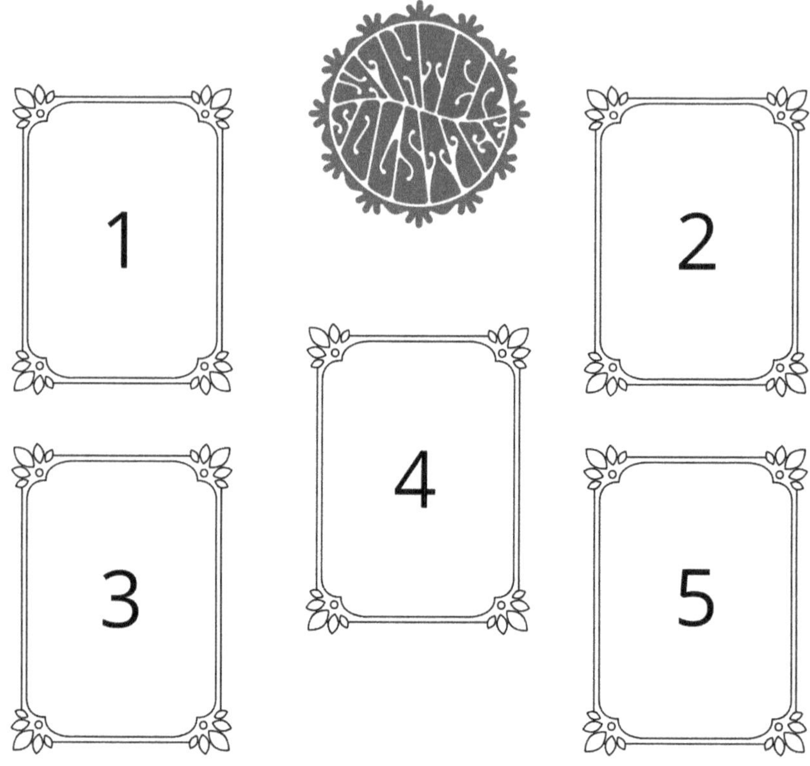

Card 1 - What must I let go of to move on?
Card 2 - What does the darkness reveal?
Card 3 - What shadows must I embrace?
Card 4 - What area of my life needs light?
Card 5 - As the light grows, where should my focus be?

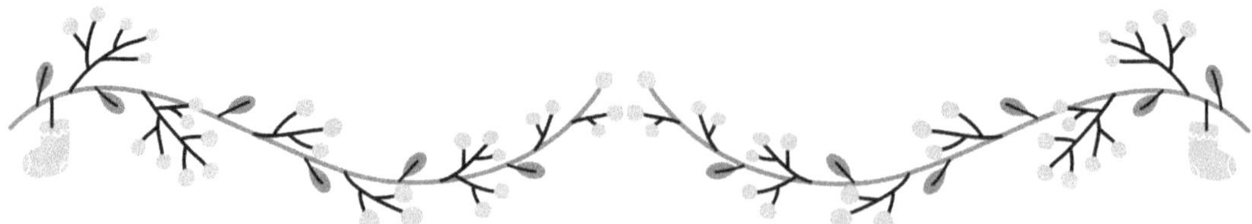

The Darkest of Nights

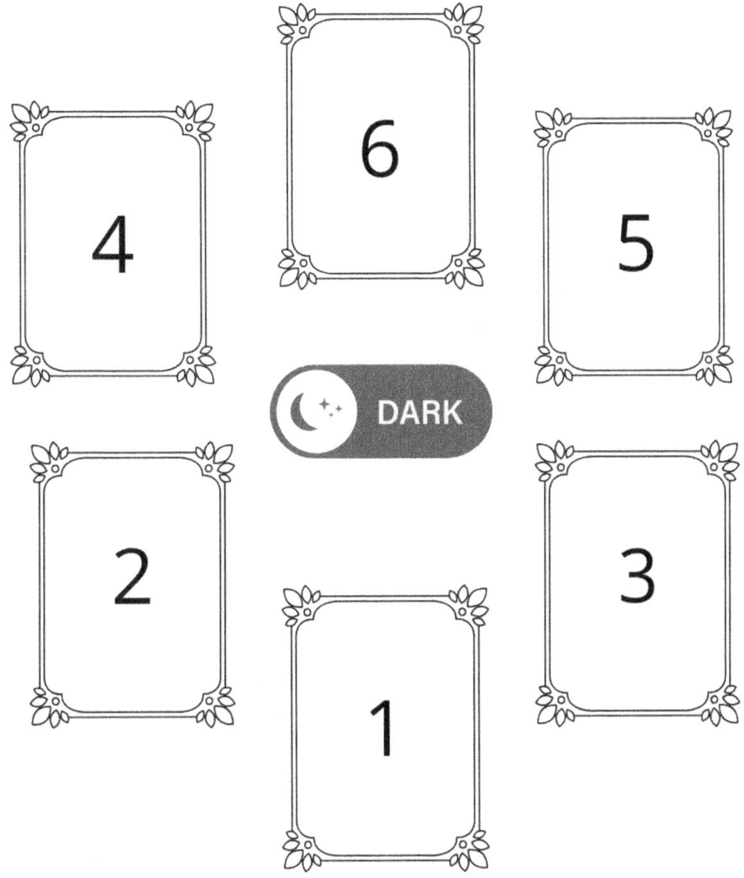

Card 1 - What's hiding in the darkness / my subconscious that I need to explore?

Card 2 - What will give me strength as I face my shadow self?

Card 3 - What must I work to release during this season of rest?

Card 4 - What aspect of my life requires hibernation?

Card 5 - How will this hibernation benefit me?

Card 6 - What lessons can I learn from this season?

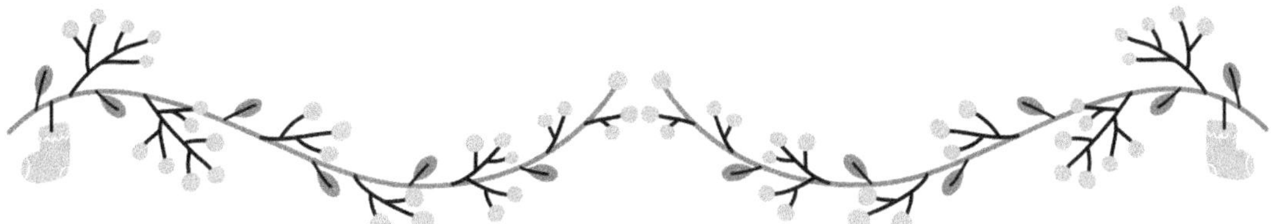

CHAPTER 17

Symbols

Symbols have played a significant role throughout history, serving as a means of communication, expression, and identity. From ancient to modern times, symbols have been used to represent abstract concepts, convey religious beliefs, and create social cohesion. They have been etched into cave walls, inscribed on tablets, and emblazoned on flags. The power of symbols lies in their ability to capture the essence of an idea in a single image. They can evoke strong emotions, inspire action, and unite people across cultures and languages. The cross, for example, represents both religious devotion and colonial domination. Symbols are not static; they evolve with society, and their meanings can change. Symbols remain a crucial aspect of communication, and understanding their meaning and context is essential for comprehending the complex ways in which humans communicate.

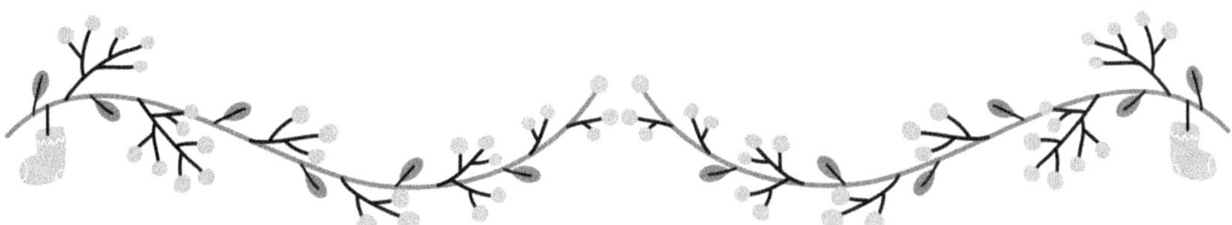

CHAPTER 18

Quicky Spirit Guides

Ascended Masters

Humans like us but who have transcended the spiritual plane (ex: Buddha)

Star Beings

Star beings are galactic entities whom you may have already known from the past

Animal Spirit Guides

Totems or Power Animals that provide healing and support during tough times

Nature Spirits

Ethereal personifications of nature who have come since the beginning of time

Ancestral Guides

They are spirit guides coming directly from our genetic lineage

Angelic Guides

Angelic Spirit Guides More commonly known as your guardian angel

Elemental Guides

Elementals Spirits who possess earthly elements such as Earth, water, fire, and air

See my previous books on Spirit Guides.

Who's Who

Spirit Companion

These spirits have chosen to form a close relationship with a human friend. They generally seek a practitioner they feel can form a bond or companionship. They are not guides or teachers; however, they may fill those roles for their practitioners if they choose to do so. Most companions are found during the natural course of a spirit worker's spiritual journey or even through spirit adoption.

Spirit Guardians

These spirits choose to protect a person, place, or item. Guardians may be assigned to an individual at birth or during different times in their life. An individual may also seek them out. In times of danger, a guardian may be called upon to help keep their practitioner safe.

Spirit Guides

There are a few different types of spirit guides. Lifetime guides are those an individual will have with them their entire lives. These guides generally appear and are assigned at birth. Depending on several factors, they may choose to leave when death occurs or continue with the individual. Temporary or short-term guides will show up from time to time in an individual's life.

Spirit Familiars

Familiar spirits have a special connection with a practitioner. They can take on one or many different forms and aid the practitioner. They share a bond regarding their craft. They also can provide companionship and protection.

HOW TO COMMUNICATE WITH YOUR SPIRIT GUIDES

Your spirit guides communicate with you using your clair abilities.
Ex: clairsentience (gut feeling), clairvoyance (clear seeing), clairaudience (clear hearing), etc.
Or through Synchronicities, downloads, and dreams.
You can communicate with your spirit guides by...
 Talking to them out loud or in your head/ thoughts.
 Asking for answers in dreams or through signs.
 Use divination tools like tarot cards and pendulum, or leave a cup/bowl of water with questions/intentions on a piece of paper. Don't drink water since it absorbs energy.

Your spirit guides always have your best interest, if it doesn't feel right to you, stop contacting said
'spirit guide'. Cleanse and protect/banish entities from your environment.

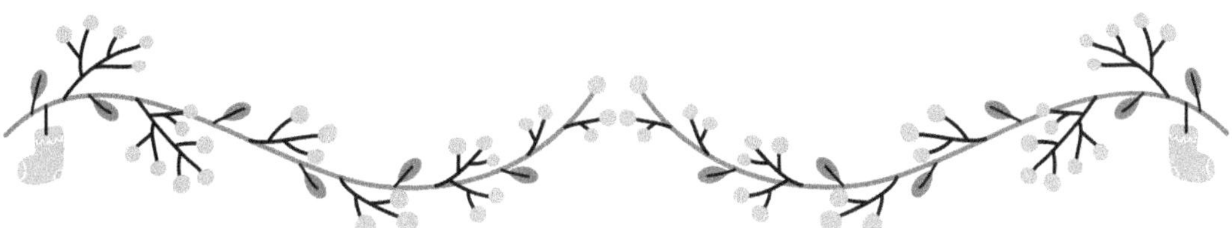

TYPES OF LIGHTWORKERS

Grid Workers - maintain the grids and gateways of the Earth.

Transmuters - have a high frequency and use it to transmute negative energy.

Lightkeepers - embody light and maintain a high vibration and loving presence.

Healers - have unique gifts that help them to heal humanity.

Seers - are clairvoyant and have their third eye opened.

Divine Blueprint Holders - are attuned to the codes needed for awakening.

Astral Travelers - are capable of lucid dreaming and astral travel.

Messengers - receive guidance from angels, ascension masters, or their higher self.

Manifestors - are powerful manifesters who can obtain instant results.

Way Showers - lead by example, influencing others to do the same.

Unifiers - look for commonalities in diverse patterns and philosophies to bring people together.

Ascension Guides - help people navigate the enlightenment process and overcome obstacles.

What Are Light Codes? Light codes are streams of information transmitted throughout the universe. They carry information from the sun, moon, stars, and from other dimensions. Light codes are also in your DNA, physical body, and human energy field (aura). They work at any and all levels of your being.

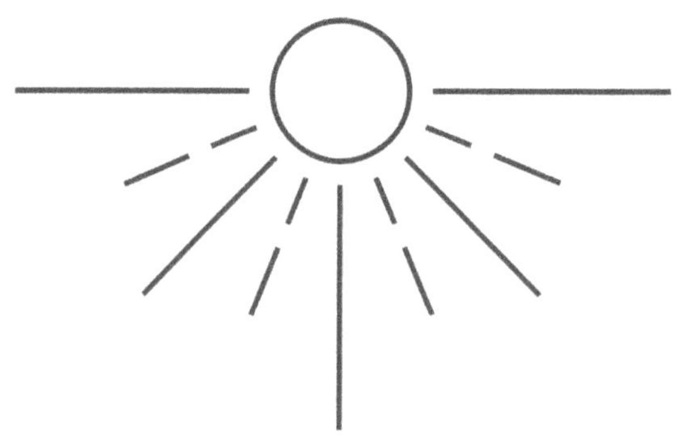

Animal Guides at a Glance

Elements: A strong connection to Mother Earth, playful humor, easy to relate to and connect with.
Talents: Alignment with our inner nature, protection, and enhanced instincts.
Traits: You're protective of family and community, physically oriented, and strongly connected to the natural environment.

Nature Spirits at a Glance

Elements: Playful creativity, manifestation skills, and the ability to heal the physical world (including our bodies and the environment).
Talents: Lightheartedness, a strong bond with animals, and a natural talent for magic.
Traits: You have a natural sense for power places and ley lines; you make an excellent peaceful warrior for the environment and are a natural healer.

Ascended Masters at a Glance

Elements: A wealth of knowledge about life on Earth, compassion for the human journey, the ability to connect people with their higher self
Talents: Discernment, wisdom, and gratitude.
Traits: You're a great teacher; you have lots of knowledge from past lives and a strong sense of responsibility.

Elemental Guides

An Elemental is a spirit that inhabits one of the earth's elements, such as earth, fire, air, or water. Elementals are not all benevolent allies for humanity, but one that is could be seen as an Elemental Spirit Guide. Gnomes are the elemental beings connected to the Earth element. Undines are connected to water. Sylphs are connected to the element of air, and Pyraustas (sometimes called Salamanders) are the elemental beings connected to the warmth ether and to fire.

Besides the 4 types of elemental beings, many kinds dwell in the etheric and astral levels of the Earth and sustain nature and humankind. Flower faeries, tree elves and nature sprites are some of these additional types of beings.

Ancestor Guide

An ancestor spirit guide is a spiritual guide connected to you through your genetic or spiritual lineage. They may be deceased loved ones you knew in your lifetime who are now guiding you from the realms of spirit. But more often the case, ancestor guides come from further back in your lineage. This could be a great, great, great grandmother. Or someone like an ancient Yogi Guru you followed in a past incarnation. Ancestor spirits guide and support you in many ways. They may step forward as guides to support you in healing, wounding, limiting beliefs or traumas that have been passed down through generations, or they may be practical day-to-day guides.

Gods and Goddesses

Gods and Goddesses are spiritual beings who, in certain cultures or spiritual traditions, are honored as being Divine. Goddesses and gods are vehicles for Divine energy, and they often have vibrant stories, personalities, and character traits that give a face to the Divine Life Force.

They are typically beings who have gone through a physical incarnation journey in another cycle, another epoch of time, and they now live in the spirit world and act as allies and often teacher guides for those still on physical incarnation journeys.

As spirit guides, they offer an example or template for how certain Divine qualities manifest

Ascended Masters

Ascended Masters are spiritual beings who have lived earthly lives and mastered their paths of spiritual transformation to ascend. They can be powerful teacher guides for us on our personal ascension paths, and their goal is our enlightenment.
Ascended Masters have been down in the trenches, so to speak. So they deeply understand the emotional and physical challenges we have and can offer powerful guidance to help us learn our lessons and more vibrantly thrive in our lives. Some ascended masters are Jesus, Buddha, Quan Yin, Merlin, Sai Baba, Sanat Kumara, and Saint Germain.

Star Beings

Star Beings Benevolent star beings can act as spirit guides for members of humanity, especially Starseed souls. A Star being spirit guide may be a being who you have known in past or future life incarnation in some other star system like the Pleiades, Arcturian, Andromedon, Lyrian, Sirian, Orion Star System, and many others.

Star Being guides are most often present to help us as humanity and individuals to evolve, grow as souls, and progress on the ascension path. The most helpful star being guides are those who have been through the ascension process, and can now help us to navigate the present ascension journey we as humanity are undergoing

Angels

Angels are spiritual beings from the angelic hierarchy who can act as Divine messengers and spiritual guides for humanity. Angels, Archangels and Guardian Angels are the types of angelic beings that most often work with humans directly.

Angels work with people by communicating messages, transmitting uplifting and inspiring energies, as well as triggering your intuition and offering nudges of guidance to keep you moving in the right direction throughout your incarnation. Your guardian angel knows your unique soul purpose, mission, and also strengths and can guide and support you in coming into your highest truth and vibrantly thriving in your life.

Animal Spirits

Animal Spirit Guides, also known as Power Animals, or Totems, are types of spirit guides that show up in animal form.They guide us in our lives through relaying inspiration, offering healing, and even lending direct support in challenging times.

Animal guides spiritual focus is around helping you to thrive as a physical being which includes staying grounded, centered and in tune with the earth. This does not mean that they don't have powerful spiritual wisdom, magic and power to relay though.

Certain animal spirit guides like Jaguar, Vulture, or Snake are well known for traveling through the veil between the physical and spirit world, and when they show up in your life it may be to help you to the same.

Familiar Spirit

A non-corporeal entity that is known (familiar) to a witch. This can be the spirit of a deceased person or animal (common), or a spirit that has always existed as a non-corporeal entity (rare), and can take any form they choose. These spirts can neip the practitioner with their magical workings, serve as a guide, or even protect from magical attacks. This is the traditional definition and usage in the practices of witchcraft.

Familiar Pet

Familiar (pet) A corporeal pet animal belonging to a witch. Can be any animal that is living that the owner must care for by feeding, grooming. and cleaning up after. This usage was created by 14th - 17th century witch hunters as a means to manufacture 'evidence' against a person accused of witchcraft by the Christian church.

This usage has also been popularized by fairytales, Hollywood, and other pop-culture, further distorting the definition.

Archangels

Archangels are revered in various religious and spiritual practices worldwide, yet their existence transcends any particular belief system. They are not gendered, but they embody both masculine and feminine energies, which sometimes cause them to be referred to as "he" or "she." However, the Archangels are not defined by such labels; you may use whatever name or pronoun feels most appropriate to you. Remember, they are beings of pure energy, not physical attributes.

The Archangels are devoted to spreading love and harmony. They were specifically created to assist human beings in their earthly journey. Whenever you feel uncertain or fearful, call upon the Archangels for guidance. They will provide you with the blessings you need. Take a moment to express gratitude to the Archangels for the love and light they bring into your life.

Ariel
Azrael
Chamuel
Gabriel
Haniel
Jeremiel
Jophiel
Metatron
Michael
Raguel
Raphael
Raziel
Sandalphon
Uriel
Zadkiel

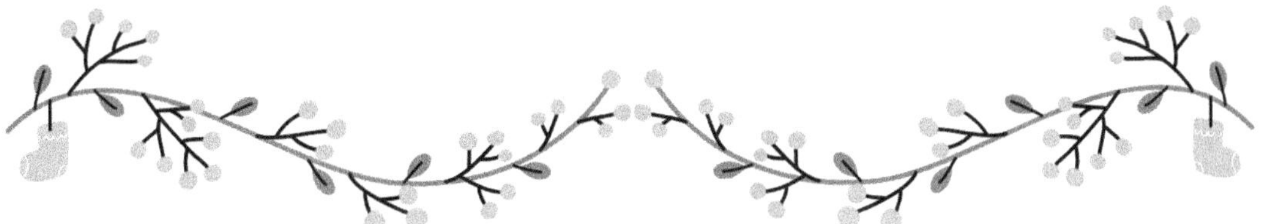

Star Beings

Star beings are galactic entities whom you may have already known from the past.

The Pleiadian Starseed
The Andromedan Starseed
The Lyran Starseed
The Sirian Starseed
The Orion Starseed
The Arcturian Starseed
The Mintaka Starseed
The Venusian Starseed
The Reptilian Starseed
The Martian Starseed
The Avian Starseed
The Polarian Starseed

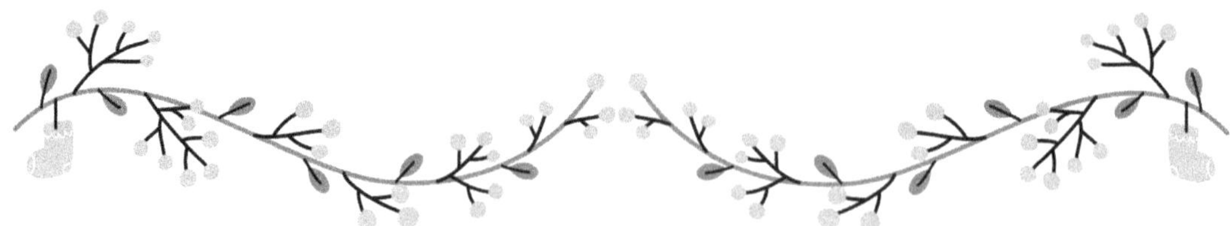

Types of Starseeds

Orion Starseeds - from the Orion constellation, likely incarnated elsewhere before coming to Earth.

Arcturian Starseeds - from Arcturus, an advanced, other-dimensional star being.

Pleiadian Starseeds - from the Pleiades star system, familiar with Earth and here to elevate humanity.

Draconian Starseeds - from the Draco constellation, linked to dragons and reptiles, some here to wake up humanity.

Sirian Starseeds - from the Dog Star Sirius, the brightest star in the night sky.

Lyran Starseeds - from the Lyra constellation, where the first humans and ancient beings called Felines and Avians originated.

Starseeds - are believed to have originated from other planets and dimensions. The different types of starseeds include Venusian, Martian, Andromedan, Polarian, Hadarian, and Alpha Centaurians.

Venusian starseeds - are Hathors who teach love and compassion. Martian starseeds participated in human evolution. Andromedan starseeds are rare guardians of the seventh dimension. Polarian starseeds were giants in height. Hadrian starseeds spread unconditional love. Alpha Centaurians are advanced civilizations who seeded some of their souls on Earth to aid our planet's development.

Agarthan Beings - According to the Hollow Earth theory, the Earth is hollow with another civilization living inside it called the Agarthans. Nowadays, Agarthans are said to be incarnating on Earth's surface to help us.

Anunnaki Starseeds - They are a branch of the Sirian civilization and were involved in creating humans in the beginning. They lived on a planet called Nibiru and are often referred to as Sumerian gods. The Anunnaki Starseeds are a new type of incarnating beings.

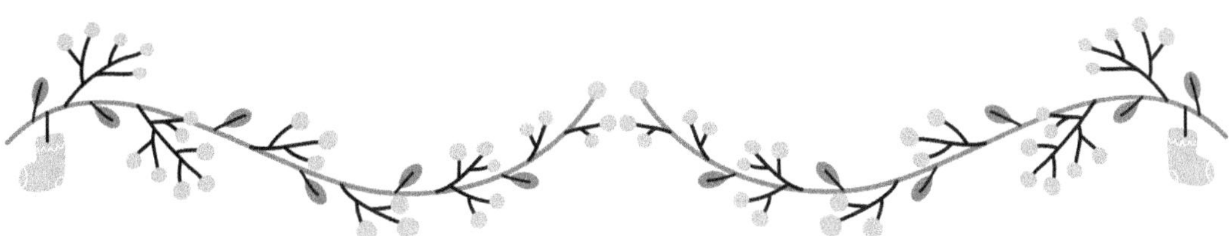

CHAPTER 18

Correspondence Flowers and Herbs

These worksheets can help you organize and personalize correspondences for your Sabbat celebration. You can use them to research and document correspondences that are meaningful to you and your unique way of celebrating the Sabbat. Feel free to add other herbs and flowers to personalize your unique celebration of this Sabbat. In addition, there is a section on how to dry herbs and make an infusion oil.

The author and publisher cannot take any responsibility for any adverse effects of using plants. Always seek advice from a professional before using a plant medicinally.

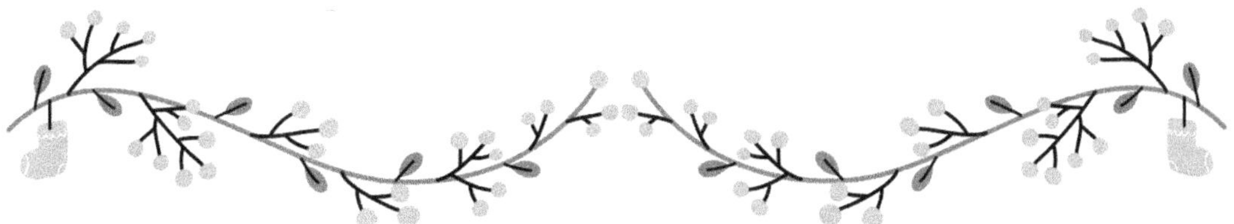

Foraging Calendar

January, February, and March
Chickweed, Common Mallow Leaves, Common Sorrel, Cowberry, Crow Garlic, Dandelion Root, Garlic Mustard, Ground Elder, Hairy Bittercress, Nettles, Pignut, Sheep's Sorrel, Silver Birch Sap, Wild Garlic, Winter Cress, and Wood Sorrel

April, May, and June
Beech Leaves, Borage, Broom, Chickweed, Cleavers, Common Poppy, Dandelion Leaves and Roots, Dog Rose Flowers, Elderflower, Garlic, Mustard, Ground Elder, Hawthorn Blossom, Hops, Nettles, Pignuts, Sheep's Sorrel, Spearmint, Sweet Cicely, Watercress, Wild Garlic, Wild Thyme, Wood Sorrel, and Yarrow

July, August, and September
Acorns, Apples, Beech Nuts, Bilberries, Blackberries, Burdock, Chamomile, Chickweed, Chicory, Cleavers, Common Mallow, Dandelion Leaves and Flowers, Elderberry, Fat Hen, Garlic, Mustard, Gooseberries, Hawthorn Berries, Hazelnuts, Horseradish, Juniper Berries, Nettle, Plums, Rowan Berries, Sheep's Sorrel, Spearmint, Sweet Chestnuts, Sweet Cicely, Walnuts, Wild Cherries, Wild Strawberries, Wild Thyme, Wood Sorrel, and Yarrow

October, November, and December
Chestnuts, Chickweed, Crab Apples, Hawthorn Berries, Horseradish, Nettles, Rosehips, Sheep's Sorrel, Sloes, Spearmint, Sweet Chestnuts, and Walnuts

I live in the North Eastern United States; you may find different species depending on where you live.

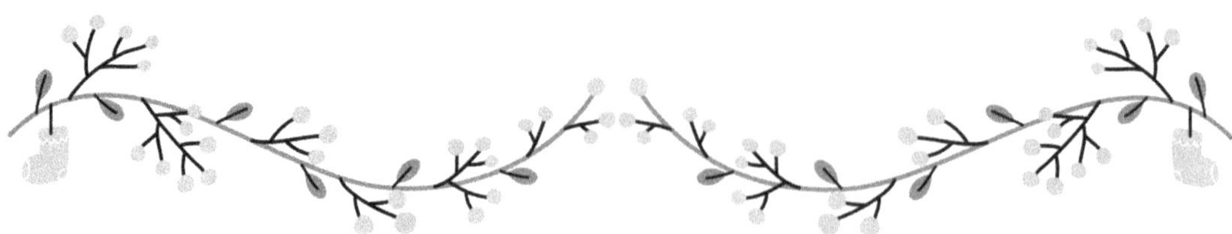

Indoor Herbs

Growing Schedule

January + February
Start perennial herb seeds indoors.

March + April
Start annual herb seeds indoors.
Pinch perennial herbs.

May + June
Move perennial herbs outdoors.
Pinch annual herbs.
Set overgrown annuals outdoors.
Second seeding of annual herbs.

July + August
Pinch second planting of annuals.
Take root cuttings of perennials.

September + October
Move perennial herb cuttings to soil indoors.

November + December
Grow + harvest perennial herbs.
Move large perennial herbs to larger pots.

Mistletoe
Viscum album
Folk Names: Birdlime, Drudenfuss, Golden Bough, Thunderbesom

Magical Properties: Mistletoe is often considered a symbol of love, protection, and fertility. Hanging mistletoe is believed to bring good luck and blessings to those beneath it. In some traditions, it is thought to possess the power to ward off negative energies and enhance spiritual connections.

Physical Properties & Essential Oil It Is/It May:
Help Hypertension.
Tonic for the nervous system.

Use Caution: Mistletoe contains compounds that can be toxic, so it should only be used under the guidance of a qualified herbalist or healthcare provider.

Mistletoe is perhaps one of the most iconic Yule plants. It has been revered in various cultures for its evergreen nature and is often used as a symbol of love and fertility. Hanging mistletoe in doorways is a popular tradition during the Yule season.

Holly

Ilex aquifolium
Folk Names: Bat's Wings, Christ's Thorn, Holm Chaste, Hulm

Magical Properties: Holly is associated with protection, especially against negative forces and ill-wishing. It symbolizes the triumph of light over darkness, making it a powerful representation of the return of the sun during the winter solstice. Holly is also believed to bring good fortune and joy.

Physical Properties & Essential Oil It Is/It May: Have astringent properties, and some historical accounts suggest it may have been used for digestive issues.

Use Caution: Holly is not commonly used in modern herbal medicine.

Holly is another evergreen plant with shiny, spiky leaves and bright red berries. It is associated with protection and good fortune. In Yule traditions, holly is often used for decorating and creating wreaths.

Pine

Pinus spp.
Folk Names: Longleaf Pine, Yellow Pine, Sweet Pine

Magical Properties: Pine is connected to endurance, purification, and rebirth. The evergreen nature of pine trees symbolizes vitality and eternal life. Pine is often used to cleanse spaces, promote healing, and attract positive energy.

Physical Properties & Essential Oil It Is/It May: Pine has been used in traditional medicine for its high vitamin C content, providing immune system support. Pine resin may also have antimicrobial properties.

Use Caution:

Pine trees are evergreen and have a strong presence during the winter months. Pine branches, cones, and needles are used in Yule decorations and rituals, symbolizing endurance and rebirth.

Juniper

Juniperus spp.
Folk Names: Aiten, Enebro, Gin Berry, Hackmatack

Magical Properties: Juniper is associated with purification, protection, and healing. It is believed to ward off negativity and invite positive energies. Juniper berries can be used in magical workings for banishing and cleansing rituals.

Physical Properties & Essential Oil It Is/It May: Juniper berries are used in herbal medicine for their diuretic properties and may be employed to support the urinary system. Juniper has historical uses for digestive issues and as an antimicrobial agent.

Use Caution:

Juniper is an evergreen shrub with aromatic berries. It is associated with purification and protection, making it a meaningful addition to Yule celebrations.

Cedar

Cedrus spp.
Folk Names: Lebanon Cedar, Tree of the Gods, Cedrus

Magical Properties:
Cedar is revered for its purifying qualities and is often used to cleanse spaces of negative energies. It is associated with protection, strength, and grounding. Cedar is used in rituals to create a sacred and spiritually charged atmosphere.

Physical Properties & Essential Oil It Is/It May: Cedarwood essential oil, derived from the wood of cedar trees, has been used in aromatherapy for relaxation and stress relief. It is also believed to have antimicrobial properties.

Use Caution:

Cedar, with its fragrant wood and evergreen needles, is often used in Yule ceremonies to cleanse and purify the space. It symbolizes strength and resilience.

Frankincense

Boswellia spp.
Folk Names: Olibanum, Frank, Luban

Magical Properties: Frankincense is considered a sacred resin with powerful spiritual properties. It is often used in rituals to enhance spiritual connection, meditation, and purification. Frankincense is associated with consecration and creating a sacred atmosphere.

Physical Properties & Essential Oil It Is/It May: Frankincense has been used traditionally for various medicinal purposes, including anti-inflammatory effects. It is sometimes used in aromatherapy and may have potential applications in joint health.

Use Caution:

Frankincense is a resin derived from the Boswellia tree. It has been used in spiritual and religious ceremonies for centuries and is often associated with purification and sacred rituals, making it a suitable addition to Yule celebrations.

Myrrh

Commiphora spp.
Folk Names: Didthin, Mirra, Bowl, Gum Myrrh

Magical Properties: Myrrh is linked to transformation, purification, and healing. It is used in rituals to banish negative energies, promote spiritual growth, and enhance meditation. Myrrh is also believed to have protective properties.

Physical Properties & Essential Oil It Is/It May: Myrrh has a long history of use in traditional medicine for its anti-inflammatory and antimicrobial properties. It has been used for oral health, wound healing, and respiratory conditions.

Use Caution:

Myrrh is a resin with a long history of use in spiritual practices. It is often associated with protection, healing, and transformation, making it a meaningful component of Yule rituals.

Bay Laurel

Laurus nobilis
Folk Names: Sweet Bay, Daphne, Apollo's Bay, Noble Laurel

Magical Properties: Bay laurel is associated with protection, success, and divination. Bay leaves are often used in rituals for psychic awareness and to attract positive energies. Bay laurel is considered a symbol of honor and accomplishment.

Physical Properties & Essential Oil It Is/It May: Bay leaves are used in traditional medicine for their mild diuretic and digestive properties. Bay laurel essential oil may be employed for its antimicrobial effects.

Use Caution:

Bay laurel is an evergreen shrub with aromatic leaves. In Yule traditions, bay leaves are sometimes used for protection and are believed to bring good luck and positive energy.

Yew

Taxus spp.
Folk Names: English Yew, Tew, Eihwaz, Yew Berry

Magical Properties: Yew is often associated with transformation, rebirth, and longevity. It is considered a powerful protective tree and is sometimes associated with rituals involving communication with the spirit world. **Caution should be exercised, as some parts of the yew are toxic.**

Physical Properties & Essential Oil It Is/It May: While yew contains compounds with potential anticancer properties (e.g., paclitaxel), it is highly toxic.

Use Caution: The medicinal use of yew should only be under the strict supervision of healthcare professionals.

Yew trees are evergreen and have a long history of symbolism in various cultures. In Yule celebrations, yew is sometimes associated with longevity and transformation, as well as protection.

Cinnamon

Cinnamomum spp.
Folk Names: Sweet Wood, Cinnamomum, Gui Zhi

Magical Properties: Cinnamon is associated with warmth, prosperity, and success. It is often used to attract abundance, enhance psychic abilities, and bring positive energy into a space. Cinnamon is also considered a powerful herb for love and passion.

Physical Properties & Essential Oil   Use Caution:
It Is/It May: Cinnamon has been studied for its potential benefits in blood sugar regulation and as an antioxidant. It is also used traditionally for digestive issues.

While not an evergreen plant, cinnamon is often used during the Yule season for its warm and comforting aroma. It is incorporated into Yule recipes, teas, and decorations.

Dehydrate Herbs

When you have more than enough fresh herbs for cooking, the BEST way to keep them is in their dehydrated form.

Sun Dry
It's called sun-dry, but do NOT dry herbs under the sun. Place in a warm spot, but avoid direct sunlight.

Air Dry
A very common method to dry herbs. It is the cheapest and most natural way of preserving your fresh herbs.

Microwave Dry
This is the fastest way, and it keeps your herbs greener.

Oven Dry
It is quicker than air and sundry, but herbs will cook a little, removing some of the potency and flavor.

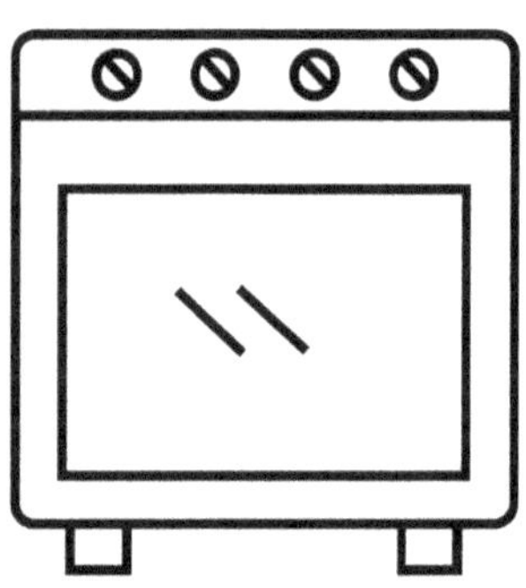

Food Dehydrator
An efficient way to quickly dry and preserve the flavor and medicinal value of fresh herbs.

Infusions

Exploring the Art of Infusion: Techniques and Methods for Infusing Plant Matter Infusion is a process that involves soaking plant matter in a liquid to create a flavored medium. This can be achieved using a variety of liquids, including water, alcohol, oil, or sweet solutions. Two primary methods of making infusions are cold and hot, each producing a unique flavor profile. Cold infusions are less bitter and have a fresh flavor, while hot infusions are more intense and offer quicker results.

How to make infused vodka, vinegar, and water. Infused vodka is made by adding flavoring agents to vodka and letting it sit for several days or weeks before straining out the solids. Infused vinegar follows the same method and can create vinaigrettes or a refreshing beverage called a "shrub." Infused water is a simple way to flavor water by adding sliced fruits or vegetables.

Several types of infusions include extracts, tinctures, glycerine, decoctions, and tisanes, each with a unique preparation method. Extracts, for example, are cold infusions typically concentrated and made with alcohol. Tinctures, on the other hand, are strong infusions used for medicinal purposes. Glycerine is a popular alternative to alcohol for those who are sensitive to it. Decoctions require simmering plant material for an extended period, while tisanes are hot herbal infusions used to differentiate herbal beverages from teas made exclusively with Camellia sinensis plant leaves.

There are two methods for infusing herbs or flowers into carrier oils: the solar infusion method and the slow infusion cooker method. For the solar method, fill a mason jar with herbs, cover them with carrier oil, and place them on a sunny windowsill for 2-6 weeks before straining the oil. For the slow-cooker method, fill a mason jar with herbs, cover them with carrier oil, place them in a slow cooker with water, and let the mixture infuse for 10-12 hours before straining the oil. Store the oil in a cool, dark place.

Freezing herbs is a simple method to keep them fresh throughout the year. This involves chopping the herbs, blending them with olive oil, and storing them in freezer bags or ice cube trays. This method is also suitable for making DIY baby food.

CHAPTER 19

Cleansing vs. Charging

Cleansing:
Removes past energies
Item is restored to its natural state
Crystal-like quartz and selenite can cleanse other crystals/tools

Charging:
Adds purpose or intention
Programs a tool for a specific energy
Charged crystals can be used to add energy to other items

Cleansing Methods

Cleansing with Water
Water Bath
Cleansing With Moonlight
Cleansing With Sound
Cleansing With Sunlight
A few crystals never need cleansing. For example, citrine, kyanite, and selenite are self-cleaning. Clear Quartz and Carnelian cleanse other crystals.
Check with which ones are safe in water

Energize and Charge

Quartz Points
Sunlight
Moonlight
Plants
Herbs

Crystal Shapes

Clusters
radiates unity
throughout the space
and
charges other crystals

Pyramids
anchoring crystal and
powerful for
manifesting desires

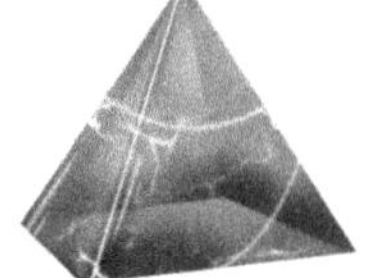

Cubes
consolidates energy,
grounding & meditation,
and connect to the
energy of the Earth

Double Terminated
absorb negative
energy,
grounding, break
down old patterns,
and
promotes psychic
ability

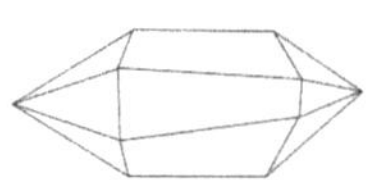

Twin
grounding &
harmonizing
energies, and
balances yin &
yang energies

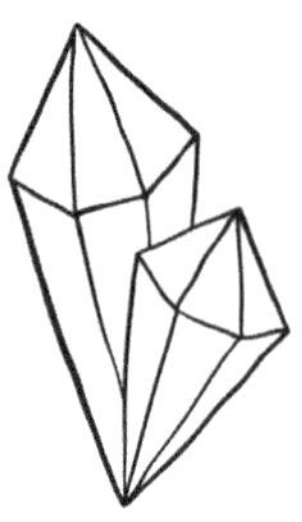

Points
concentrates &
directs energy

Crystal Shapes

Wand
healing rituals,
moving & directing
energy

Egg
healing, fertility,
and
balance

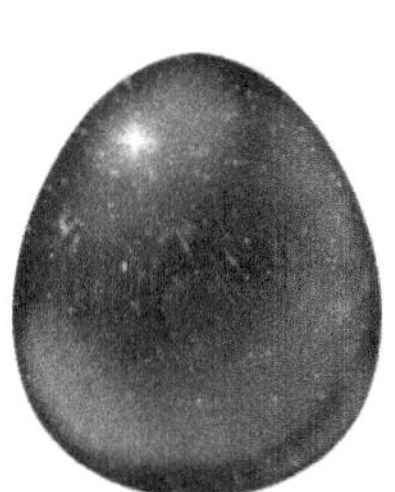

Spheres
emits energy
equally
from all direction,
and
ideal for scrying

Druzy
charging, relaxation &
harmony, purify &
amplify body's
natural healing
properties

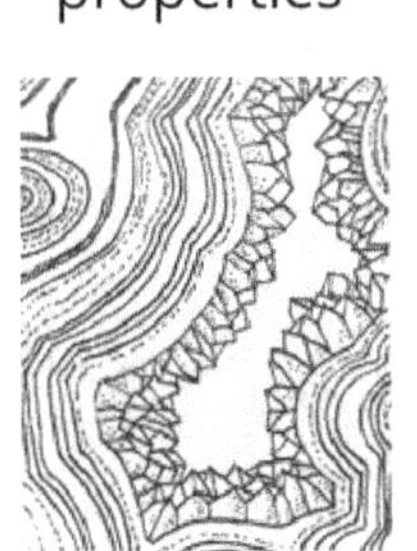

Geode
amplifies,
conserves &
releases energy,
and
Internal healing

Isis
feminine energy,
healing
emotional
hurt and distress

Choosing the Shape of Your Crystal

1 - Look up the energetic properties of your crystal.

2 - Consider the shape and if it offers benefits, such as enhancing any of the properties you are interested in.

3 - Consider if the crystal shape suits your chosen way of working with the stone.

Fuchsite

Magical Properties
Resolution
Love & Relationships
Meditation
New Beginnings
Nourishing and Rejuvenation
PTSD
Passion
Peace of Mind
Self- Healing
Self Discovery
Selflessness
Soothing
Stress Relief

Classification -
Origin - Brazil, South America, and India
Rarity - Common

Crystal Pairs With -
Don't Mix With -
Cost -
Got it from -
Planets - Mercury, Earth
Chakra - Heart
Signs - Aquarius
Notes:

Identification
Color(s) - Olive Green, Venusian-Green Green
Transparency -
Lustre -
Crystal System - masses, scales, layered plates
Chemical - $K(Al, Cr)_3Si_3O_{10}(OH)_2$

Jade

Magical Properties
Calming and Patience
Dreams
Love & Relationships
Joy
Protection
Physical Healing
Peace of Mind
Transmutation of Negative Energies
Longevity
Connection with Nature
Astral Travel
Self- Healing
Fertility and Pregnancy

Classification -
Origin - Australia,
Russia, China, Taiwan,
Canada, Zimbabwe and
USA
Rarity - Common

Crystal Pairs With -
Don't Mix With -
Cost -
Got it from -
Planets - Earth
Chakra - Heart
Signs - Aries, Taurus, Gemini, and
Libra
Notes:

Draw or Paste your crystal here

Identification
Color(s) - Green, Grey, Black, White,
Yellow, Olive Green
Transparency -
Lustre -
Crystal System -
Chemical - n{NaAlSi2O6} p{Ca2(Mg,
Fe)5Si8O22(OH)2}

Turquoise

Magical Properties
Travel
Balance
Communication
Empathy
Truth
Stress Relief
Higher Self
Expansion
Expanded Awareness
Inner Peace
Self- Healing
Peace of Mind
Emotional Understanding

Classification -
Origin - Turkey, United States
Rarity - Common

Draw or Paste your crystal here

Crystal Pairs With -
Don't Mix With -
Cost -
Got it from -
Planets - Venus, Neptune
Chakra - Throat
Signs - Scorpio, Sagittarius, Pisces
Notes:

Identification
Color(s) - Blue, Pale yellow, Light Blue
Transparency -
Lustre -
Crystal System -
Chemical - $CuAl_6(PO_4)_4(OH)_8 \cdot 4H_2O$

Iolite

Magical Properties
Psychic Abilities
Dreams
Communication
Meditation
Past Lives
Cleansing
Attunement
Higher Self
Inner Vision
Attunement With Higher Realms
Communication With Higher Realms
Self- Healing
Lucid Dreaming

Classification -
Origin - Brazil, Madagascar,
Burma, and India
Rarity - Common

Draw or Paste your crystal here

Crystal Pairs With -
Don't Mix With -
Cost -
Got it from -
Planets - Saturn
Chakra - Third Eye, Crown
Signs - Taurus, Sagittarius, Libra
Notes:

Identification
Color(s) - Blue, Violet
Transparency -
Lustre -
Crystal System -
Chemical - (Mg, Fe)2Al3(AlSi5O18)

Vanadinite

Magical Properties
Meditation
Channeling
Grounding
Self-Discipline
Focus
Manifestation
Determination
Bridging the Spiritual and Physical
Worlds
Organization
Channeling and Grounding Higher
Vibrations
Self Discovery
Sexuality

Classification -
Origin - Morrocco, Mexico, and
the U.S.A.
Rarity - Rare

Draw or Paste your crystal here

Crystal Pairs With - Carnelian or
Zincite
Don't Mix With -
Cost -
Got it from -
Planets -
Chakra - Third Eye, Solar Plexus
Sacral, Root
Signs - Virgo
Notes:

Identification
Color(s) - red, orange, and brown
Transparency -
Lustre -
Crystal System - Prismatic
Chemical - $Pb_5(VO_4)_3Cl$

Bronzite

Magical Properties
Strength
Love & Relationships
Opportunities
Transformation
Protection
Courage
Channeling
Grounding
Self-Discipline
Leadership
Focus
Determination
Self Discovery
Growth

Classification -
Origin - Brazil, Czech Republic,
Madagascar, Austria, and USA.
Rarity - Common

Draw or Paste your crystal here

Crystal Pairs With -
Don't Mix With -
Cost -
Got it from -
Planets -
Chakra - Sacral, Root
Signs - Virgo
Notes:

Identification
Color(s) - brown
Transparency -
Lustre -
Crystal System -
Chemical - $(Mg, Fe2+)2[SiO3]2$

Eclogite

Magical Properties
Strength
Leadership
Spiritual Awakening
Soothing
Sexuality
Sense of Purpose
Selflessness
Self Discovery
Self- Healing
Action
Courage
Confidence
Compassion
Claiming Wholeness

Classification -
Origin - Norway, China, Germany, Austria, and the United States
Rarity - incredibly rare

Draw or Paste your crystal here

Crystal Pairs With - Rose Quartz, Rhodonite, Kunzite, Rhodochrosite or Pink Opal
Don't Mix With -
Cost -
Got it from -
Planets - Earth
Chakra - Heart, Solar Plexus, Sacral, Root
Signs - Scorpio
Notes:

Identification
Color(s) - Red, Green
Transparency -
Lustre -
Crystal System -
Chemical - $n\{(Mg, Ca, Fe2+, Mn2+)3(Al, Fe3+, Cr3+, V3+)2(SiO4)3\}$ $p\{(NaaCabFe2+cMgd)(AleFe3+fFe2+gMgh)Si2O6\}$

Irnimite

Magical Properties
Psychic Abilities
Dreams
Transformation
Synchronicity
Channeling
Attunement
Ascension
Higher Self
Wisdom
Inner Vision
Angelic Communication
Attunement With Higher Realms

Draw or Paste your crystal here

Classification -
Origin - Khabarovsk Krai region
of eastern Russia.
Rarity - Extremely rare

Crystal Pairs With - Moldavite
Don't Mix With -
Cost -
Got it from -
Planets - Saturn
Chakra - Crown, Third eye Throat
Signs - Scorpio, Cancer, Pisces
Notes:

Identification
Color(s) - Blue, White, Brown
Transparency -
Lustre -
Crystal System - crystallizes in mass
formation
Chemical -

Celestite

Magical Properties
Retrograde
Meditation
Creativity
Psychic Abilities
Calming and Patience
Dreams
Clarity
Cleansing
Angelic Communication
Attunement With Higher Realms
Communication With Higher Realms
Elimination Toxins
Lucid Dreaming
Communication
Resolution

Classification -
Origin - Madagascar
Rarity - Extremely rare

Draw or Paste your crystal here

Crystal Pairs With -
Don't Mix With -
Cost -
Got it from -
Planets - Venus, Neptune
Chakra - Etheric, Crown, Third eye
Throat
Signs - Gemini
Notes:

Identification
Color(s) - Blue, Light Blue
Transparency - Transparent
Lustre -
Crystal System - crystallizes as small prismatic shards
Chemical - $SrSO_4$

CHAPTER 20

Årsgång: Yearwalking: A Swedish New Year's Divination is an ancient Swedish divination practice that takes place on Christmas or New Year's Eve. As far back as the 19th century, individuals would venture out on yearlong journeys, risking their minds and bodies (even encountering spirits) to obtain a glimpse of the year ahead. While there is limited information on the subject, one method involved fasting for a prolonged period without food or water, then journeying to a place of power (such as a church) in the hopes of experiencing visions.

Barbegazi: The Dwarf-Like Creatures of the Swiss Alps
The Swiss Alps are home to an extraordinary group of beings – the Barbegazi. These creatures are known for their flat feet, white fur, and long white beards that resemble icicles. They spend most of their time underground, but as soon as the snow arrives, they emerge to roam the mountains. Despite their shy nature, they have been known to assist humans in various ways, such as helping lost sheep and warning of potential dangers with their whistling. They even enjoy surfing on avalanches! Living as a Barbegazi seems to be a carefree and joyful existence.

Exploring the Scottish Myth and Folklore of the Winter Goddess, Beira
Beira, the winter goddess of Scottish mythology and folklore, is often referred to as the "Queen of Winter." She is also known as the "Cailleach," which means "veiled one." According to some tales, Beira is depicted as a one-eyed hag with blue skin who possesses the ability to see into the singularity of all things.

A famous Queen of Winter story tells of her search for a heroic lover. Should the hero accept Beira in her hag form, she will transform into a beautiful young woman. This transformation mirrors the dormant seeds of winter that blossom into young shoots in the spring. Another version of the tale describes Beira carrying a magical staff capable of freeing the ground wherever she taps it. When she throws the staff under her sacred trees, the holly and gorse bush, it serves as a sign that winter has come to an end.

The Legend of Belsnickel: Belsnickel is an imaginary elderly man from German folklore. He is depicted wearing ragged clothes, and animal skins and visiting children before Christmas. If they're well-behaved, he brings them tasty treats, but if they're not, he frightens them by brandishing a switch to make them behave by Christmas. Nowadays, Belsnickel still visits children, but fortunately, the switch is only used to make noise, not to punish them.

Boreas is the Greek god of the north wind. He is the one who brings winter and all its chills to the land. His daughter, a nymph called Khione, is the Greek goddess of snow.

The Tale of Ded Moroz: A Slavic Equivalent to Father Christmas, also known as Dzied Moroz and by many other names, is a beloved Slavic folklore figure who resembles Father Christmas. His name, "Old Man Frost," suggests that he may have been a pre-Christian winter wizard (life goals, indeed) and possibly the offspring of Slavic gods Mara and Veles. He wears long robes in pale blue, and his head is adorned with a furry hat or a crown featuring a snowflake design. Ded Moroz visits young children on Christmas Eve, bearing gifts he often delivers.

Frau Perchta is the Christmas Witch of Eastern Europe. She is often depicted as having a goose foot, and it's believed that goose fat helped witches fly. She likes to reward the hard-working and generous with gifts during the twelve days of Christmas. Equally, she loves to punish the idle and greedy. One of her favorite punishments involves ripping out your intestines to replace them with rocks, rubbish, and straw. Gruesome. Never cross a witch.

Holming, or Holly-beating: The thankfully extinct old Welsh tradition of holming, or holly-beating, was carried out on the day after Christmas (St Stephens Day). It could refer to the practice of beating the last person out of bed in the morning with holly sprigs. Holming also referred to young men beating the arms or legs of girls with holly until they bled.

The Mythical Jack Frost: The Personification of Winter: "Look out! Look out! Jack Frost is about!" It is a well-known rhyme that personifies the frosty winter season. Jack Frost embodies the cold, frost, and winter's stinginess. The image we have of him today comes from the 19th-century poem "Jack Frost" by Hannah Gould, although it wasn't referred to as such at the time of its publication. He is considered the youthful counterpart of Old Man Winter, known for his mischievous qualities. Jack Frost playfully nips at our noses, leaving patterns resembling ferns on cold windows while turning leaves brown. Surprisingly, as a personification, he is relatively recent but has an everlasting presence.

The Kallikantzaroi: Greek Underground Goblins: The subterranean goblins from Greece pose a threat to the world tree by sawing away at its roots. However, during the 12 days of Christmas, they emerge from the depths to create chaos among mortals. Oddly enough, this is beneficial because it means they forget about the world tree, allowing it to heal. Nonetheless, their above-ground Christmas visit can cause immense trouble for us humans. One method of thwarting them is to place a colander outside your door, since they can't count higher than two and will waste their time counting the holes in the colander repeatedly. Burning a Yule log in your fireplace all night will also prevent the Kallikantzaroi from coming down your chimney. Legend has it that individuals born on a Saturday have the ability to see and speak to these creatures.

Exploring Mari Lwyd, the Mythical Welsh Christmas "Pony Zombie" Mari Lwyd is a well-known figure in Welsh folklore, described as a skeletal mare that rises from the dead during the winter season. Her ultimate goal is to gain entry into people's homes, flanked by her undead followers. Volunteers often participate in this tradition by parading around the streets with a horse skull mounted on a pole and covered in white cloth. On New Year's Eve, locals engage in a poetic battle of wits with Mari Lwyd to keep her at bay.

Exploring the Tradition of Mumming: Mumming is a unique practice involving traveling around streets, pubs, and homes to perform folk plays, typically during Christmas. The performances often include a mix of broad comedy and traditional characters, such as Saint George the Dragon Slayer and Beelzebub. Additionally, the acts feature a staged fight and a doctor character who brings the hero back to life with a magical potion.

In Finland, the name given to the Northern Lights is **Revontulet**, which is associated with the Arctic fox. Folk tales depict the fox running north and brushing against the mountains with its fur, causing sparks (the Northern Lights) to fly into the air.

The Northern Lights are known as the **Merry Dancers or the Nimble Men** in Gaelic folklore. They're said to depict glorious fights among celestial warriors in the sky.

The Tale of Snegurochka, the Snow Maiden: Snegurochka, the beloved Snow Maiden, is often described as Ded Moroz's daughter or granddaughter. The name Snegurochka comes from the Russian word for snow, "sneg." When Ded Moroz embarks on his annual gift-giving mission during the winter season, Snegurochka is always by his side.

However, there is a more somber story behind Snegurochka's origins. According to legend, she was a snow statue carved by an elderly couple who were unable to have children of their own. She joined the local children in playing and jumping over a fire, but when it was her turn to jump, she melted away.

In certain areas of Russia, a tradition still exists where a straw figure is drowned in a river or burned on a bonfire to symbolize the end of winter and the beginning of spring.

It is traditional in Poland to leave an extra space at the table for the unexpected guest on Christmas Eve. It could be a family member or friend you never expected to show up at your door. It could be someone you don't know. It's a practice rooted in charitable goodwill... and a certain level of gambling spirit.

Wren Day is celebrated in Ireland and elsewhere on 26 December, on St Stephen's Day. The wren is a symbol of the old sun and the senior year. The wren (once a live wren, but these days a fake one) must be hunted down and paraded through the town to symbolize the sacrifice of the old year so that the new year can come into being. Wrenboys and mummers dress up in motley costumes, masks, and suits of straw to parade the 'wren' through the town.

Wild Hunt: There is an ancient Norwegian belief that the dead walk among the living during Yule – no, Samhain isn't the only time for such things to occur. The Wild Hunt taps into this. It's a name given to gods or fierce spirits who lead their celestial comrades in a hunt across the sky. It's most commonly associated with Norse mythology and the Wild Hunts led by Odin riding his eight-legged horse Sleipnir. The Wild Hunt can occur at any time (often before times of trial and outbreaks of war). However, it is said to happen most frequently on winter nights, especially between Yule and Twelfth Night. During this time, ancestors are honored, and food is left out for them. Farmers may also leave harvested grain for the hunters' horses in the fields. The Wild Hunt during this time is said to be linked to ancestors returning to collect their earthly gifts and tokens of respect in return for a good harvest next year.

In Germanic folklore, the leader of the Wild Hunt will shout, "Midden in dem Weg!" ("Middle of the Road!") if they see you in their path. If you hear this call, it is best to lie down in the middle of the path immediately. This will save you from the worst of the trampling, though you may still feel the cold feet of the hunting dogs run along your spine. If you are very unlucky, you will be swept up in the Wild Hunt... and who knows when you will return to earth again, or in what condition?

CHAPTER 21

Magical Water

Water is a revered element with transformative and purifying properties, making it sacred to life. In the realm of spirituality and magic, different types of magical water hold immense power and are utilized for various purposes. Each enchanted kind of water has unique qualities, making it a versatile tool for spellwork, rituals, and energetic practices. Moon water offers soothing and healing properties, while holy water is potent and protective. These enchanted waters serve as conduits for intention and manifestation.

When combined with intention, visualization, and focused energy, the power of water is amplified in magic and spirituality. These different types of magical water serve as potent tools that allow practitioners to connect with the natural forces and energies around us. Whether seeking healing, protection, purification, or manifestation, the versatile uses of magical water offer a profound connection to the mystical realms.

Magical Water Properties

Rain Water: Growth and rebirth spells, cleansing, scrying, altar water, and ritual baths.

Storm Water: Vitality, self-esteem, courage, mental strength, strengthening spells, and protection.

Dew Water: Healing, beauty, eyesight, love, fertility, working with the fae, and cleansing.

Snow Water: Unthaw a situation, transformation, balance, peace, consecrating, and endings.

Moon Water: Charging, blessing or cleanse, bath rituals, powering spells, healing magic, curses, and hexes.

Sun Water: Protection, healing, clairvoyance, happiness, fertility, and creativity.

River Water: Moving on, focusing energy, warding, breakthrough, power, and charging.

Sea Water: Cleansing, banishing, protection, emotional balance, healing rituals, and manifestation.

Spring Water: Growth, holy water, cleansing, abundance, potions, and beauty.

Lake Water: Peace, joy, contentment, relaxation, self-reflection, and self-discovery.

Wellwater: Healing, wishes, intuition, manifestation, connection to otherworldly beings.

Swamp Water: Banishing, binding, hexing, cursing, and reversing.

To add more magic to your recipes, use clean, filtered water like distilled or spring water.

Rain Water

Catch the rainwater any time of day and bottle it up for your craft usage. Good for rebirth, cycles, transformation, cleansings, protection, altar water, ritual baths, peace, tranquility, purification, scrying, divination, and asperging.

Lake Water

Good for peace, happiness, contentment, joy, relaxation, reflection, personal journey, and growth.

Swamp Water

Good for revenge magic, binding, hexing, curses, and banishing

Dew Water

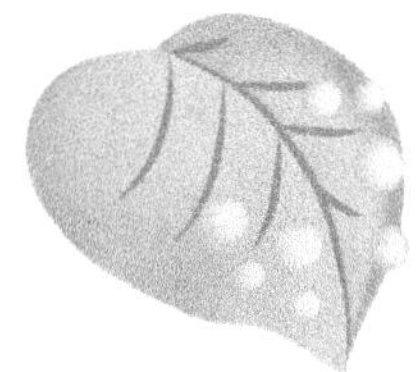

Collect dew water during the morning from windows, leaves, or flowers. Good for healing, cleansing, beauty, love, passion, fertility, and fae magic

Well Water

Good for connecting with elemental spirits, sprites, and the fae healing, intuition, scrying, manifestation, and wishes.

Spring Water

Good for growth, cleansing, abundance, fae work, love, fertility, healing, positivity, strength, purify altars, divination tools, endurance and grounding

I Got a Jar of Dirt!

Types of Dirt and Their Magical Uses

Graveyard

Traditionally used in divination, cursing, love & protection spells
Avoid collecting from an unclean spirit's grave for most workings
Leave an offering in exchange for the dirt
Try to collect from an ancestor's grave to ensure the energy you are collecting is safe.

Churchyard

Traditionally used for many intentions and spells:
Healing
Prosperity
Purification
Protection
Mending relationships
Justice workings

Crossroad

They are traditionally used in road-opening spells
Used in journeying to the underworld, as it helps open the gate to the other realms
Used as offerings to guardians and gods of the crossroads: Hecate, Hermes, Papa Legba, etc.

Backyard

Traditionally used in workings for the family, home, and property:
Purification
Protection
Peace
Collect from the 4 corners of the property if possible.

Graveyard

Working with Graveyard Dirt: Traditional Use in Healing, Protection and Prosperity Spells.

Graveyard dirt has long been used for its mystical properties, particularly in healing, protection, and prosperity spells. However, following certain guidelines when collecting graveyard dirt is essential to avoid negative energies. Here are some tips:

Avoid collecting dirt from the grave of an unwell spirit. Always leave an offering in exchange for the dirt gathered. Collecting dirt from ancestors' graves rather than from unknown ones is recommended. By following these guidelines, you can safely and effectively work with graveyard dirt in your practice.

Churchyard

Churchyard dirt is a versatile substance that can be utilized in magic and witchcraft for various purposes. Some of the most popular intentions and spells include:

Healing
Prosperity
Purification
Protection
Mending relationships
Justice workings

Crossroads

The Power of Crossroads Dirt in Road Opening Spells
Crossroads dirt has been used in road-opening spells for years and is particularly helpful in journeying to the underworld. This is because it helps to open the gate to other realms. Additionally, it's a great offering to guardians of the crossroads, such as Hecate and Papa Legba.

Leave

Things to leave at the crossroads for power or ritual.

Offerings

Spiritual offerings and prayers can be left at the crossroads to show thanks or strengthen your relationships with spirits. Be sure to leave appropriate offerings for the particular spirits you are working with or for the specific prayer/work.

Active Spells

The crossroads is a perfect place to anchor spells related to the power of that crossroads. Burying a spell designed to work long term here will allow the work to stay strong and progress without being actively worked at home.

Spell Remains

Most spellwork remains can be buried, burned, or left at the crossroads. This brings their energy to full completion. It lets any leftover prayer or intent in the plants, petitions, or other remains of the work be fully and safely released. Use mindfully.

Take

Things to take from the crossroads for spells or charms.

Dirt

Crossroads dirt brings the power of manifestation from the crossroads. Dirt from male crossroads is excellent to manifest customers to a business. Dirt from a divine crossroads mixed into a garden or field attracts good spirits and increases harvest.

Stones

Crossroads stones carry the power of the crossroads itself with them. Pregnant women can carry stones from a female crossroads to protect the baby.
Stones from damned crossroads may be left in a house, yard, or field to curse it and make it barren.

Coins

Coins found at the crossroads are especially powerful. Silver coins found here protect from haunting nightmares and evil spirits. Copper coins protect one who carries them from love spells and binding. You may leave coins on purpose to pick up later but found is always best.

Spiritual Water Properties

Fast Luck - Brings fast luck, money luck, quick outcomes, and aids manifestation.

Love Water - It brings love and resonates with love, harmony, and compassion.

7 African Powers - Draws strength from the 7 African Orishas.

Protection - Protects you, your space, your place, and your things.

Road Opener - Removes obstacles, brings new opportunities, and opens pathways.

Peruvian FL Water- Help with spiritual work, purification, rituals, and cleansing.

Destroy Everything - Destroys all conditions, jinxes, and curses and removes all things that do not serve you.

Attraction or Come To Me - Attracts the things you want, need, or desire in your life.

Tobacco Water - Draws spirits of nature, helps communication between worlds, and honors ancestors.

Success & Prosperity - Attracts success, abundance, money, and positivity.

Florida Water - It brings protection, spiritual cleansing, and positive vibes.

Florida Water Recipe

Ingredients:
16 oz of vodka
3-5 tablespoons of floral water (orange, rose, lavender, etc.)
8 drops of Lavender EO
10 drops of Lemon EO
10 drops of Orange EO
5 drops of Bergamot EO
5 drops of Cinnamon EO
5 drops of Clove EO
3 drops of Benzoin EO
Fresh rose petals and fresh rosemary (optional)

Directions:
Add your vodka and floral water to a bowl and smell each EO before adding it to your bowl. Let your nose and spirit tell you if you should add more or less than the recipe.
Combine all ingredients in a spray bottle.
Shake well before each use.
Remove rose petals and rosemary if you wish.
Keep your customized Florida Water on hand, too.

Rosemary Water

Protection Spray

Rosemary is known for its cleansing and purifying properties. It can help to eliminate negativity and create a more positive environment.

Ingredients:
Rosemary sprigs
Salt

Directions:
Add 6 ounces (if using an 8-ounce bottle) of boiling water to the rosemary in a bowl.
Add some salt.
Allow to cool down.
Strain and fill the 8-ounce spray bottle.

Mood-Boosting Spray

Ingredients:
10-15 drops of Lavender EO
5-10 drops of Clary Sage EO
10-15 drops of Chamomile EO
3 tablespoons of Distilled Water
3 tablespoons of Witch Hazel or Grain Alcohol

Optional:
Amethyst crystals for balance, clarity, and calming
Magical Water: Distilled water that has absorbed the power from the elements
Lemon or Orange Peel in fresh or EO form or fresh herbs that you find to be mood-boosting and can cleanse negative energy.

Directions:
Add to a 4 oz spray bottle.
Shake after each use.

Cascarilla Powder

Cascarilla powder is an essential ingredient in protective magic that's easy to make. The powder is made from powdered eggshells and is primarily used for spiritual cleansing and protection. Originating from Hoodoo and Santeria, it has become increasingly popular throughout America due to its accessibility. Cascarilla powder can also help create spiritual barriers similar to salt, add blessings, aid in protection, and make a great nutritional addition for plants in the garden. For added protection, try complementing the cascarilla powder with Florida water.

Tip: To make a higher-quality powder, run the eggshells under a kitchen faucet to remove the membrane before drying them.

Ingredients:
2 dozen eggshells, dried
A food processor or mortar and pestle
½ teaspoon of Florida water (see recipe)
A small glass jar or sealable container

Directions:
Bake the eggshells at 200 degrees for approximately 30 minutes to further dry them. This step allows excess moisture to cook off, making for a more delicate powder. This step is significant if you grind the shells by hand using a mortar and pestle! You might notice the color change slightly if you're using white eggshells. Don't worry - your powder will still come out white.

When the eggshells are dry, grind them into a fine powder using a mortar and pestle or food processor.

Add about 1/2 teaspoon of Florida water and process until you have a fine, sand-like consistency.

Store the cascarilla powder in a jar or pack it into chalk.

For Cascarilla Chalk:
Mix 1 tablespoon of flour and 1 tablespoon of loose cascarilla powder thoroughly.
Add a tablespoon of warm water and mix until the ingredients combine to form a ball in your hands.
Roll the mixture into sticks about 1/2 to 1 inch in diameter and let them dry for 3 to 5 days. Alternatively, you can roll the mixture into balls and place them in a small-pack paper condiment cup.
Store the chalk in a glass, plastic, or metal container to protect it from breaking, and keep it in a cool, dark place.
Note: Be careful not to add too many additional or specific herbs, as this may stop the mixture from sticking together and forming chalk. You can use cascarilla powder in spells, as well as making sigils and magical symbols.

Salt for Magic

Himalayan/Pink Salt - ("purest salt on Earth" because of maturing for 250 million years) is used for love, removing negative blockages and curses, and cleansing.
Hawaiian Black Salt - (harvested from the evaporated water on Hawaiian Island Molokai) is used for its extra strength.
Table Salt - Used for purifying, protecting, and cleansing, and used in culinary recipes.
Kosher Salt - (blessed by a Jewish Rabbi)
Used to draw out negativity or absorb negativity
Black Salt -(leftover ashes or scrapings from cast iron)
Used for banishing and protection.
Alaea/Hawaiian Red Salt - (From iron-rich volcanic clay)
Used for love and sex, blocks negative energy, protects aggressively to defend an area that has been set with or encircled with it, and is used in culinary recipes (high in nutrients 80+).
Sel Gris Sea Salt - Used for blessing.
Celtic Sea Salt - Used for protection and attracting financial abundance.
Sea Salt - (carries the power of the sea and water elements)
Used for purification and cleansing, it helps to balance emotions.
Cyprus Black Salt - (sea water dried in lava beds mixed with charcoal)
Used to evoke properties of the pyramids, energy from heaven, used in culinary recipes.
Rock Salt - Used for return to sender, used to reflect negativity to sender.
Fleur de Sel Salt - (sea salt from France) is a gentler salt used with fairies and elementals.
Gray Salt - (developed in clay pools) Used in liminal workings.
Blue Salt - (sea salt mixed with blue flowers) Used for protection from the Evil eye, justice, and healing. That being said, you can make any color salt by mixing colored herbs with it.
Herb Infused Salts - (salt infused with edible herbs)
Choose an herb that aligns with your intentions.
Epsom Salt - Use in the bath to reduce inflammation and muscle pain and to help you de-stress.
Pickling Salt - (purest form, no added agents)
Used for purification, preservation of love, prosperity, etc., and used in culinary recipes.

CHAPTER 22

Magical Oils

Essential oils have been used in magic and pagan traditions since ancient times. Today, they still play a vital role in modern-day witchcraft, promoting healing, relaxation, love, and prosperity. Whether new to witchcraft or an experienced practitioner, incorporating essential oils into your practice can help you connect with the natural world. Discover the fascinating uses of these powerful plant extracts in magic and pagan traditions.

Uncrossing Oil

Uncrossing oil is a powerful potion that helps to remove negative energy, bad luck, and curses.

Feeling "crossed" or under a spell can affect your life in many ways, causing you to lose your energy, positivity, and focus. Uncrossing magic is the perfect remedy to eliminate these negative effects and bring back good vibes into your life.

Most Uncrossing Oils are made from natural ingredients with high spiritual vibrations and cleansing properties. These include Verbena, Hyssop, Lavender, and Rose, commonly used for their aroma and mood-lifting benefits.

These ingredients combine to break up stagnant energy, purify your surroundings, and create a positive and uplifting atmosphere.

Van Van Oil

Van Van is a traditional New Orleans Voodoo oil that serves as a lucky all-purpose oil, a protective ointment, and a signature fragrance of Bayou Witch.

The scent of Van Van oil is unique and recognizable once you have smelled it; according to Cat Yronwode, the scent of this oil used to be so widespread that one could not walk down a street in the Algiers district of New Orleans without smelling it. You can use it to anoint lucky charms and magical tools. Dress candles, cleanse and bless, mix into floor washes and room sprays to banish negativity, and add some to a cleansing bath to boost your mojo before doing any spell work.

Spiritual Oil Properties

Black Cat Oil

Black Cat Oil is a traditional New Orleans preparation that is believed to bring good luck to those who practice witchcraft, engage in trickery, have a charismatic personality, or prefer to be alone. In the European tradition, black cats are considered unlucky, but in Afro-American folk magic, they are believed to be the wise man or woman's helper and a symbol of good fortune. You can use Black Cat Oil as an anointing oil to enhance your magical powers, protect yourself from bad luck, and work spells related to invisibility, enthrallment, clairvoyance, and charisma. For best results, use Black Cat Oil during the waning or dark moon.

Abramelin Oil

The recipe for Abramelin Oil, the oldest on this list, dates back to the late medieval grimoire known as The Book of the Sacred Magic of Abramelin the Mage. Later, in the 19th century, members of the Hermetic Order of the Golden Dawn adopted the formula. Nowadays, Abramelin Oil is widely used in modern high magick traditions, especially in Thelma, and has also found its way into the practices of Pagan and folk-magick conjurors.

Abramelin Oil has versatile uses, such as consecrating altar tools, evoking or communing with malevolent spirits, and anointing the body for high magick rituals. It has stimulating and purifying properties. When applied to the brow or other chakras, it creates a warming sensation that enhances focus and energy flow during rituals.

Yule Sabbat Oil

2 drops of cinnamon oil
2 drops of clove oil
1 drop of mandarin oil
1 drop of pine oil
2 drops of frankincense oil
2 drops of myrrh oil

Essential Oils

Essential oils have been used for centuries in natural and spiritual practices. In witchcraft, they offer many benefits and are utilized for various purposes, each with a unique signature. By incorporating these oils, practitioners can connect deeply with the natural world, tap into its limitless potential, and align themselves with elemental forces and ancient wisdom. To explore the mystical world of essential oils, you can incorporate them into your practice in various ways, such as anointing candles, creating personalized blends, or incorporating them into meditation or energy work. Always approach essential oils with reverence and respect, research their properties, and allow their aromatic essence to guide your magical voyage where the natural and the mystical intertwine in harmony.

Oil Correspondences

Oils are used for magic to anoint candles, tools, talismans, spell bags, amulets, and the body. They can be a substitute for incense and combined with herbs. To infuse oil with intentions, add a few drops onto a handkerchief or cotton ball. To charge it, focus energy while holding it at the third eye, using a tool, or burying it. Alternatively, expose it to starlight, moonlight, or sunlight.

Almond - Prosperity, Wisdom, Abundance, Divination, and Luck

Amber - Success, Confidence, Fertility, and Sexuality

Anise - Psychic Awareness and Clairvoyance

Basil - Conscious, Mind, Happiness, Peace, and Attracts Money

Bay - Purification of the soul when used on the body

Bayberry - Attracts Money - Back to the home

Bergamot - Peace, Happiness - Restful Sleep and Soothes Stress

Cedarwood - Spirituality, Self-Control, Healing, and Anti-Hex

Cinnamon- Physical Energy, Clairvoyance, Good Luck, Prosperity, and Protection

Clove - Healing, Memory, Protection, and Courage

Eucalyptus - Health, Healing, and Purification

Frankincense - Spirituality, Meditation, and Astral Strength

Ginger - Energy (magical and physical), Love, Sex, Money, Confidence, and Business Success

Hyssop - Purification, Protection, and Money

Jasmine - Love, Calming, Peace, Spirituality, Sex, Sleep, and Psychic Dreaming

Carrier Oils and Their Uses

To use essential oils on our bodies, we need to dilute them with carrier oils. Carrier oils dilute the oils and make them absorbable by the skin. Use ½ teaspoon of carrier oil with 5-8 drops of essential oil per application. Avoid sensitive areas such as mucus membranes and open wounds.

Experiment with your carrier oils to find the ones you like. Check the label before purchasing to ensure that the carrier oil is 100% pure and not mixed with cheaper oils. Make sure it's fresh and doesn't have a bitter aroma.

Where To Apply Your EOs

For Energy & Focus
Crown of your head, back of your neck, chest, or forearms.

For Respiratory Support
Behind your ears, down the spine, chest, neck, and throat.

For Immune Support
Down the spine and bottoms of the feet.

For Restful Sleep
Big toe, forearms, forehead, and wrists.

For Head Tension
Temples, the back of your neck, and around your ears.

For Emotional Support
Rub the oil in your hands and breathe deeply; apply over the heart and behind the ears.

For Feeling Overwhelmed
Lower back, back of neck, shoulders, and neck.

For Digestion
Belly button,1-2 drops, and rub clockwise on the stomach.

Types of Carrier Oils

Sweet Almond Oil
This carrier oil is cheap and readily available. It's also loaded with vitamins, so it's good for your skin. Almond oil will last a year on the shelf. It has lots of protein and is excellent to use in massage oils.

Apricot Kernel Oil
This carrier oil is excellent for dry, aged skin (like mine). It works wonders as a moisturizing lotion and is used in antiaging products worldwide. In addition, it's loaded with vitamin A and is a good base for healing products.

Grape Seed Oil
This carrier oil is inexpensive but has a short shelf life. However, it has vitamins A and E, so it's perfect for your skin.

Jojoba Oil
This carrier oil is my favorite and is terrific for all skin types, plus it's perfect for skin conditions. It will keep forever on the shelf and mixes beautifully with EOs. It's great for the hair, scalp, and skin.

Sesame Oil
This carrier oil works well for sensitive skin because it has protein, vitamins, and minerals, which are very good for the body and the skin.

Other Carrier Oils
Aloe vera, Apricot, Avocado, Borage, Calendula, Coconut, Evening Primrose, Hazelnut, Macadamia, Meadowfoam, Olive, Pumpkinseed, Rosehip, Safflower, Soybean, Sunflower, Walnut, and Wheat germ.

How Different Scents Influence Our Mood

When I smell certain scents, I know it brings back memories and can totally change my mood for the day.

Citrus: Promotes productivity and calmness.
Orange: Reduces anxiety.
Vanilla: Strong relaxation effect.
Peppermint: Boosts physical energy and alertness.
Cedar: Reduces tension.
Lavender: Promotes relaxation and sleep.
Jasmine: Improves sleep and reduces anxiety.
Rosemary: Improves long-term memory and boosts mood.
Grapefruit: Increases energy.
Lemon and Jasmine: Improves cognitive performance.
Cinnamon and vanilla: Improves creativity.
Frankincense: Reduces anxiety and depression.
Rosemary and Grapefruit: boost long-term memory and energy.
Ylang-Ylang: Reduces stress and promotes calmness.
Lemon: Reduces stress and improves mood.
Geranium plant: Reduces stress.
Bergamot: Reduces anxiety.
Chamomile flowers: Promote calmness and relaxation.
Valerian: Reduces anxiety and improves sleep.
Chocolate: Increases theta brain waves and relaxation

CHAPTER 23

Introduction to Spells

Discover the power of spells, which are rituals crafted using intention, symbolism, and energy manipulation to achieve desires and intentions.

From candle magic and herbal spells to sigil work and crystal enchantments, spells offer endless possibilities for those seeking to deepen their connection with magic. Find the methods that resonate with you, personalize them, and infuse them with your unique style of spelicasting to manifest change in alignment with your highest good.

Types of Spells

Banishing- Banish means to cast something or someone out of your life. If it's a person, the spell will stop them from seeing you or even thinking about you. Some practitioners use banishing spells to get rid of negative entities in general. Banishing spells are popular among folk magic circles such as Hoodoo.

Sweetening - Commonly known as honey jars, sweetening spells try to sweeten or mellow someone's attitude toward you. They can be cast on a specific person or situation (such as a legal case, a career problem, or a relationship). A representation of the target is placed in a jar (a name, personal belonging, sigil), and honey is added on top.

Binding - To bind means to control or limit the target's power. The idea behind this type of ritual is to symbolically tie up someone or something to restrict their actions and prevent them from harming themselves or others. While casting these spells on a person is not advisable, you could cast a binding spell on yourself, for example, to break a bad habit.

Protection - Feeling safe and protected is our most valuable gift. In ancient times, shamans and healers would help people to cure diseases, remove ailments, and feel stronger. These rituals were complemented in many cases with the use of remedies such as food, beverages, cleanses, and more.

Freezing - Similar to binding spells, a freezing spell is typically used when we want to silence somebody. We call this to freeze someone's words or actions. The most common method is to write down the target's name and put it in the freezer.

Good Luck - Inviting good luck is a way to empower ourselves. These spells can open doors by removing fear and increasing our willingness to take risks that lead to success. Attract good fortune by consecrating a lucky amulet such as a coin or a gemstone.

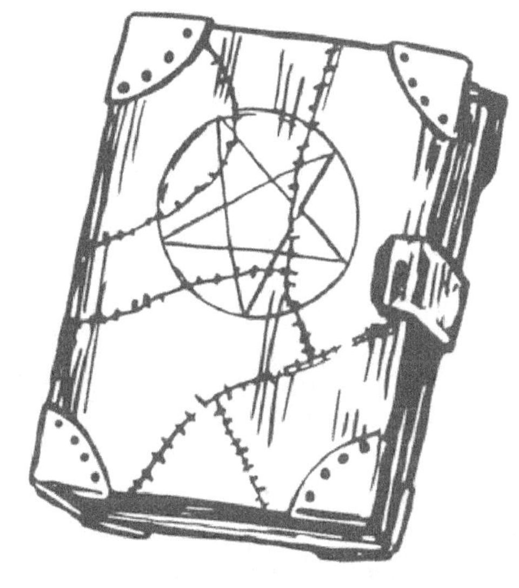

Types of Spells

Candle: The most accessible form of magic for beginners. It can be as simple as burning a candle in the color that supports your intention

Spray: An easy burst of magic on the go made with herbs or essential oils

Jars concentrate the energy of your spell in one place for extra power

Oils are made from a base or carrier oil and a blend of essential oils or herbs left or infuse the base

Pouches contain the spells energy similar to a jar spell. Use a ribbon to tie the pouch when you've filled it

Potions are liquid spells that are consumed or put externally on the on the body

Spell Jars

Anxiety Be-Gone Spell Jar
This can be used to help you feel calm and in control of your life
Lavender
Chamomile
Sage
Magical Water
Amethyst
And your petition on a bay leaf or paper wrapped around a bay leaf

Protection Spell Jar
Salt
White Rice
Common Sage
Lavender
Rosemary

Healing Spell Jar
Salt
Honey
Mint
Sunflower Petals
Agate
Amethyst

Quicky Spell Jar Correspondence

Prosperity

Cinnamon, clove, mint, chamomile, citrine, green aventurine, coins, and green sealing wax

Happiness

Honeysuckle, lemon, balm, marjoram St John's wort, carnelian, sunstone, and yellow sealing wax

Insight

Mugwort, bay leaf, sweetgrass, moonstone, labradorite, lapis lazuli, and purple sealing wax

Banishing

Cayenne pepper, black pepper, garlic rosemary, rue, black tourmaline, jet, and black or grey sealing wax

Love

Rose, jasmine, lavender, basil, pink salt, rose quartz, garnet, and pink sealing wax

Healing

Lavender, calendula, eucalyptus, turmeric, amethyst, clear quartz, sea salt, and blue sealing wax

Success

Lemon balm, bergamot, cinnamon, ginger, tiger's eye, pyrite, citrine, and gold sealing wax

Protection

Angelica, nettle lavender, bay leaf. obsidian, smoky. quartz, black salt, and black sealing wax

Element Spell Jars

Air
Star Anise
Mint
Lavender
Lemongrass
Salt
Flourite
Amethyst

Earth
Mugwort
Patchouli
Corn Kernels
Primrose
Some dirt
Unakite
Tiger's Eye

Fire
Cloves
Rosemary
Pepper Flakes
Calendula
Red Salt
Garnet
Carnelian

Water
Chamomile
Roses
Eucalyptus
Sea Salt
Aquamarine
Lapis Lazuli

How to personalize your spell jar

Include handwritten intentions, sigils, or doodles.
Add an inspiring quote or poetry.
Use several items that resonate with you.
Use locally grown herbs and flowers that you have foraged.
Personal things related to your desired outcome.

Spell Jars

Introduction: Within the realm of spellwork, where intention meets ritual, one finds a fascinating and versatile tool known as the spell jar. These enchanting vessels encapsulate the essence of intention, allowing practitioners to blend their desires with tangible and visually captivating symbolic items. In this concise exploration, we will delve into the art of spell jars, understanding how these small, intricately crafted containers can serve as conduits for focused energy, manifestation, and personal transformation.

Spell Jar Anatomy

Smoke
Infusing and trapping the smoke of dressed candles, herb bundles or incense cleanses as well as embuing your jar with the element of air.

Crystals
Choose crystals that correspond to your intention.

Intentions & Sigils
Add a written intent or sigil to your spell jar.

Earth or Sand
Adding a base layer of sand, earth or pebbles can help to ground the overall energy of your spell jar

Herbs
The following ingredients form the basis of a spell jar however. there is no set recipe so always feel free to add or remove ingredients using your intuition as a guide.

Yule

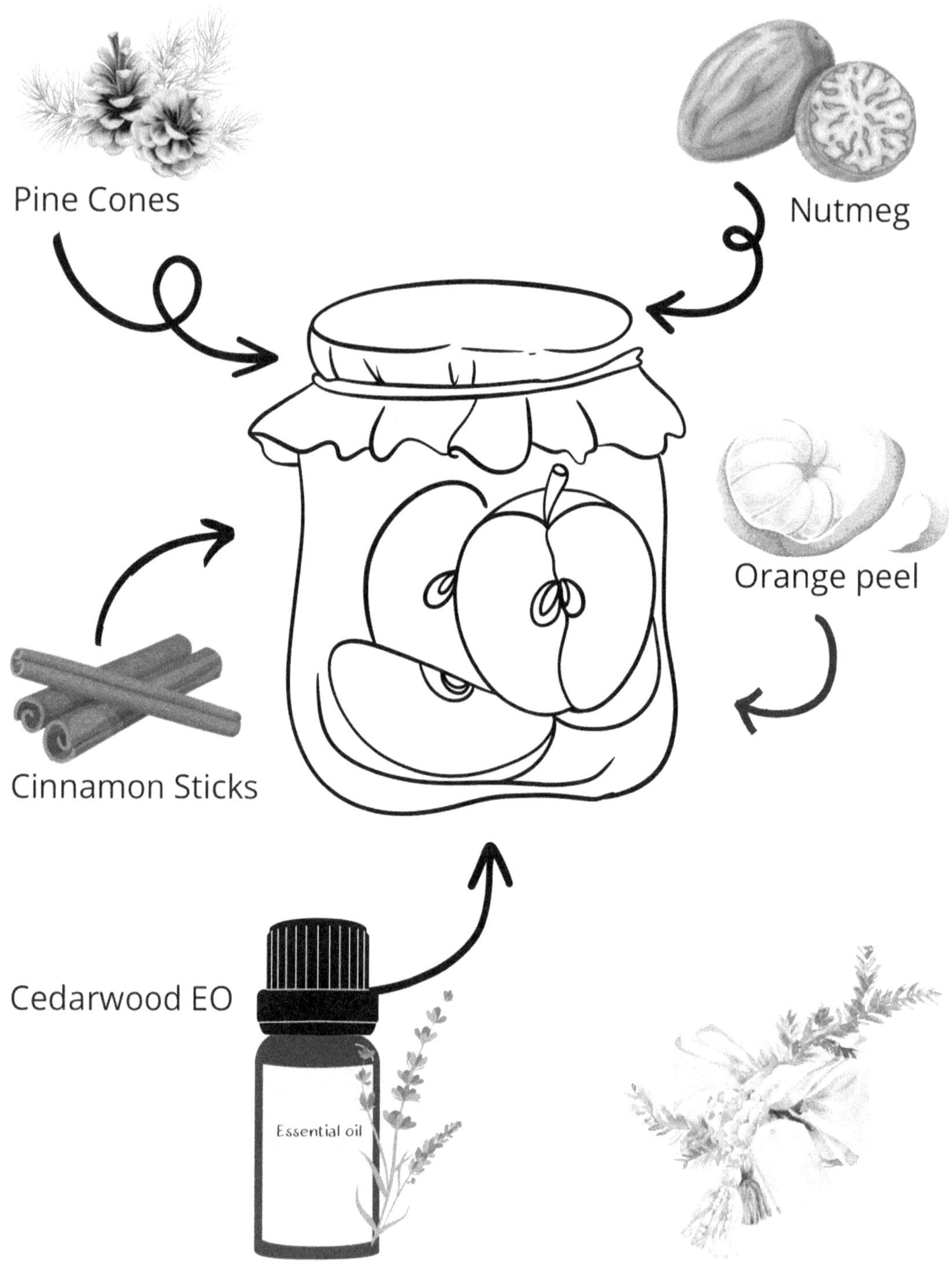

Pine Cones
Nutmeg
Orange peel
Cinnamon Sticks
Cedarwood EO
Essential oil

Yule Spell Jar

Winter Solstice Blessing

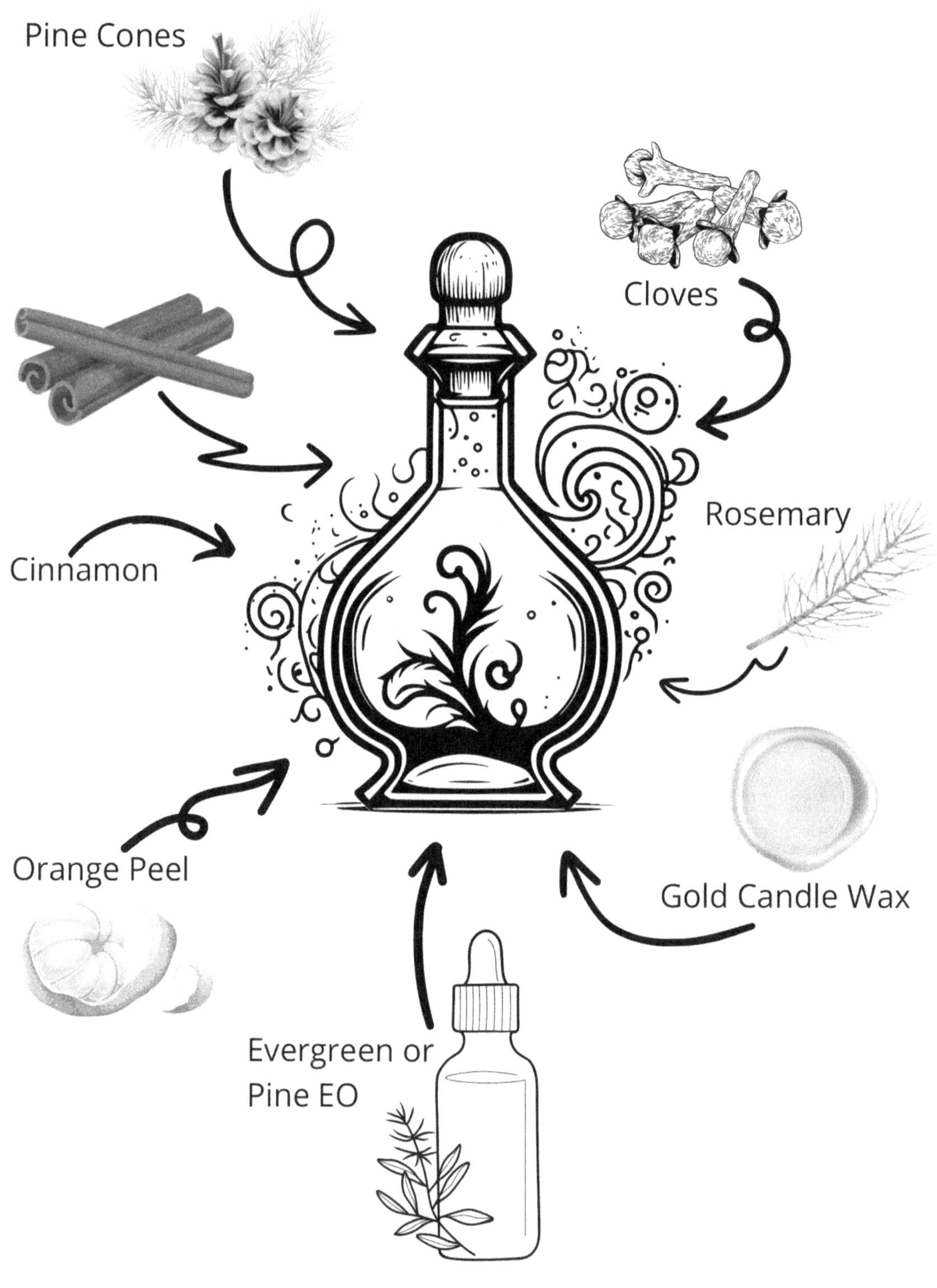

Yule Mini Altar Jar

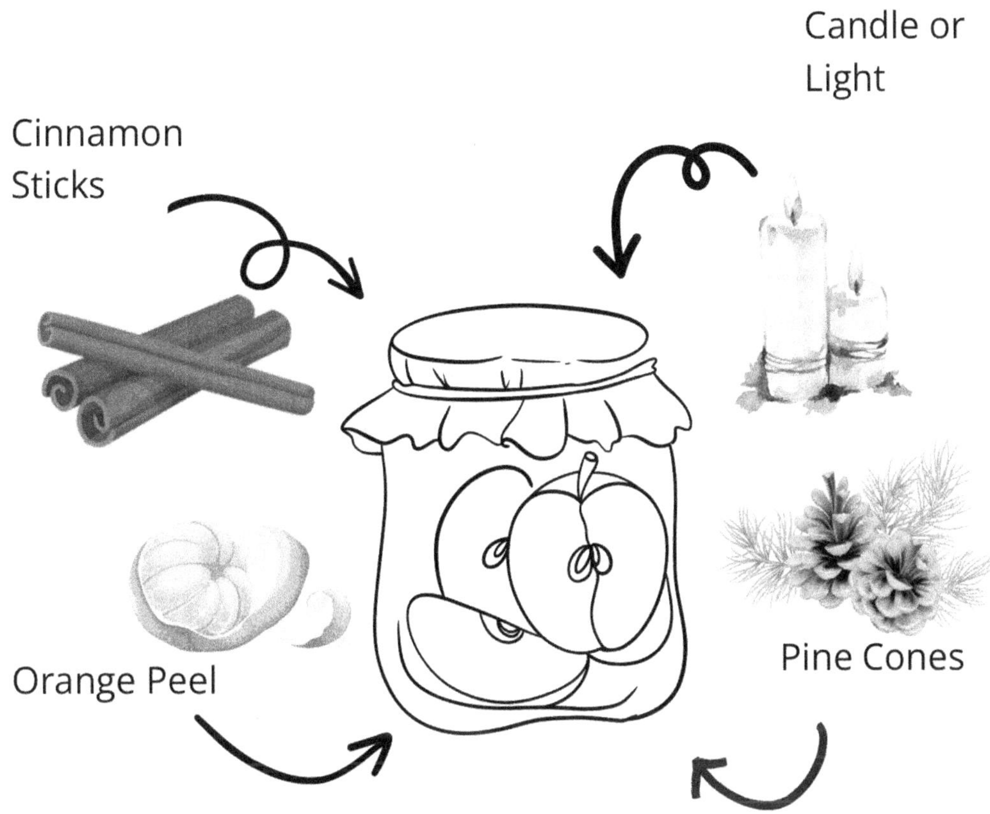

Home Protection Corner Jars

Prepare four jars.
Place them on your home's North, South, East, and West corners.

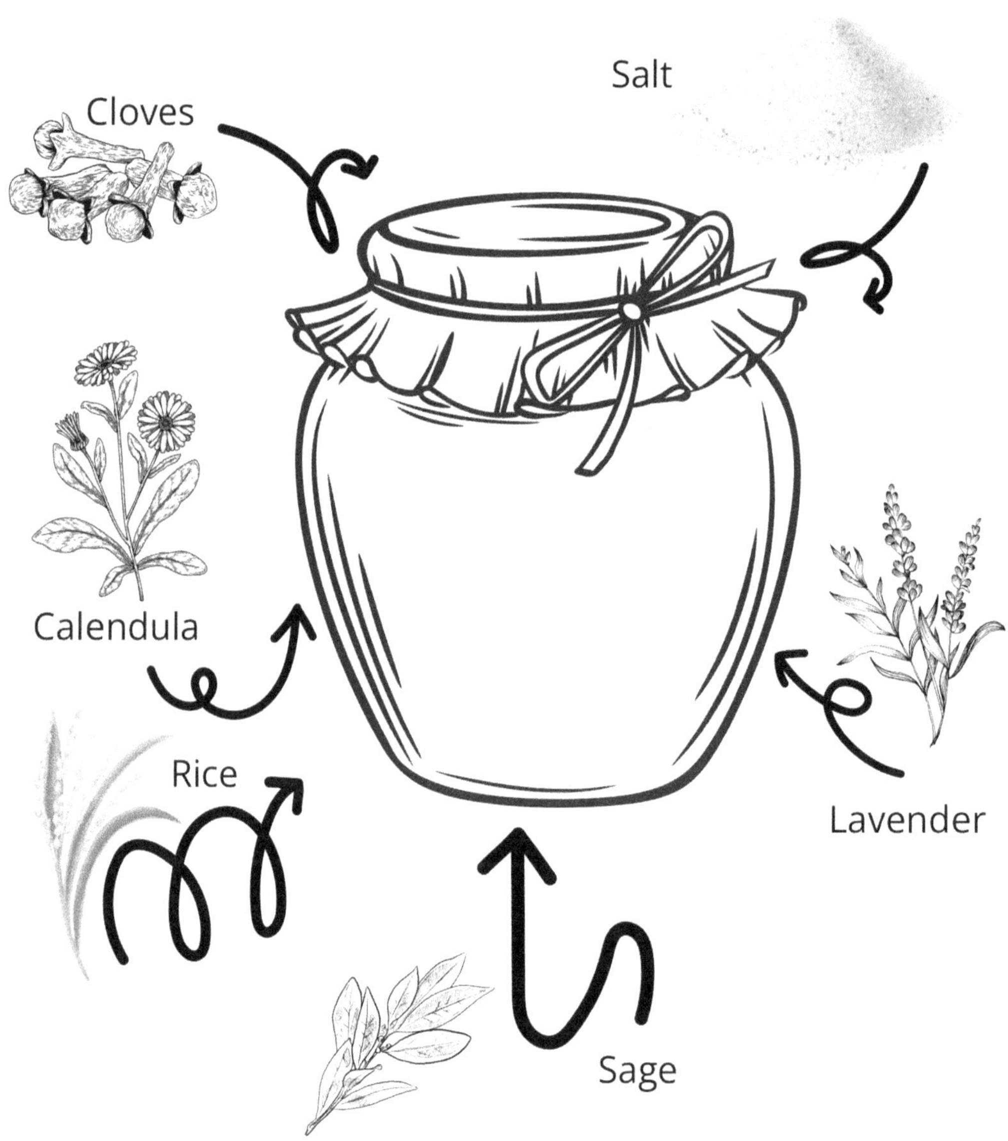

Manifestation Spell Jar

A Spell Jar to help you Manifest with ease.

Ingredients:
Glass Jar
 Clear Quartz Crystal
 Citrine Crystal
 Cinnamon
 Bay Leaves
 Orange Essential Oil
A Marker

Directions:
Cleanse and charge your tools with your intentions.

With a marker, write on the bay leaves the things you wish to manifest.

Then place them in the jar and add the rest of your ingredients.

Close the jar, shake it to activate its energy and hold it in your hands daily while you visualize your desires.

Money Jar or Bag

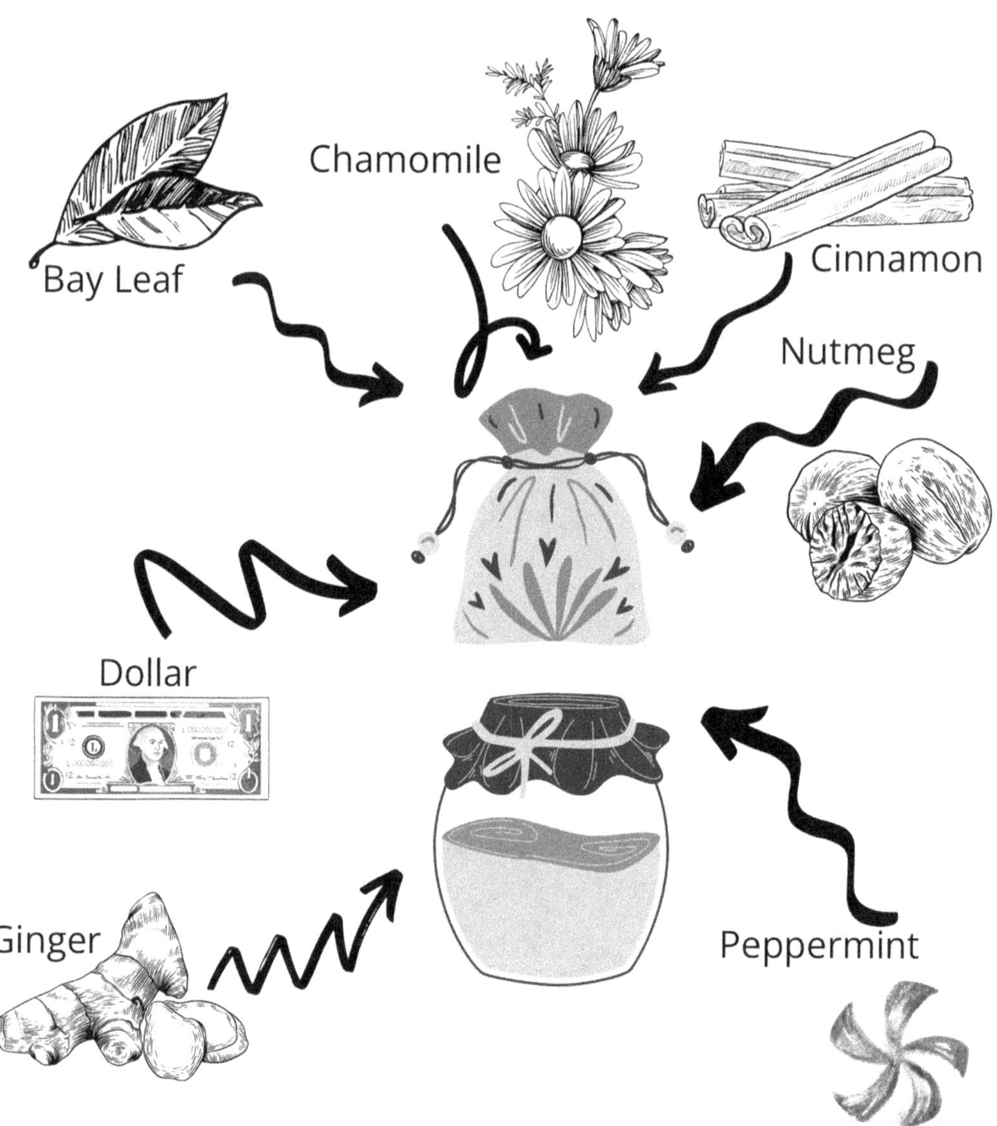

Emotional Protection Jar or Bag

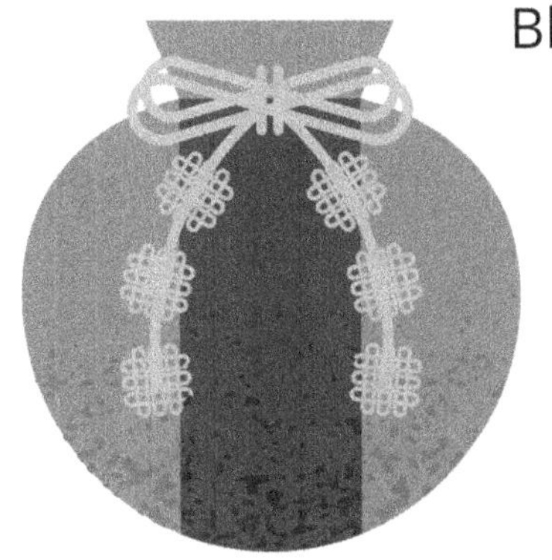

Black tourmaline
Smoky Quartz
Lemon balm
Chamomile
Bay leaf
Rosemary
Calendula

Room Spray
Remove Negative Energy

Amethyst
Moon Water
Common Sage
4 Drops of Lavender Oil
Sea Salt
3 Drops of Eucalyptus Oil
Clear Quartz

Self Love Spell Jar

Pink Candle Wax to Seal the Jar
Honey
Rosebuds
Rosemary
Rose Quartz
Dried Lavender
Himalayan Pink Salt
A Love Note to Yourself
Essential oils:
Rose
Jasmine
Bergamont or Ylang Ylang

Home Blessings Spell Jar

Jar with a lid
Common Sage for good vibes
Sea Salt for purity
White Rice
LAVENDER for peace

Protection & Positivity

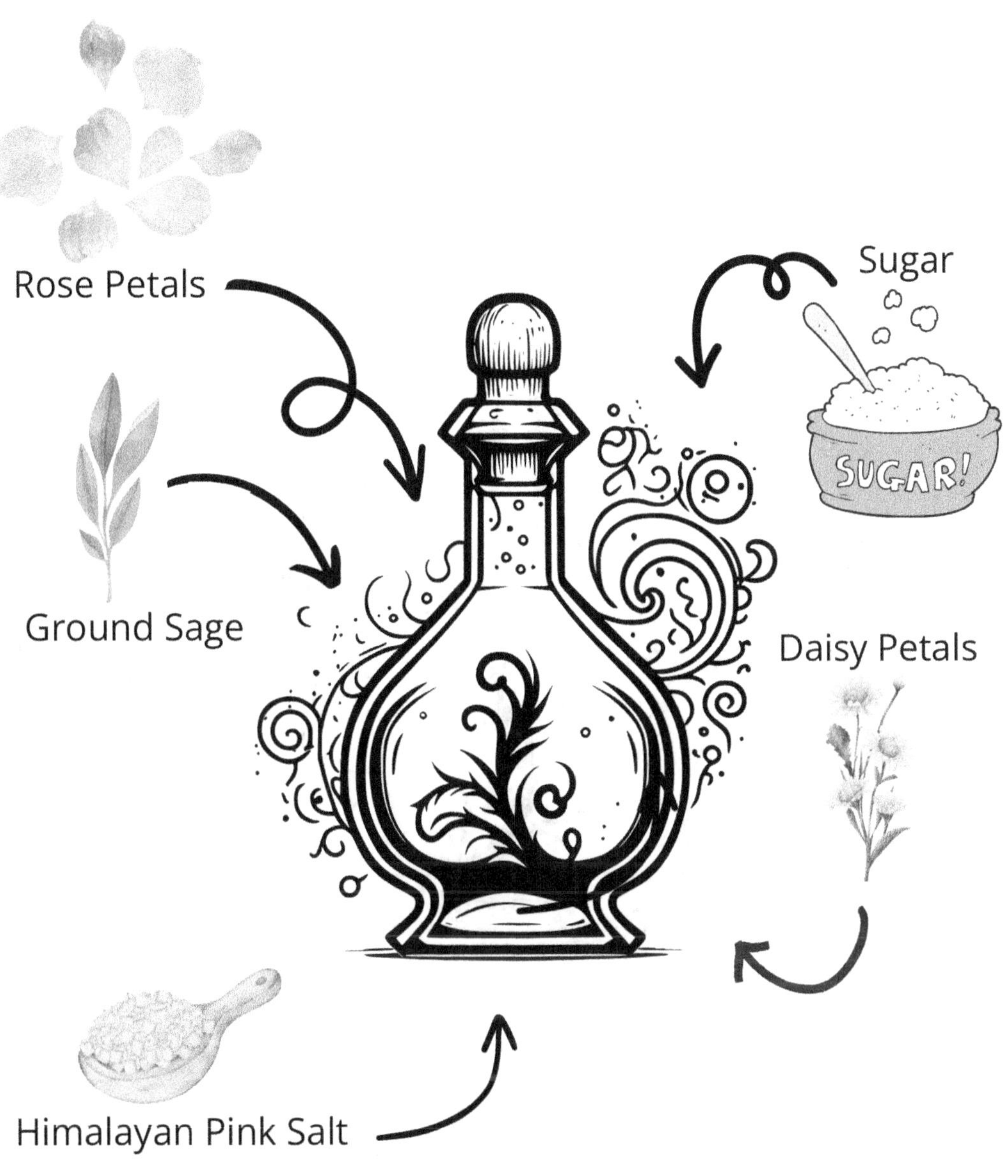

Money

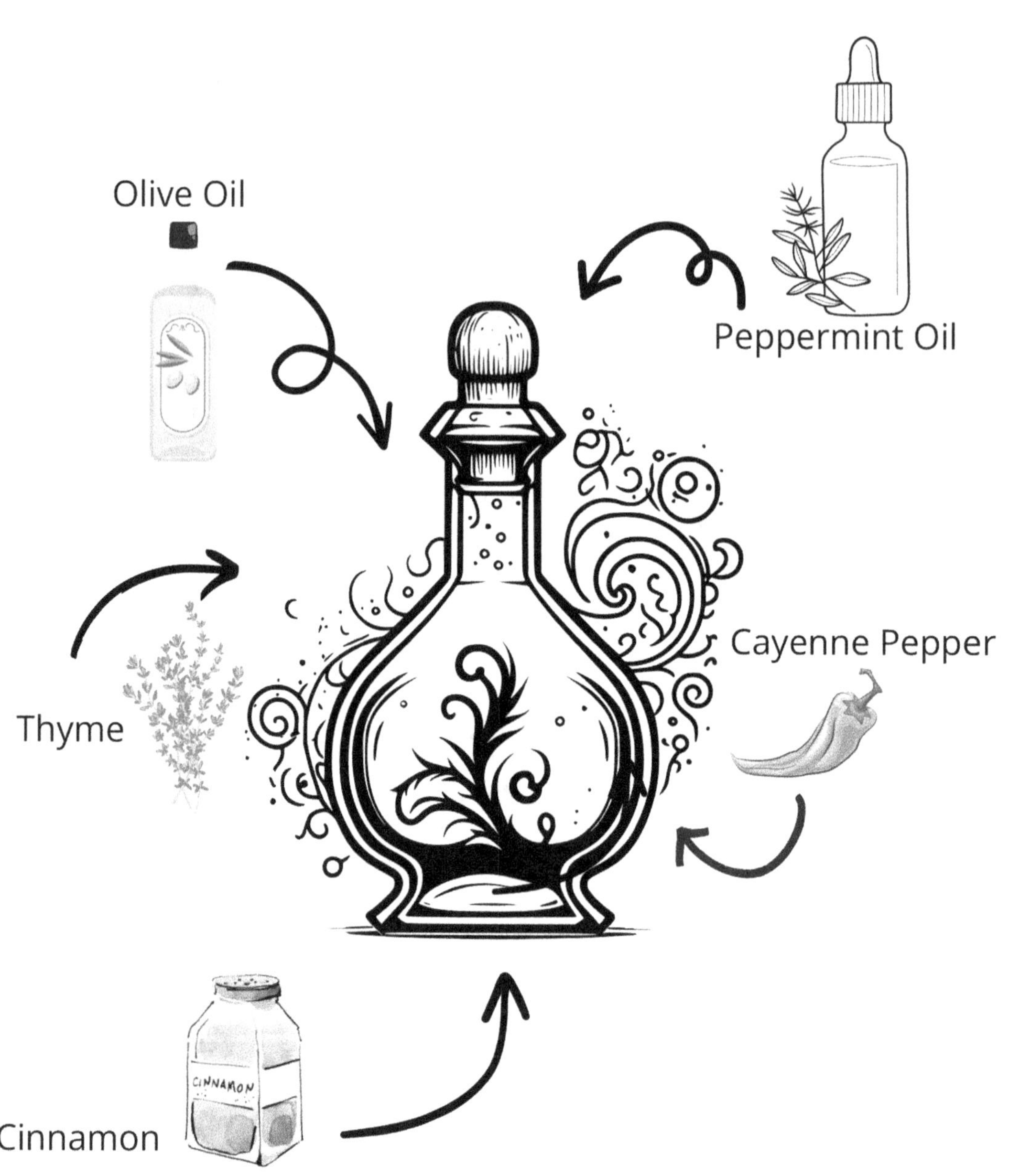

Prosperity Spell Jar

Perform during New Moon
Honeysuckle
Written Intentions
Basil
Lucky Charm
Almonds
Ginger
Seal with green candle wax

Sweet Dreams Spell Jar

Ingredients:
Jar with a lid
Chamomile
Thyme
Amethyst
Jasmine Oil
Anise
Lavender
Purple Candle Wax seal on the lid.

Sleep Spell Jar

Ingredients:
Lavender for calming
Black Salt for protection
Rosemary for preventing nightmares
Aquamarine for serenity
Black pepper for banishing negativity
Seal with purple wax for wisdom, authority, and hidden knowledge

Spell Jar for Anxiety

Ingredients:
Lavender
Chamomile
Sage
Amethyst
Salt
Rose Quartz

New Year Wishing Jar

A wishing jar is said to help encourage wishes to come true protect and cleanse a space from unwanted energies. "Wishing jars are glass vessels filled with salt, cinnamon, herbs, crystals, and items found in nature. Simply place a wishing jar near your own entryway to trap unwanted energies and welcome abundance, fresh new energies, and encourage wishes."

Protection Spell Jar

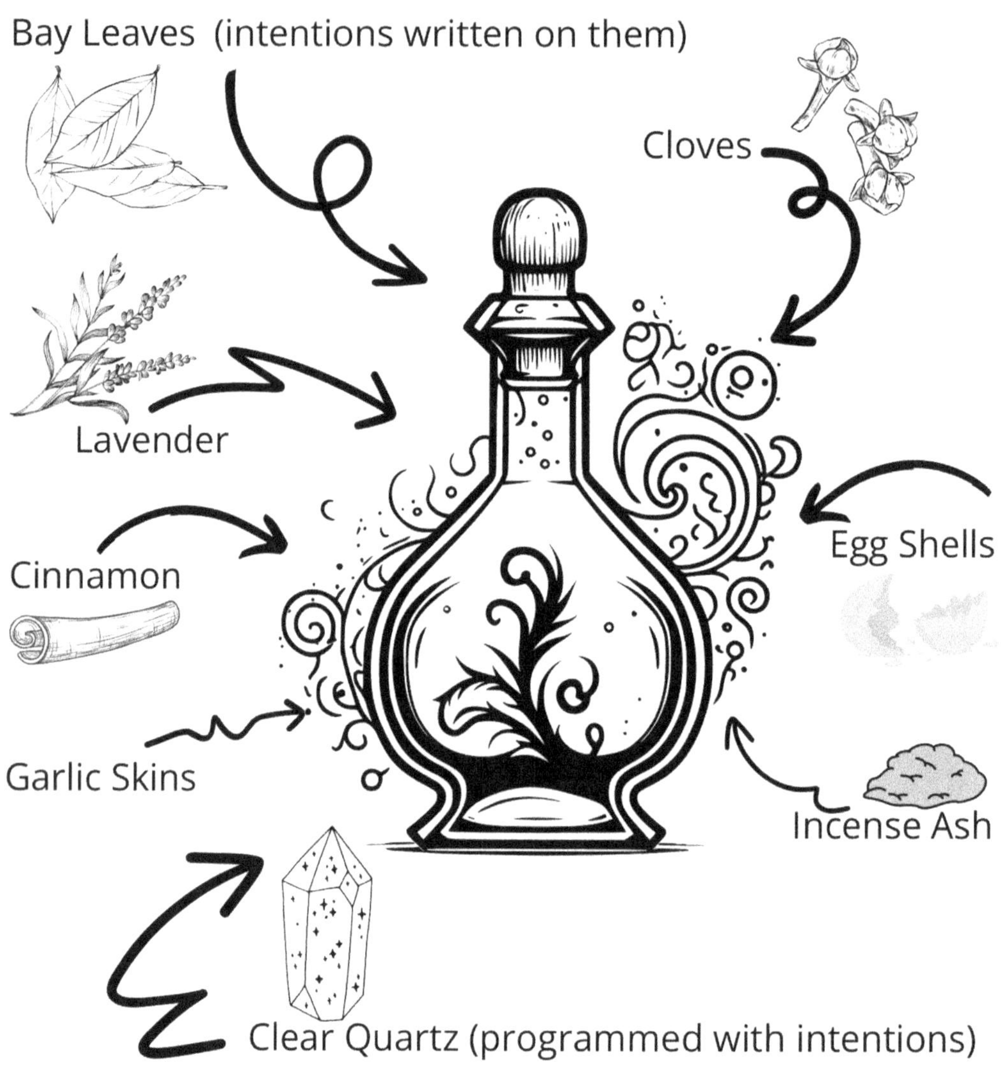

Offering Oil

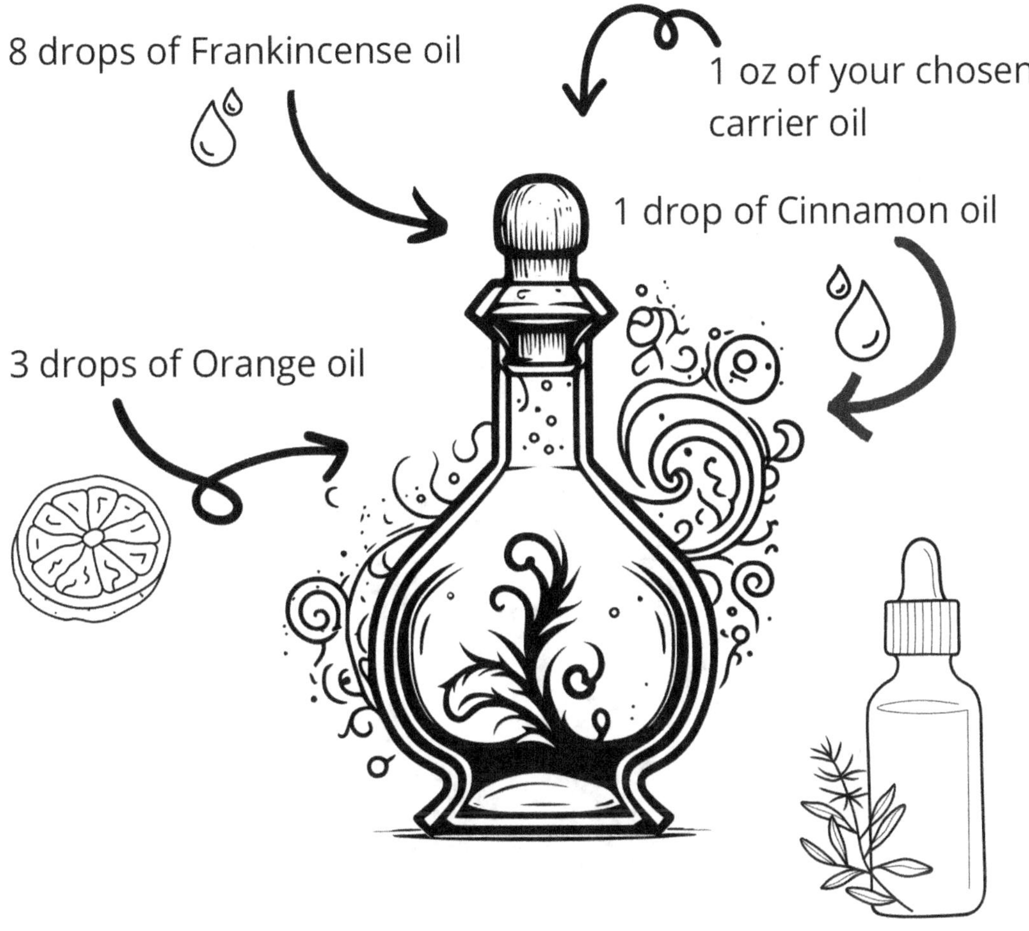

Spirit Oil

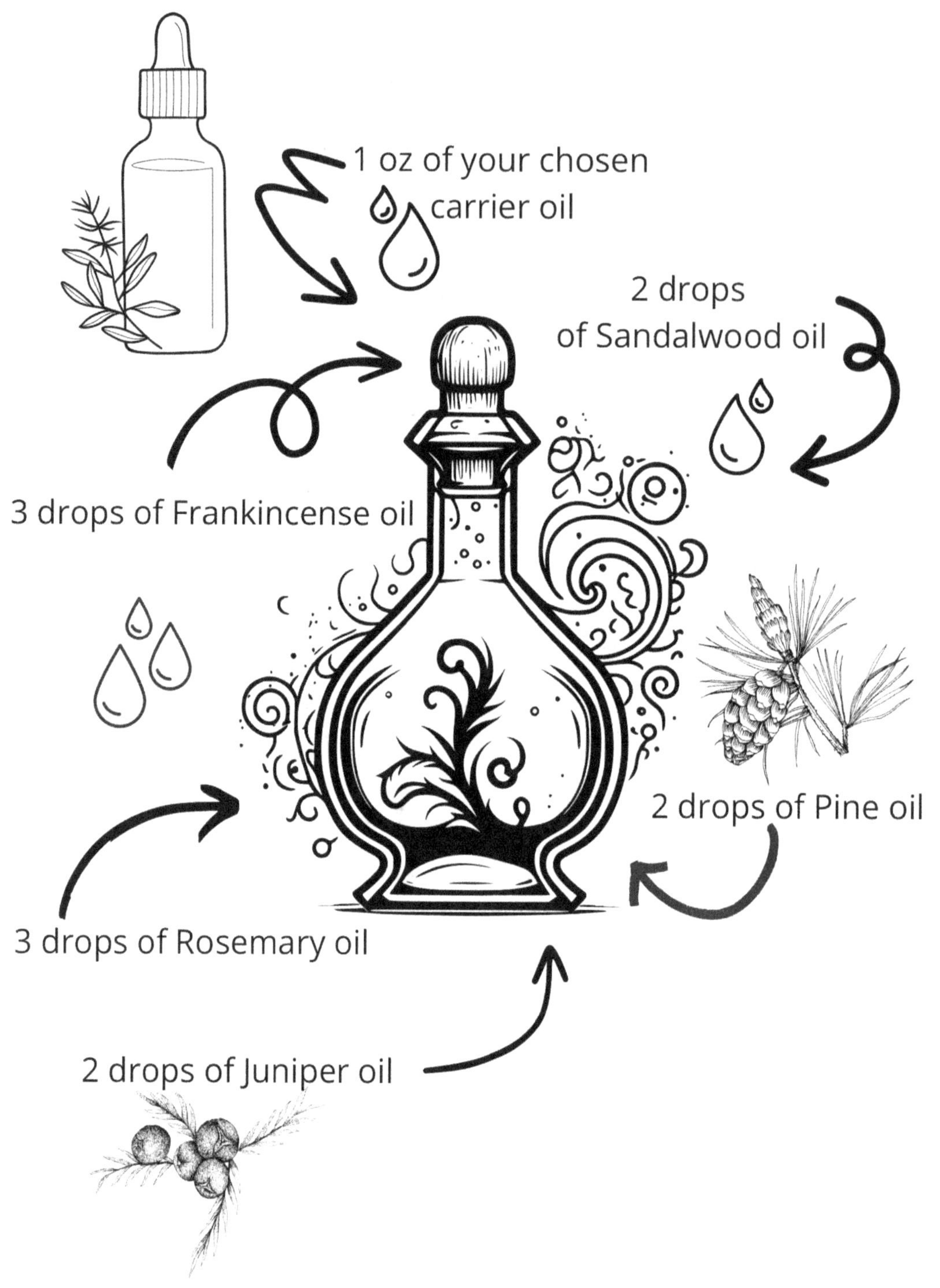

1 oz of your chosen carrier oil
2 drops of Sandalwood oil
3 drops of Frankincense oil
2 drops of Pine oil
3 drops of Rosemary oil
2 drops of Juniper oil

Psychic Oil

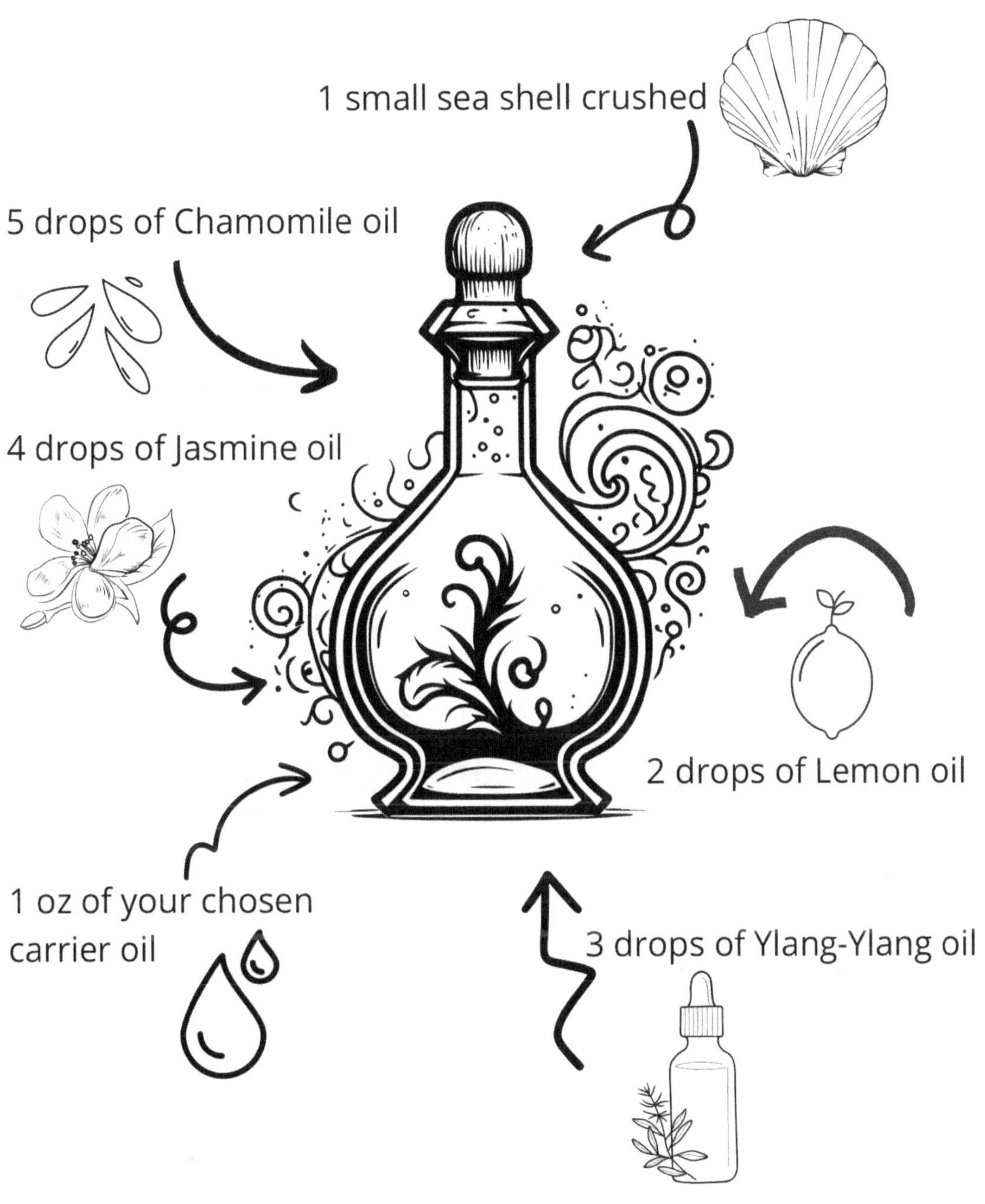

1 small sea shell crushed
5 drops of Chamomile oil
4 drops of Jasmine oil
2 drops of Lemon oil
1 oz of your chosen carrier oil
3 drops of Ylang-Ylang oil

Emotional Stability Jar

Vervain
Rose petals
Lemon balm
Lavender
Black obsidian chips
Rhodochrosite chips
Sealed with black wax

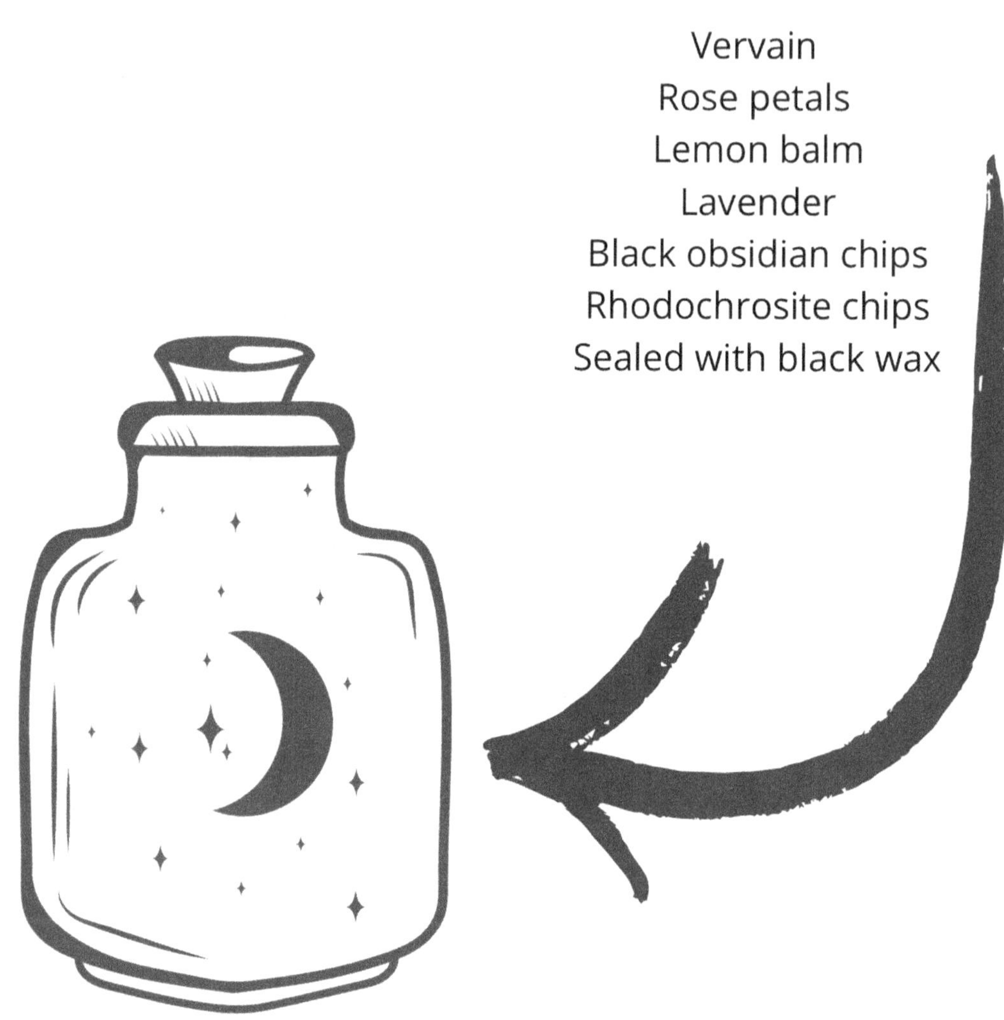

CHAPTER 25

Yule Sachets

During the holidays, sachets make a charming and fragrant gift that is simple to create.

Yule Sachet
Ingredients:
7 parts Juniper
4 parts Cinnamon
4 parts Allspice
4 parts Ginger
4 parts Caraway
2 parts Nutmeg
2 parts Rosemary
2 parts Lemon peel
2 parts Orange peel
1 part Clove
1 part Bay
2 pinches Orris root **
Directions:
Tie up in a green or red cloth and give as a gift on Yule or Christmas.

**When using orris root, especially for medicinal or magical purposes, it's crucial to exercise caution and be aware of potential allergies or sensitivities.

Yule Protection Bag
Ingredients:
1/2 Teaspoon of Dried Peppermint
1/2 Teaspoon of Dried Rosemary
 1 Small Piece of Amethyst
Red Cord or Yarn 1
Piece of Black Fabric

Directions:
Place the herbs and amethyst in the center of the fabric, grab the corners together, and tie the sack closed. Continue to tie nine knots while saying the following," Protection and safety, peace of mind, herbs, and stone, their magick I bind.!" Place them in your car, backpack, purse, or anywhere for protection. You can even give them as gifts.

Personal Protection Bag

Carry with you or place in your car, purse, wherever you want to place protection.

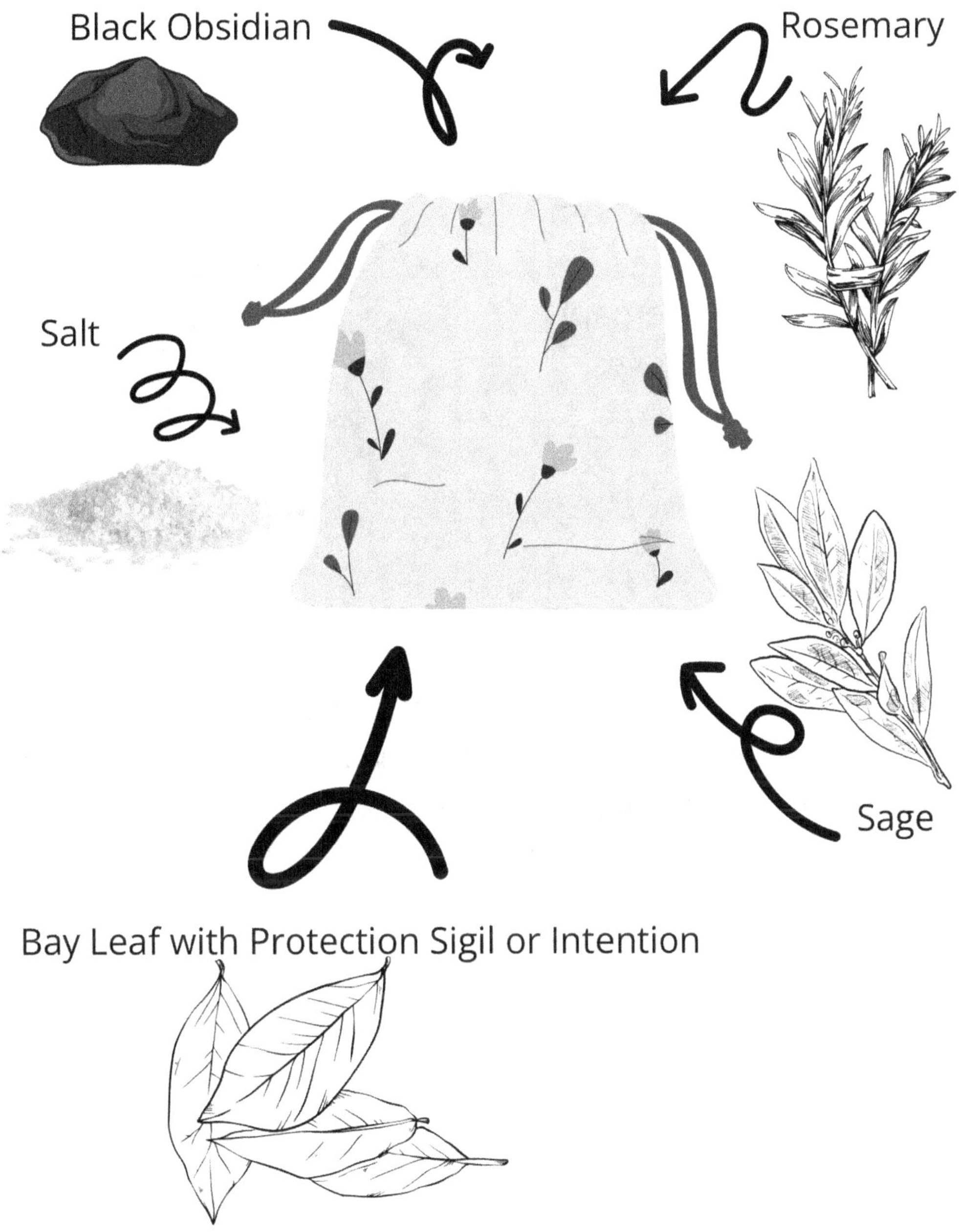

Black Obsidian

Rosemary

Salt

Sage

Bay Leaf with Protection Sigil or Intention

Yule Mojo Bag

Ensure all herbs are dry before putting them in your Mojo Bag

Lavender
Thyme
Cinnamon
Cardomom
Bay
Rosemary
Cloves

Feeding your Mojo bag simply means giving it an extra power boost 2 to 3 times a week.
You can do this by dropping essential oils inside or smoking it with incense.

Yule Charm

Place the powder in a green cloth and bind it with red thread. Carry it with you through the Winter Solstice All 3 herbs are ruled by the Sun.
This charm is a good protector for travel, justice, psychic awareness, luck & positive energy.

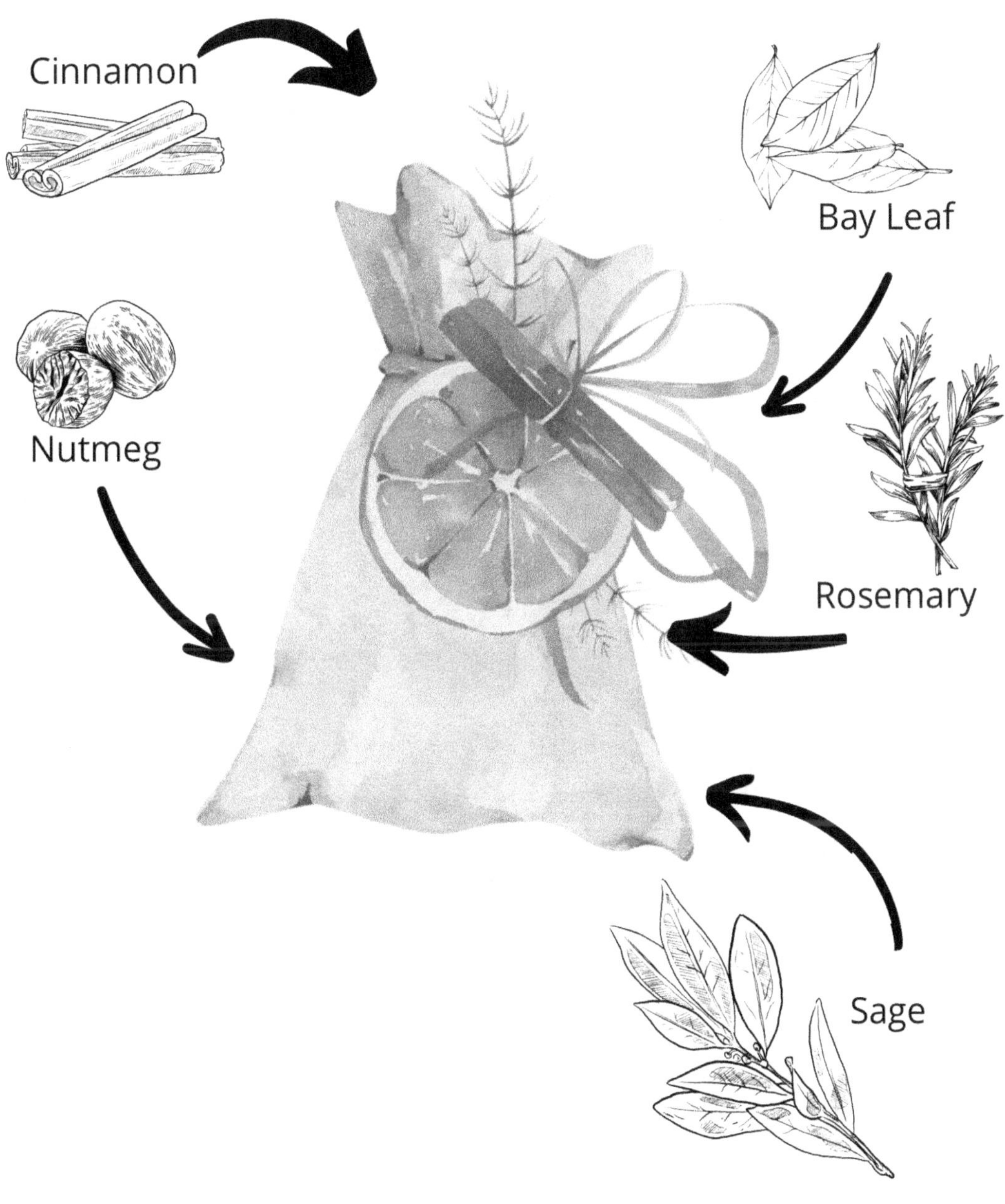

Anti-Nightmare Bag

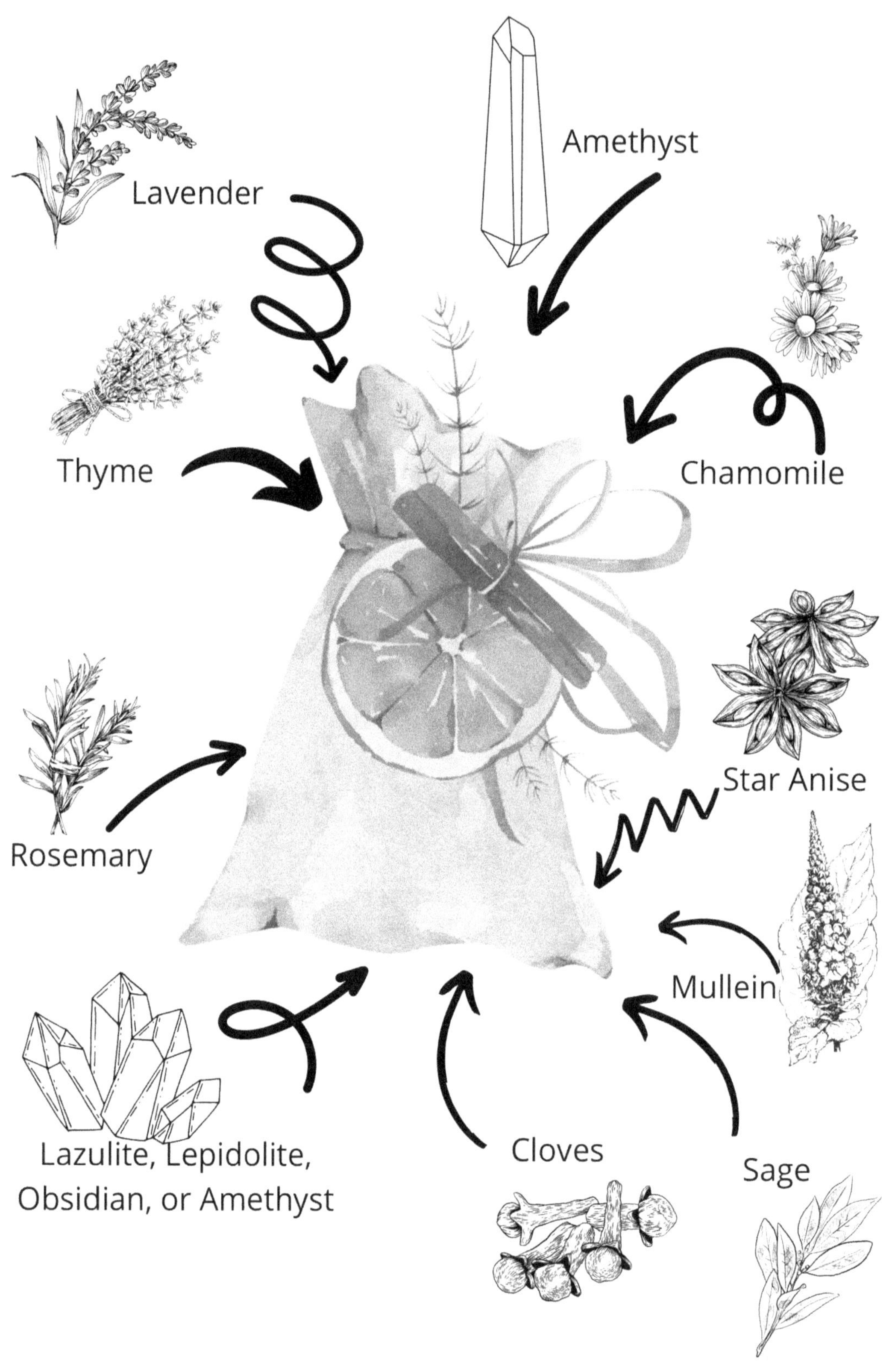

Restful Sleep Bag

Charge under Full Moon

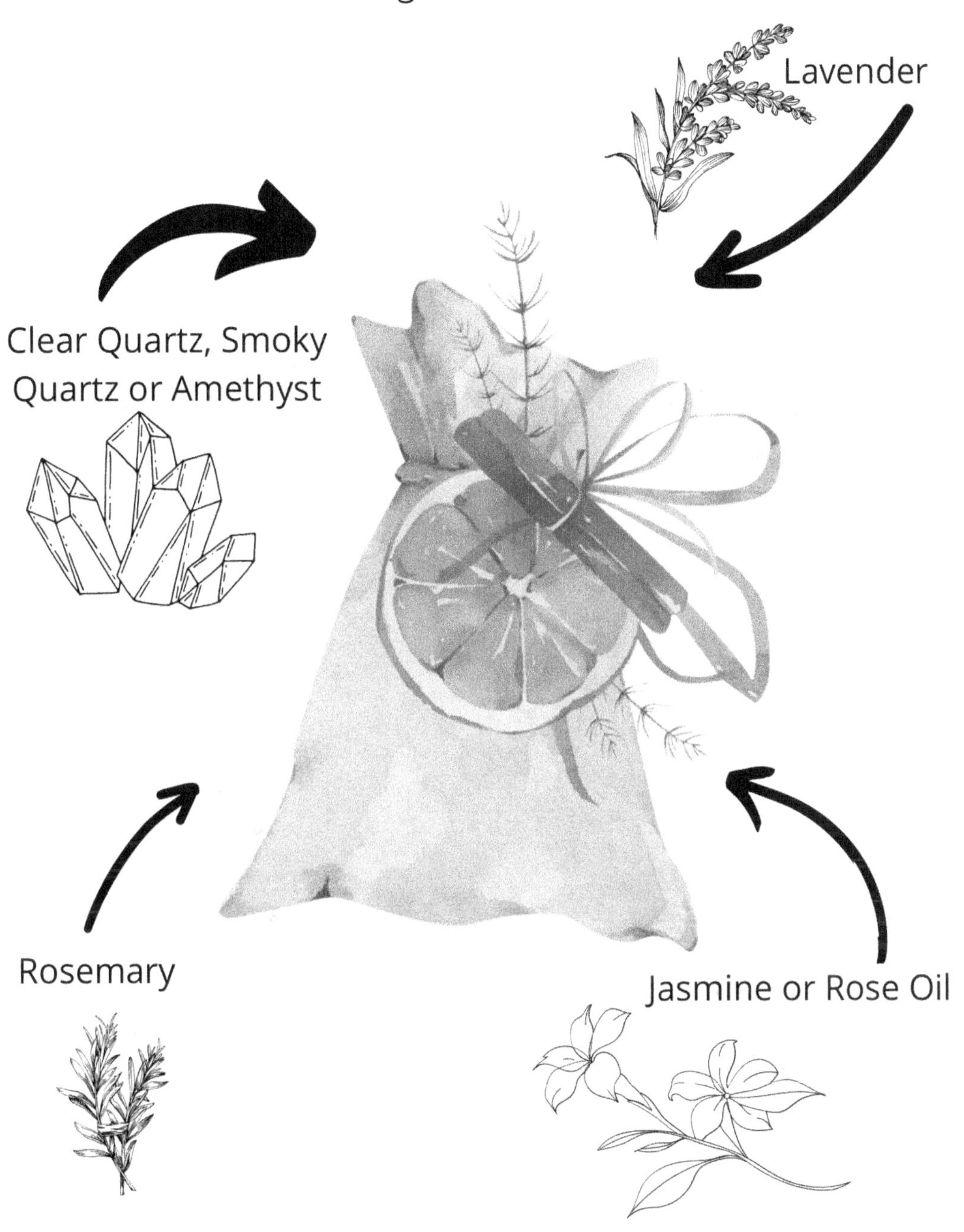

Sleep Potion Bag

Sleep Potion Oil
10 Argus Rose Oil
10 drops Ylang Ylang Oil
5 drops Cedarwood Oil
1 ounce Grapeseed or Olive Oil

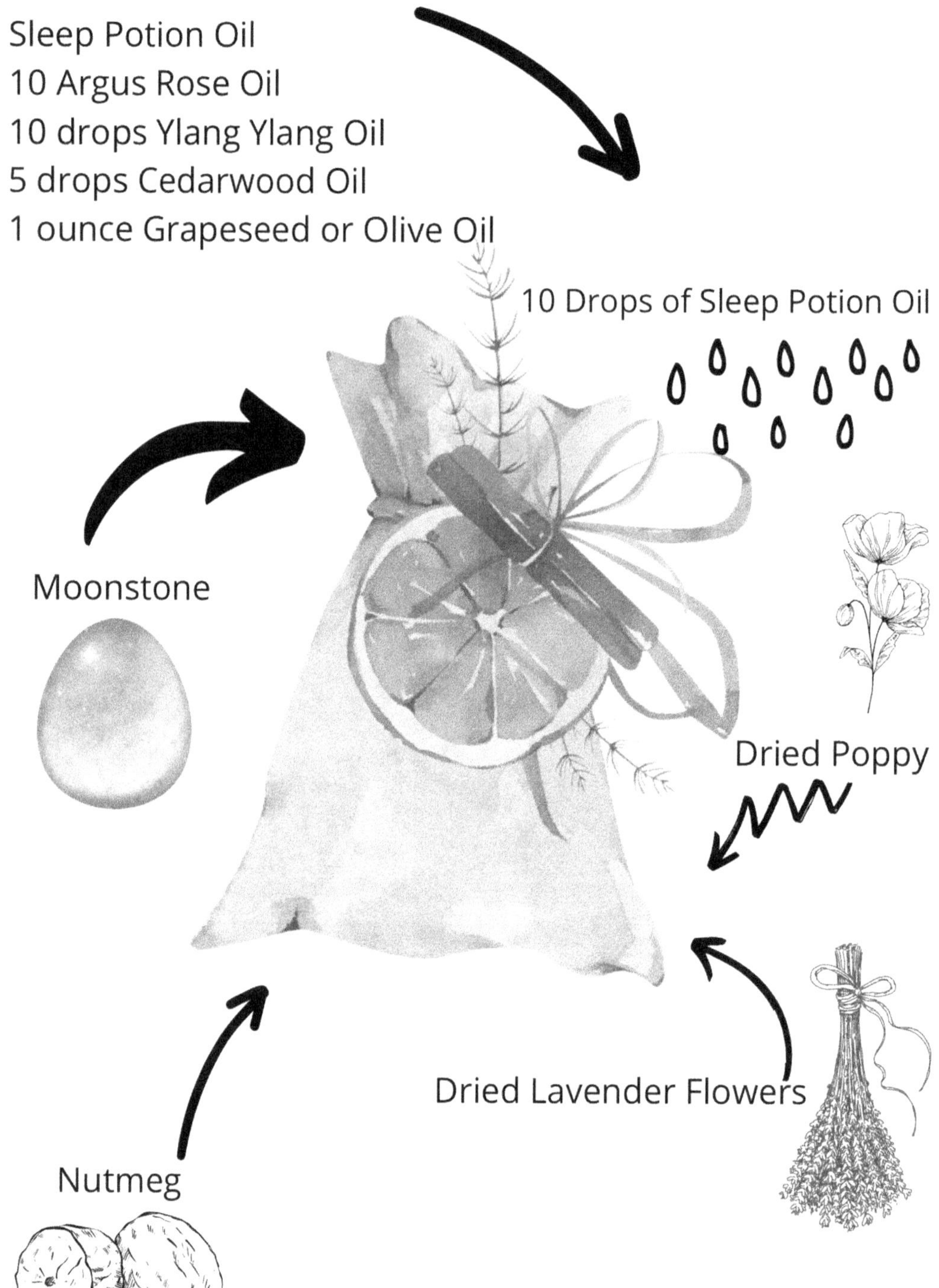

Sleep Mojo Bag

Ensure all herbs are dry before putting them in your Mojo Bag

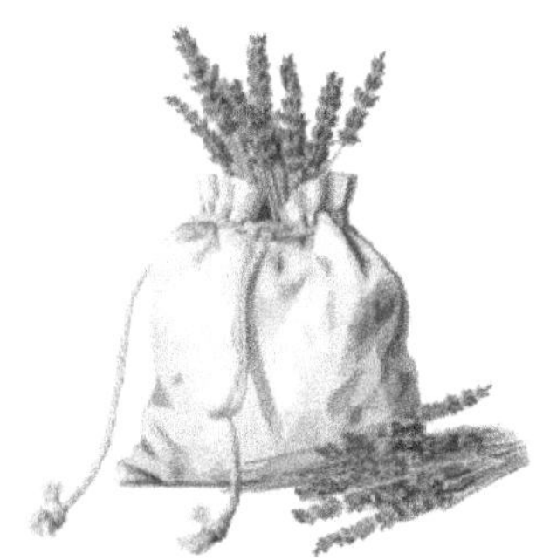

Hops
Lavender
Lemon balm
Lepidolite
Clear Quartz
Chamomile

Feeding your Mojo bag simply means giving it an extra power boost 2 to 3 times a week. You can do this by dropping essential oils inside or smoking it with incense.

Freezer Spell

Best Under a Waning Moon
Banishing
Binding
Protection

Write what you want to banish or bind on paper—place in a
jar or freezer bag.
Add water or moon water.
You can use a photo (if more appropriate)
Add protective herbs.
Seal the jar/bag and place it in the freezer.

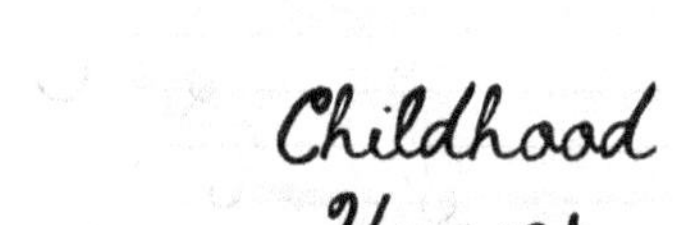

Childhood
Hunger

Money Bowl

STEP 3:
Add coins and
bills

STEP 2:
Place a green
candle in the
center

STEP 4:
Light candle. Do
not leave
unattended

STEP 1:
Add salt in a fire
safe dish

STEP 5:
Focus intentions
on money
arriving

Scrying Mirror

Scrying is a technique to obtain insights from images perceived in reflective, translucent, or luminescent surfaces. However, this is not simply observing one's reflection in a bathroom mirror; the images obtained during scrying represent inner spiritual visions. Various materials, including crystals, glass, or water, can create a scrying mirror. The term "scry" is derived from the word "descry," which means to catch sight of or detect something. The origin of "descry" can be traced back to the Old French term "descrier," meaning "to call out."

History: In modern times, scrying is believed to reveal visions from one's subconscious or inner spirit, whereas, in the past, it was attributed to gods, spirits, or other divine influences. Persian mythology tells the tale of the famous Cup of Jamshid, a scrying mirror said to contain an elixir of immortality that reflected the entire world. Nostradamus, a renowned French apothecary and seer from the 16th century used a bowl of clear water for scrying and documented his visions. Joseph Smith Jr., who lived from 1805 to 1844, founded the Mormon religion based on insights from seer stones.

Uses: Despite the belief held by some that scrying abilities are reserved only for a special few, it is widely accepted that anyone can attain proficiency in this ancient practice through dedication and practice. To commence your journey, acquire a scrying mirror, which can be purchased or crafted using various materials and designs. Stones such as malachite, obsidian, and tourmaline are particularly suited for scrying purposes. Alternatively, you may explore Nostradamus's technique involving a bowl of water. Additionally, achieving a state of deep inner focus and exploration through meditation or trance is essential. With continuous practice, vivid visions will manifest themselves before you. Countless resources, including books, websites, and organizations, provide specific methods to learn from and offer guidance on interpreting the visions that unfold during your scrying endeavors.

Worry Water

Water is the element of the ocean. It will absorb the feelings and emotions you release into it. Use this energy transmutation ritual to help release stress and anxiety from inside the body into a pool of water and then disperse back to newer, neutral energy. Tell your secrets, fears, and worries to the water pond open up. Don't hold back and pour the water out, either down the drain or into the Earth, not directly onto plants, though perhaps for the concert; trade it, or I'll worry water on undesirable weeds in your garden.

Wealth Attraction Spell

Ingredients:
Green Candle
Bay Leaves
Olive Oil
Cinnamon

Directions:
Anoint each of your 3 green candles with olive oil while you rub it from top to bottom.
Mark each of the candles with a relevant currency sign.
Grind your cinnamon and bay leaves, then rub the candles with it.
Light the candles, and chant 3 times: "The winds of change 1 feel tonight, The waters are calm, and the sky is bright, Wealth be mine, come for me, My desires are true, so mote it be."
Let your candles burn down completely.

Yule Cleansing Sticks

Smudging is a great way to cleanse a sacred space, and most people use smudge sticks made of sweetgrass or sage for this purpose, but why not use more seasonally appropriate plants at Yule?

Supplies:
Scissors or garden clippers
Cotton string
Seasonal plants such as evergreens (pine, fir, juniper, balsam, and cedar) and other scents that you find appealing.

Directions:
Trim your clippings to a manageable length, between four and six inches. Next, cut a length of string about five feet long. Put several branches together and wind the string tightly around the stems of the bundle. Tie a knot to the end and make a loop to dry them. Depending on how fresh your branches are - and how much sap they have - it can take a few weeks to dry them out. Once they're done, burn them in Yule rituals and ceremonies or use them for cleansing sacred space.

If you want to get frisky, use cinnamon and pine the same way.

Yule EO Blend

Ingredients:

1 /8 cup of grapeseed oil or your chosen carrier oil 4 drops of pine EO
2 drops of orange EO
2 drops of cedar EO
2 drops of juniper EO
2 to 3 small lumps of frankincense, finely ground

Directions:
Blend the oils and put them in a sealed container-label, date, and store them in a cool, dark place.

Cleansing Spray

Ingredients:
A Spray bottle
Sage
Rosemary
Sea Salt
Spring or rainwater
A couple of drops of lemon juice

Directions:
Boil the water and pour over the herbs and salt.
Leave covered until cool.
Strain and add to a dark spray bottle.
Add a couple of drops of lemon juice.

Use this spray to cleanse objects, people, or an area, just as you would use smudge sticks.

For a house, start from the corner furthest from the front door and work your way forward, making sure to get corners.

Energy Clearing Spray

Ingredients:
2 drops of palo santo EO
2 drops of sage EO
2 drops of bergamot EO
1 drop of lime EO
30 ml distilled water

Directions:
Use a 4oz spray bottle and fill most of the way with distilled water.
Add the EO's and shake well to mix.
Add a small chip of Amethyst or other protecting crystal of your choice.
Shake well before each use.

Use to clear a room of negative energy or spray your hands and arms before, during, and after energy sessions.

Warding

Warding is a form of defensive magic that offers a gentle approach to protection. Its purpose is to safeguard against negative energies, redirecting them away from you or your surroundings in a general sense.

Methods
Guardians
Create a guardian to guard your home or space against negative energies.

Crystals
Corresponding crystals can be worn on jewelry to protect against negative energy. Place crystals in a room or around your house to create a protective barrier.

Salt
Black salt can be used in rituals or just used alone. Sprinkle salt around your doors and windows, or make protection jars with it.

Herbs
Burn protective herbs and pass the smoke through your space or tools. Sprinkle herbal oils and tinctures on yourself and your space for protective barriers.

Visualization
Use your intention and energy to visualize a powerful barrier of protecting light around yourself or your space.

Trust your instincts and rely on methods that resonate with you. Avoid using techniques that don't feel right or that you haven't thoroughly researched.

Spell for Warding

Ingredients:
Small white candle
Protection herbs (e.g., rosemary, basil, sage)
Protective crystals (e.g., black tourmaline, obsidian, clear quartz)
Sea salt
Anointing oil (e.g., olive or coconut oil)
Fire-safe bowl or cauldron

Instructions:
Clear and prepare your sacred space. Light a white candle.
Crush protection herbs and roll the white candle in anointing oil. Coat the candle in crushed herbs.
Place a circle of protective crystals around the candle and sprinkle sea salt in a circle around them.
Light the white candle and state your warding intention.
Visualize a protective shield forming around you and your space.
Let the candle burn down completely in a safe manner.
Express gratitude and close your sacred space.

Banishing

Regarding defensive magic, banishing is a much more targeted and forceful approach than warding. Its purpose is to eliminate a specific energy, spirit, or individual. However, it's essential to carefully consider the consequences before resorting to banishing.

Methods
Use the Elements
Burn a slip of paper with your target's name on it or throw a leaf with your target's name on it in a running river/stream. Burn corresponding herbs and pass the smoke through your space.

Candles
Anoint your candle with corresponding herbs and oils, then burn it when the candle has burnt out; the banishing is complete.

Sigils
Make your own banishing sigil, or find one that resonates with you; place it in the space or on the item you are banishing energy from.

Herbs & Tinctures
Use herbal smoke to force energy out of a space or object; make a spray or herbal tincture to sprinkle around your home.

Trust your instincts and rely on methods that resonate with you. Avoid using techniques that don't feel right or that you haven't thoroughly researched.

Spell for Banishing

Ingredients:
Small black candle
Pinch of sea salt
Handful of dried sage leaves
Piece of paper
Black pen or marker
Fire-safe bowl or cauldron

Instructions:
Clear and prepare your sacred space.
Write down what you want to banish on the piece of paper.
Place the black candle in the center and sprinkle a pinch of sea salt around it.
Light the black candle and recite your banishing incantation.
Hold sage leaves over the flame to smolder and let the smoke surround you.
Visualize the negative energies leaving and into the flame.
Burn the paper and affirm your release from what you wish to banish.
Let the candle burn out safely.
Bury or scatter the cooled ashes.
Express gratitude and close your sacred space.
Remember to approach the spell with respect, focus, and sincere intentions for positive change.

CHAPTER 26

Introduction to Manifestation

Manifestation turns desires into reality through focused thought, belief, and action. Aligning thoughts, emotions, and energy with desired outcomes leads to positive changes. It's based on the idea that our thoughts and beliefs shape our reality. By directing energy towards desired outcomes, we tap into universal energy and co-create. Manifestation empowers individuals to harness universal forces and fulfill dreams, goals, and aspirations. It opens doors to limitless possibilities, bringing about profound transformation.

Manifestation Mantras

I attract massive amounts of happiness.

I accept myself unconditionally.

I have plenty of time and energy to do the things I need to do.

All I need is within me.

I have enough. I do enough. I am enough.

I attract love, success, freedom, and health into my life.

My money is an unlimited resource and is constantly flowing my way.

My wildest dreams are coming true.

I am in the right place at the right time.

The Universe is bringing good things my way, and I am already thankful for them.

Magic will always surround me.

Opportunities will always come my way.

I can see the future that I want to have and know that it is on its way.

Manifestation Methods

3 6 9 Method
Write your desires 3 times in the present tense. Write your intention 6 times. Write the outcome 9 times.

Manifestation Meditation
Every spiritual person practices some form of meditation because it is how you connect with your higher power. Meditation allows divine wisdom and spiritual guidance to come through.

Manifestation Jar/Box
A manifestation jar is a container that holds all the desires you want to manifest. The things you put into the jar represent your requests to the Universe, and anything you put in will manifest in your reality.

Manifestation Journal
A manifestation journal is a dedicated journal to manifest what you want into reality. Write about the goals and life that you want to attract.

Scripting
Scripting is a manifestation technique that describes the experience you would like to manifest as if it has already happened.

Gratitude
Be grateful for what you have right now. Manifestation happens when you're vibrating at a high frequency.

Subliminals
Subliminals can help you gently reprogram your subconscious mind by releasing the limiting beliefs that no longer serve you and filling them with new beliefs that do serve you.

The Pillow Method
Write your intention on paper and tack it under your pillow. Then, every night, read what you've written and focus on it while falling asleep.

Visualization
Visualization helps you get into vibrational alignment with your desire by cultivating the feeling of experiencing your desire as if it has manifested.

55x5 Manifestation
Write your affirmation 55 times for 5 days to manifest your desire. This helps you become a vibrational match for what you want and attract it into your life.

CHAPTER 27

How to Dry Potpourri

Moisture causes spoilage and rot. To prevent this, dry or dehydrate anything moist. Use a dehydrator or oven to dry fruits and herbs.

Drying Sliced Fruit Oven Method

For oranges, lemons, limes, and other citrus fruits, first preheat your oven to 200 degrees. Slice your citrus into 1/4-inch thick slices. Arrange on a parchment paper-lined baking sheet. Cook in the oven for about 6 hours or until dry.

Stovetop Potpourri Ingredient Suggestions

To enjoy simmering stovetop potpourri, fill a pot halfway with water and potpourri. Simmer on low heat, and keep an eye on the water level as it dissipates and spreads the scent throughout your home.

Tip: If all the water evaporates, the fruit burns and emits an unpleasant odor. To avoid this, you can add more water or turn off the stovetop.

Combine any amount of the following:

Dried Oranges
Dried Cranberries
Cinnamon Sticks
Vanilla Bean
Cloves
Dried Lemons
Dried Limes
Dried Rosemary
Star Anise
Dried Pomegranate
Dried Apples

Simmer Pots

Introduction: In the world of spellwork, where the senses intertwine with intention, simmer pots have emerged as a captivating technique that marries the power of fragrance with the art of magic. Simmer pots, much like modern cauldrons, offer a unique and sensory-rich way to infuse spaces with intent, utilizing aromatic ingredients to conjure an atmosphere ripe for spells and manifestations. In this brief exploration, we'll uncover the transformative potential of simmer pots in spellwork, where the gentle dance of steam becomes a conduit for weaving intentions into the fabric of reality.

Simmer Pots

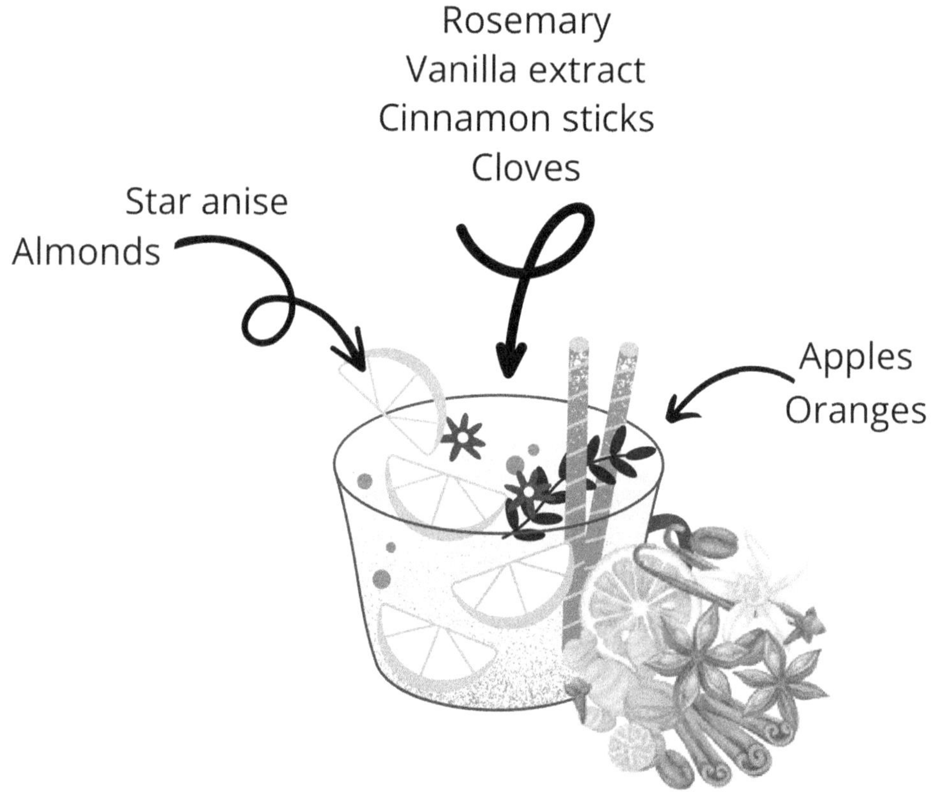

Prosperity Simmer Pots

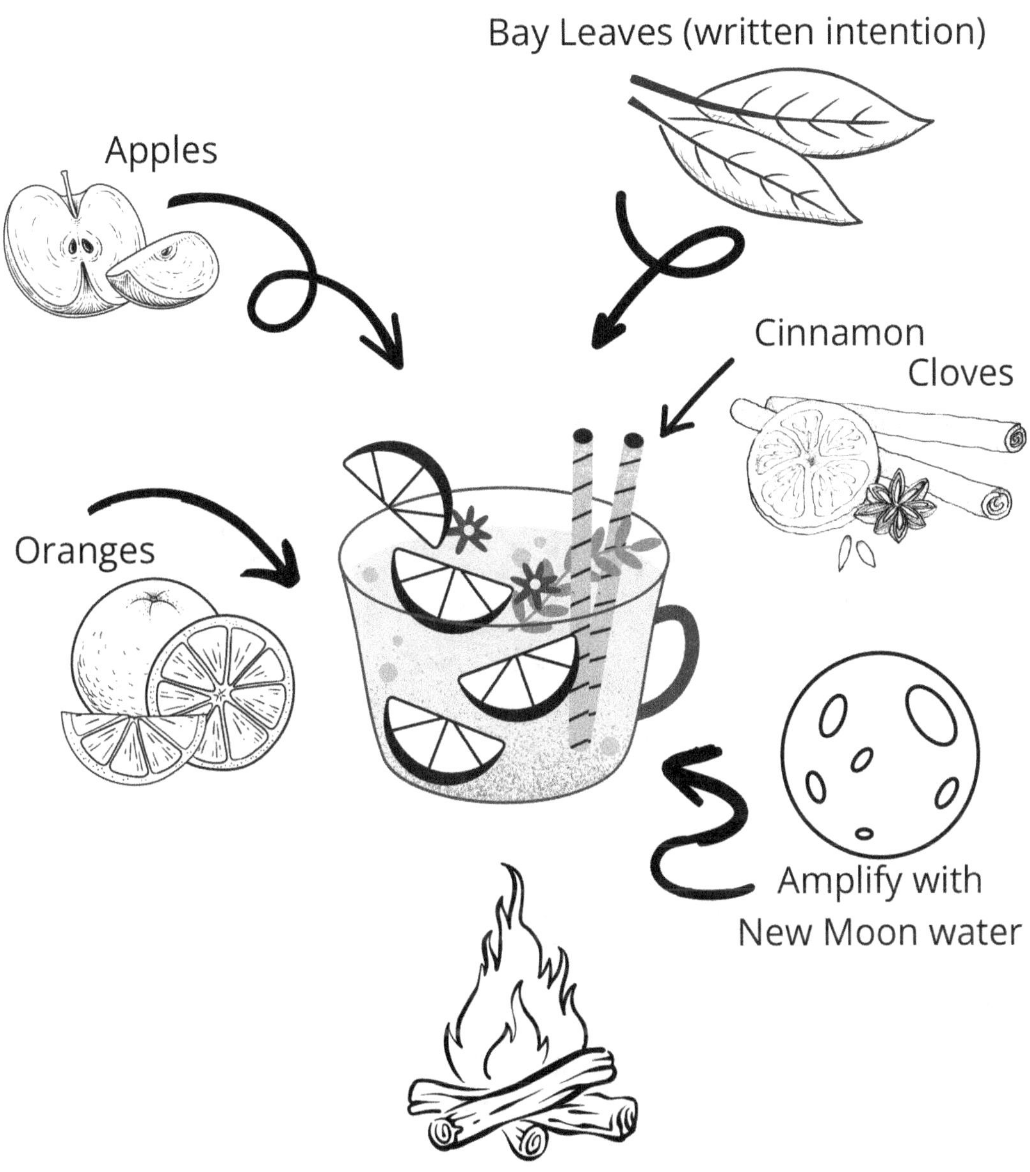

Calm Simmer Pot

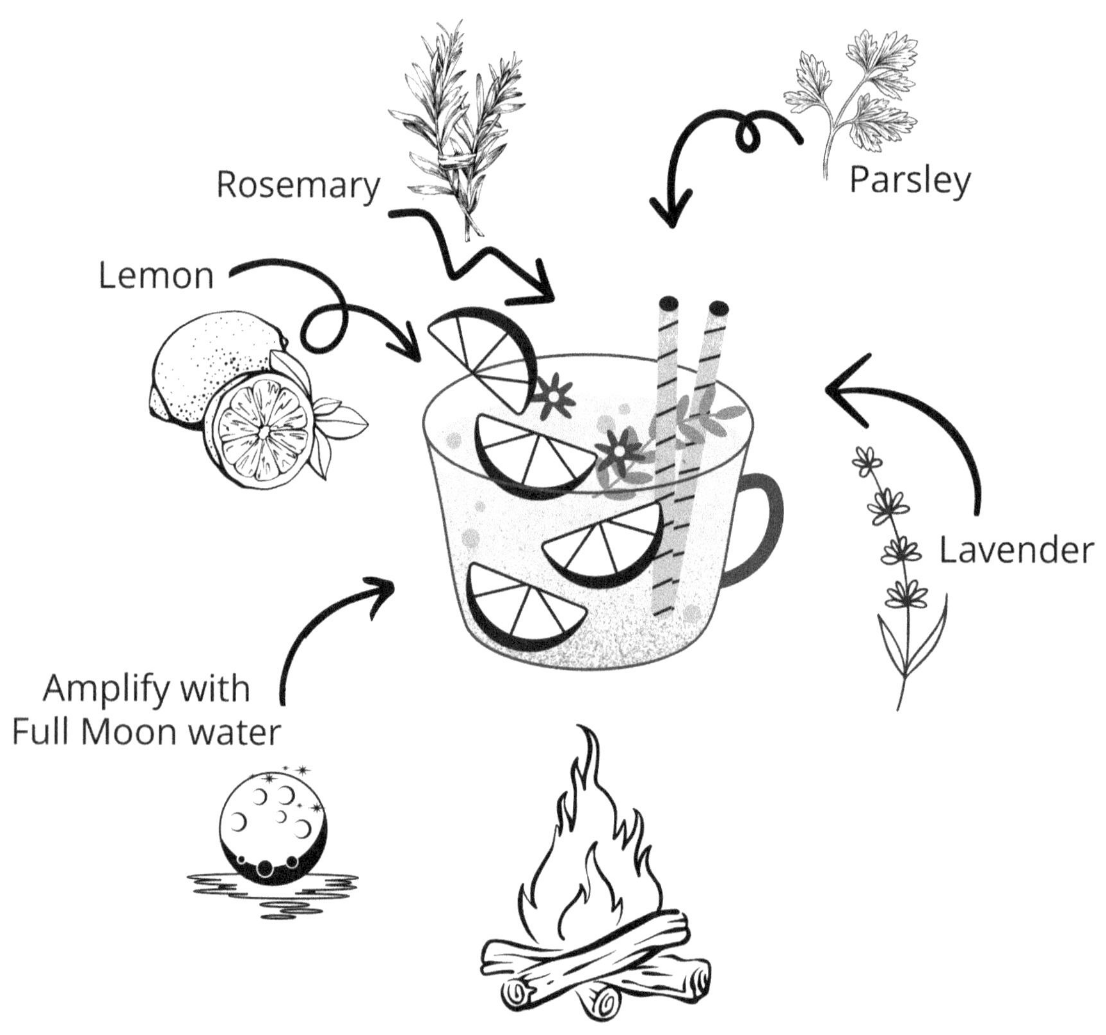

Harvest Simmer Pot

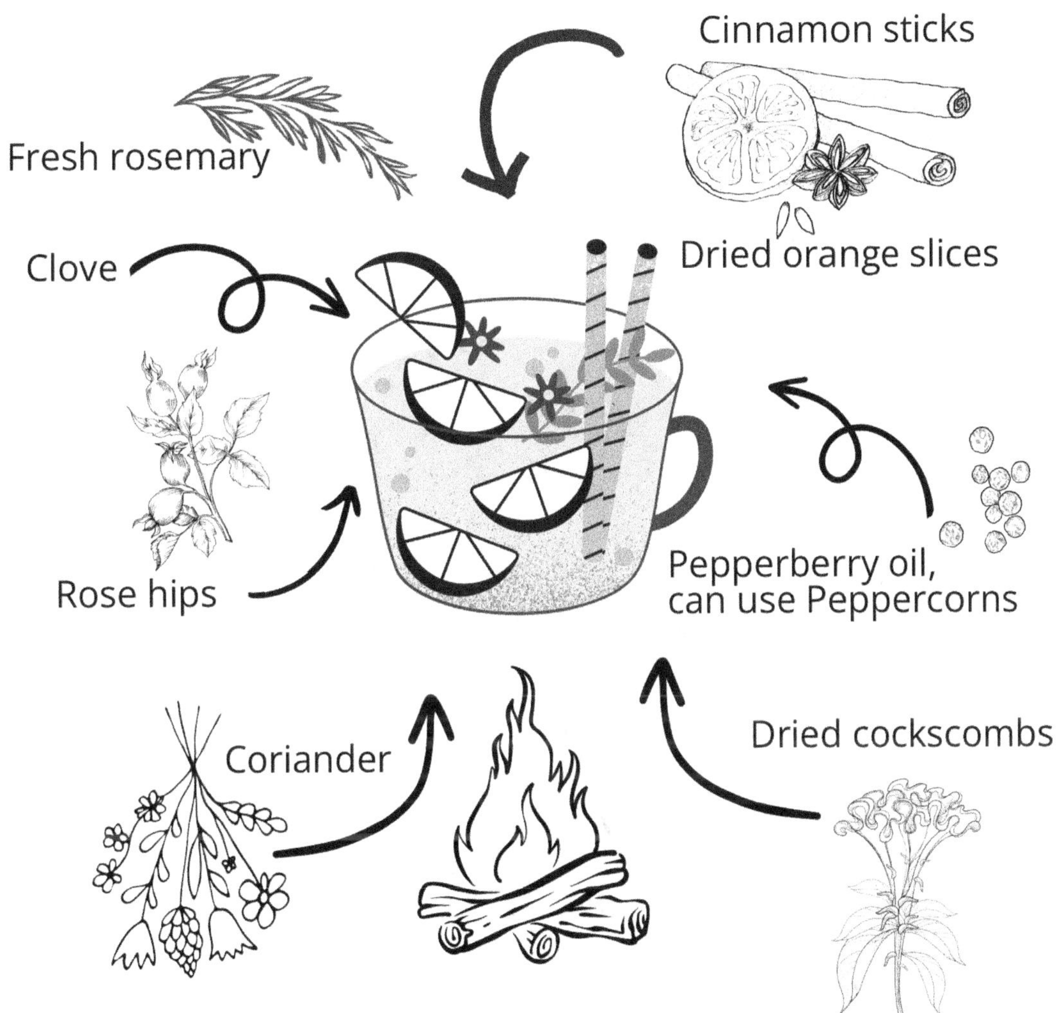

Purification & Abundance

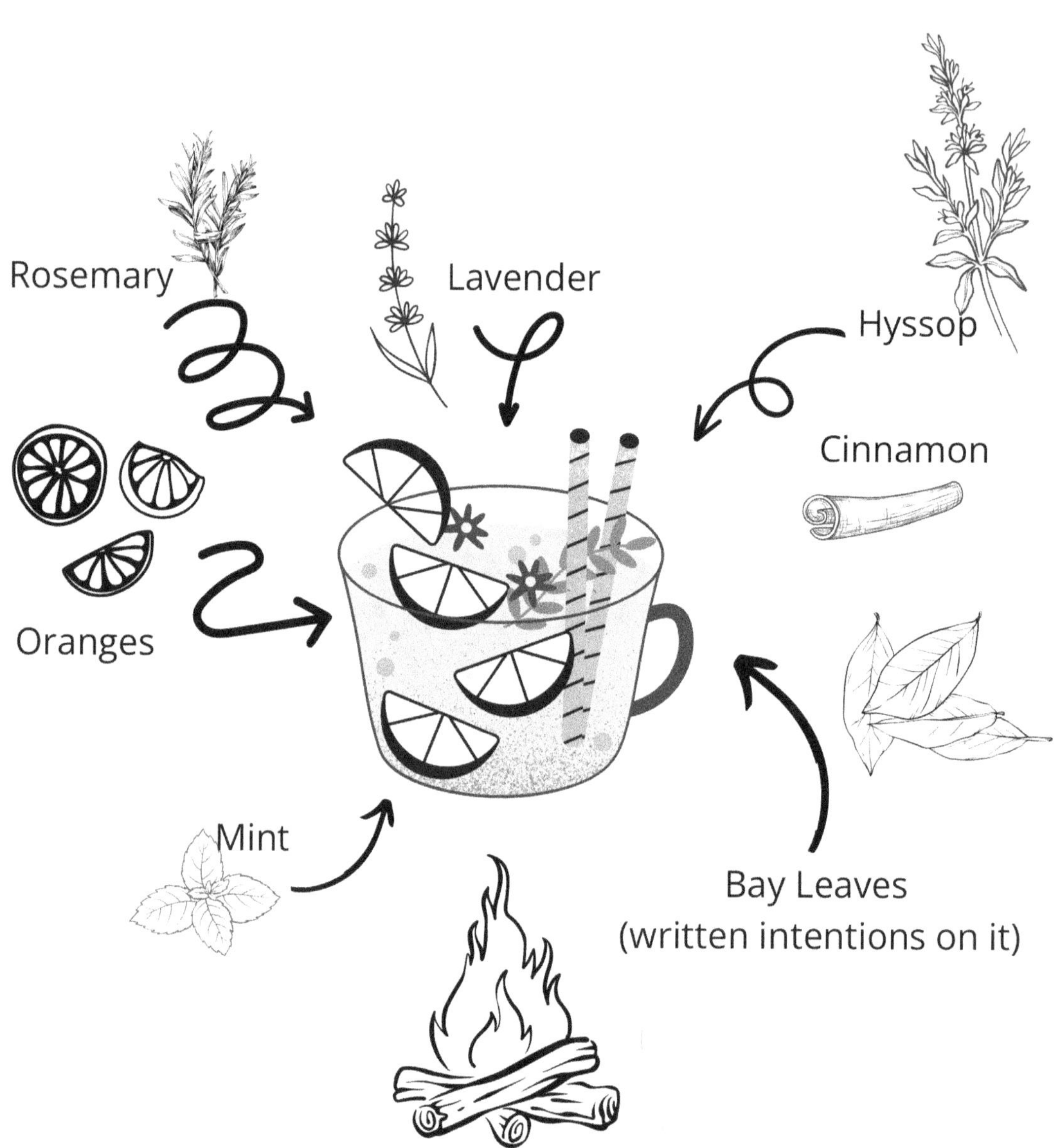

Love & Happiness Simmer Pot

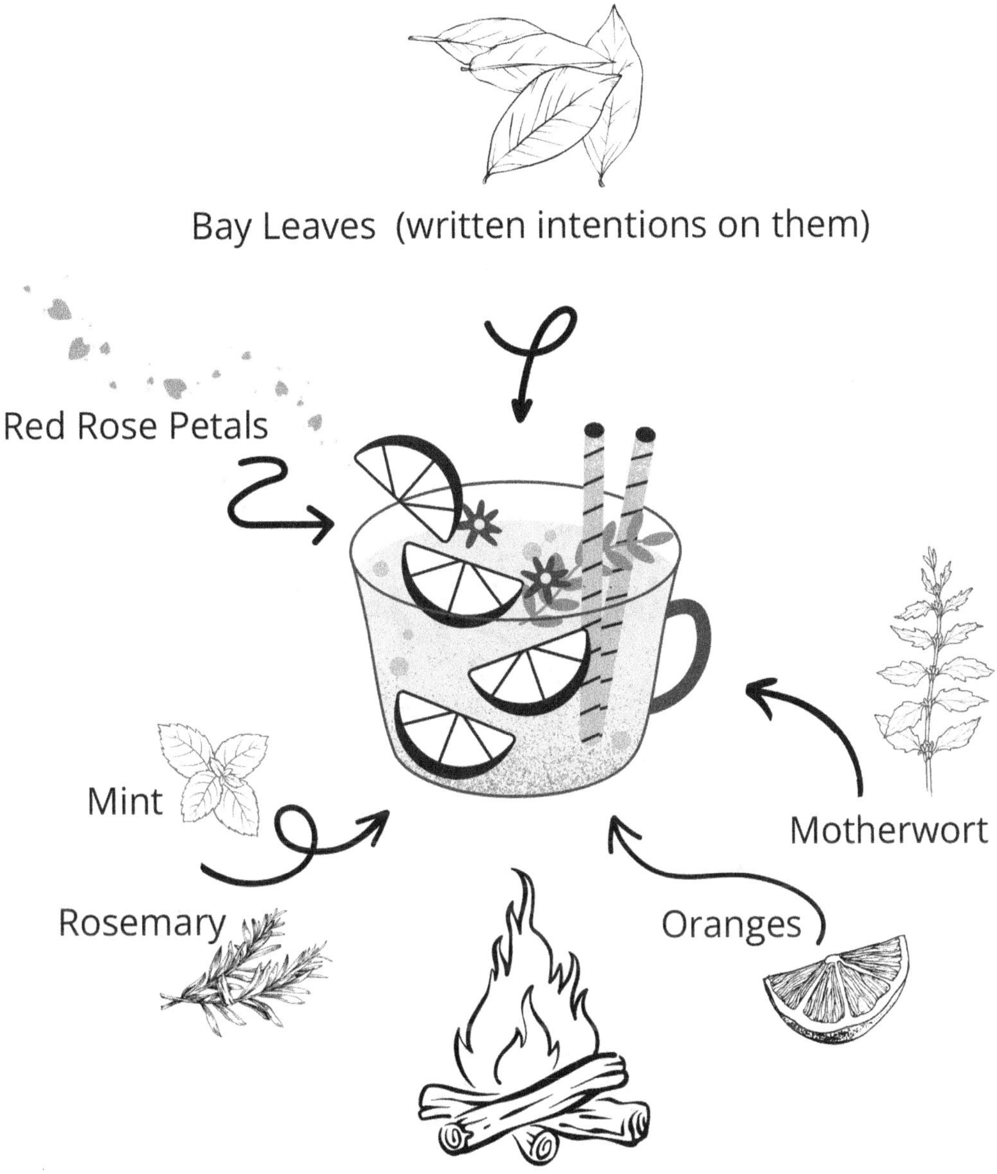

Bay Leaves (written intentions on them)

Red Rose Petals

Mint

Rosemary

Motherwort

Oranges

Cleansing Simmer Pot

Prosperity Simmer Pot

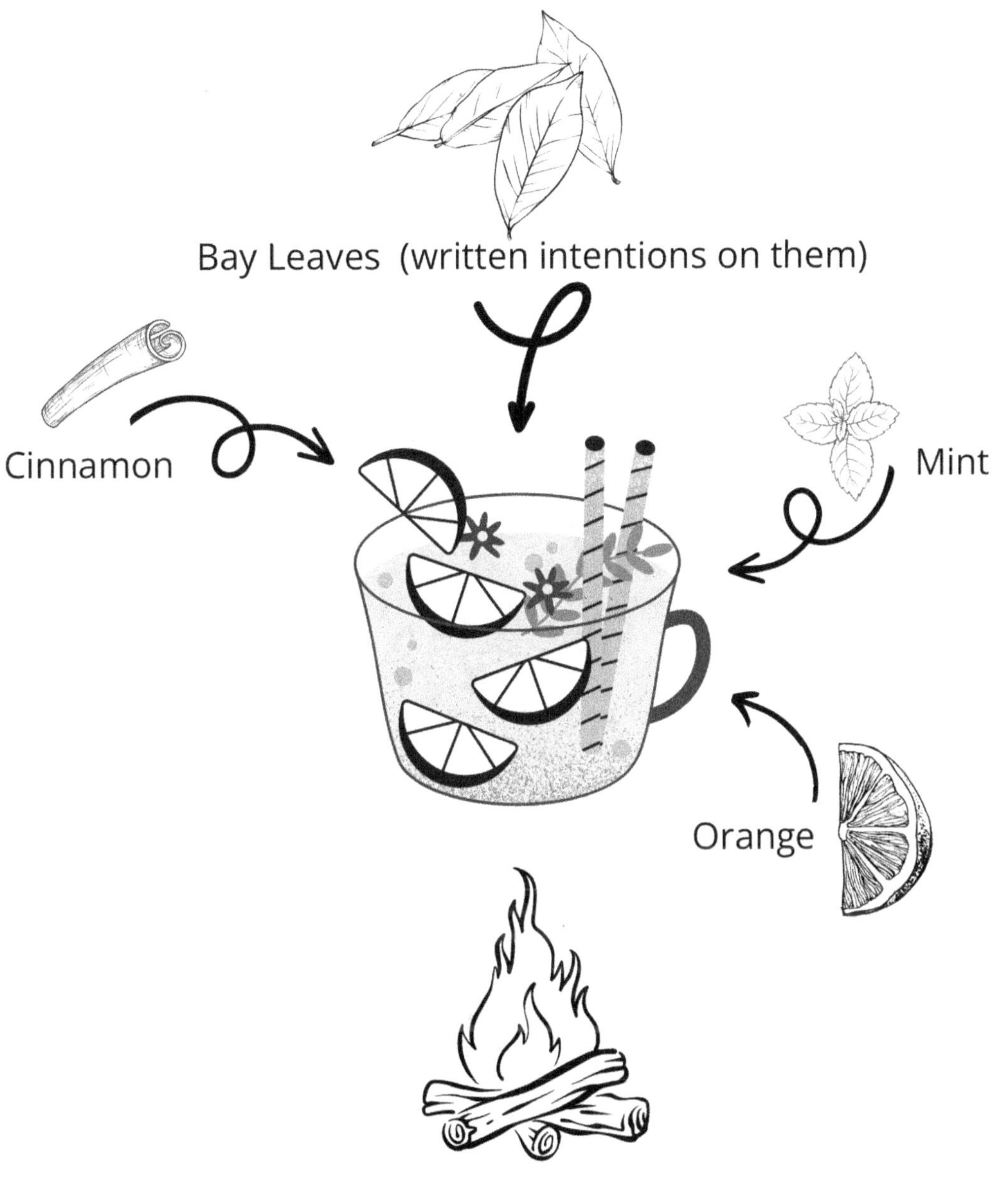

Holiday Simmer Pot

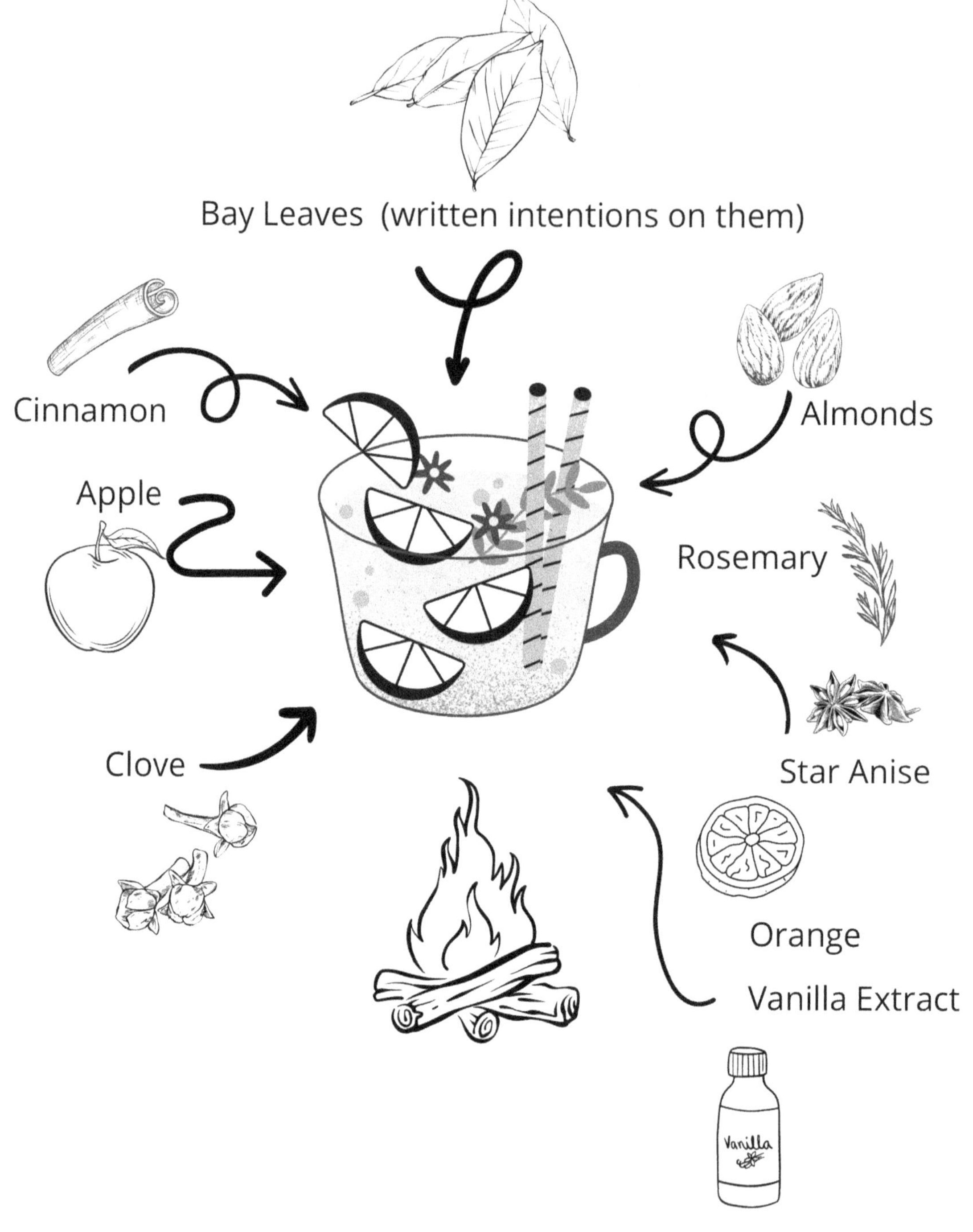

Cold and Flu Fighter

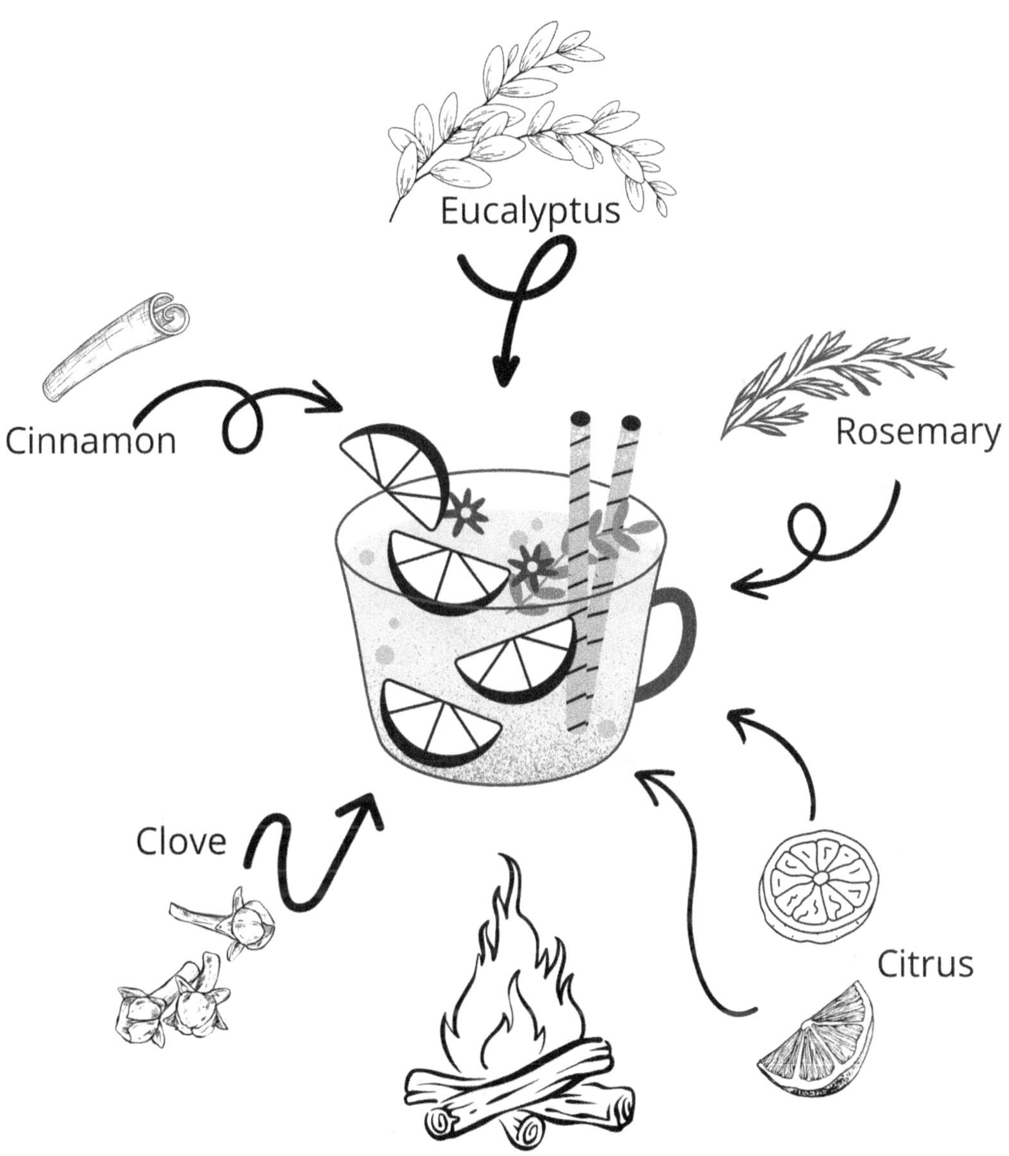

Spiritual Connection

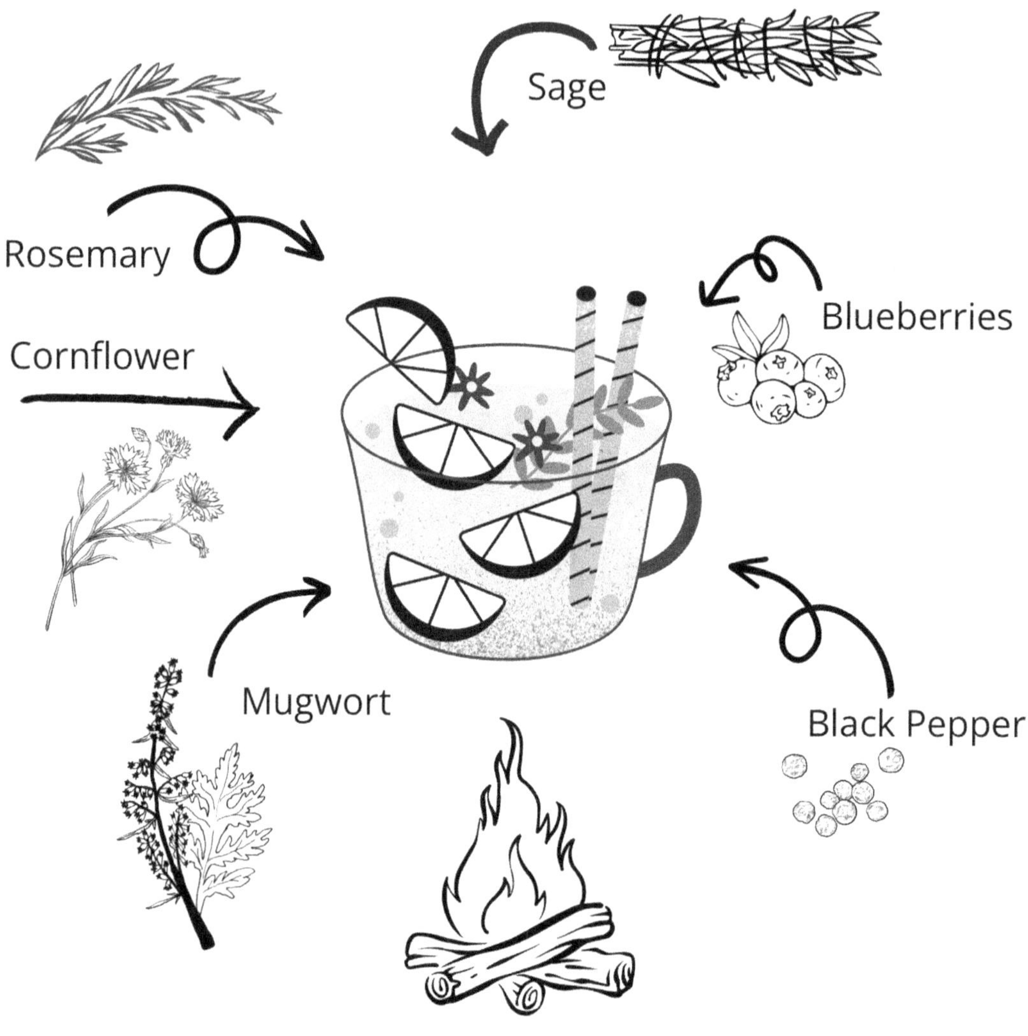

CHAPTER 28

What is a Closed Practice?

There have been a lot of harmful misconceptions about what constitutes a "closed practice" within spirituality. Simply put, a closed practice in witchcraft and the Occult refers to a practice in which you can only take part in their craft if you were specifically born into the practice, or went through an initiation process. One of the most common fallacies regarding closed practices is that if you weren't initially born into the community, you will never be able to practice, which can be the case in various instances, but there are some exceptions. It is essential to note that these practices are closed until the individual is vetted and the designated initiation process has been completed.

There is always a cause for some religions to be closed. Some reasons may include that it is founded on specific cultural values and beliefs that would never be understood by outsiders who were not truly immersed in the community. Brujería and Santería are examples of this.

Closed Communities and Race-Locked Spirituality

While it is critical to analyze specific practices within some religions, it is even more vital to address, on a larger scale, how entire communities can be closed. Differentiating between closed communities and closed practices reduces the likelihood of gatekeeping and reinforces marginalization. Some closed communities include the Amish, the Roma, Judaism (along with their type of mysticism, Kabbalah), Hoodoo, and Haitian Vodou. A reason a variety of communities may close their practices is that they are deemed as "race locked", indicating that these communities were created as an attempt to unify together during times of hardship, with their beliefs formed around their shared experiences.

Closed Objects

White sage: A sacred herb used in Indigenous American practices and currently endangered. Used in smudging rituals.

Palo Santo: An aged wood that is burned in South American practices and is currently endangered. Palo Santo is important to Hispanic/Latino culture and is currently endangered. Commercial buying of this wood is generally looked down upon by those not belonging to this group of people.

Dream catchers: A hand-made woven willow hoop adorned with sacred items made by Indigenous Americans. Any that are not made by an indigenous American is not a true dream catcher.

Sweetgrass: Considered sacred to Indigenous Americans and is used in smudging rituals. Also is currently endangered.

Rituals and Divination

Smudging: A sacred, elaborate, exclusively Indigenous American ritual using smoke. Very different from smoke cleansing an area.

Spirit Animals: A purely Indigenous American belief/ part of the religion of certain tribes. Nobody not belonging to this group simply does not have one.

Egg Limpia: A South American practice to cleanse oneself using an egg.

Karma: A Hinduism belief/concept that the energy someone builds in their life (good or bad) affects how their later lives turn out.

Chakras: A term specific to Hinduism and Buddhism referencing various focal points on the body used in meditation practices. Within Kundali yoga, breath exercises, visualizations, mudras, bandhas, kriyas, and mantras are focused on manipulating the flow of subtle energies through chakras

Sour Jars: A spell belonging to hoodoo, vodou, and various other closed practices using a jar to hex.

Groups of people

Haitian Vodou: A polytheistic, syncretic religion coming from West African (Yoruba and Fon) Roman Catholicism. Developed among Afro-Haitian communities amid the Atlantic slave trade, and the main religion in Haiti as well as Catholicism.

Hoodoo: A syncretic religion created by enslaved Africans, this religion is practiced in the Caribbean and in southern America, an amalgamation of spiritual practices, traditions, and beliefs that were held in secret away from white slaveholders.

Santeria: a polytheistic, syncretic religion originating in Cuba and combines Yoruba and Roman Catholic beliefs. Also developed during the Atlantic slave trade.

Groups of people (cont)
Many Native American cultures
Many African cultures
Saami (in Finland)
Shinto (There are branches of Shinto practice that are open, but this kind of practice should be approached with a high level of respect, and some branches are definitely closed. Jinja Shinto would be to most prominent example of an open denomination)
Druidism (proper, not neo)
Gardnerian and Alexandrian Wicca

Some parts of African Vodou (It depends on the section/group/family etc.)
Hinduism (There are denominations of Hinduism that are open and available, just as there are sects that are closed. Some of the "open sects are highly problematic, and so it does one to be very careful when looking at joining a sect of the Hindu faith. Dharmic law is part of what makes this a little sticky to navigate, so best to be approached with deference and caution.)
Hopi
Inuit
Judaism (You must earn the right to be called Jewish)
Rastafari Movement
Tribal (almost all)
Voudon
Zoroastrianism
Kemetic Orthodox - This does not require an initiation per se but does require a rite of passage of sorts, and there is a series of coursework that should be completed.

Though I am a writer and, by extension, a researcher, I am still trying to find clear answers for closed practice or closed items. It is with a kind heart that I say, please do your research and always be respectful of others' race, heritage, nationality, religion, and or practice.

CHAPTER 29

What is Holding Space?

The Concept of Holding Space for Someone: Understanding and Execution
"Holding space" is a term for being wholly present for someone both mentally and emotionally. It involves supporting them as they work through their feelings without judgment. To convey that you are holding space for someone, tell them you're there to listen and offer a space for them to express themselves if they choose to do so. Respecting their emotional boundaries and reassuring them that you believe in them is vital.

When holding space for someone, there are key elements to remember. These include:

- Practicing Loving Kindness: a term rooted in Buddhist tradition, describing the cultivation of compassion and love for another living being, the earth, or the self.
- Using Deep Listening: going beyond the act of hearing and seeking to understand someone with your heart.
- Having Unconditional Positive Regard: a practice of holding another person with absolute respect, compassion, and positive regard, regardless of what they have done or who they are.

Ultimately, holding space is about creating a safe and non-judgmental environment, akin to a metaphorical bucket for someone to emotionally and verbally release into.

Essential Elements

Holding space for others can be challenging, especially for those from Western cultures. Here are some fundamental elements to keep in mind when holding space for someone:

- Sit With What Is: It means to be present for the person you're holding space for without trying to change anything. Create a safe space where they can express and feel their emotions.
- Allow: Let others feel their emotions and hold them when they cry.
- Breathe: Check in with your breath to remain grounded and connected to your body.
- Ground: Find a way to ground yourself to ensure that you remain centered while holding space for someone.
- Be Present With Yourself: Be present for yourself before you can be present with others.
- Don't Usurp Their Pain: Although holding space for someone in pain can be challenging, it's important to remember that it's not about you. Focus on being there for the other person without making their pain your own.
- Practice Non-Judgment: Don't judge yourself or the person you're holding space for.
- Don't Try To Fix It: Resist the urge to fix their feelings or make everything better. They don't need fixing; they need you to listen and support them.

Practicing these essential elements can help you hold a safe and supportive space for others. However, if you find yourself struggling to hold space for someone or need the pure and clear attention provided by unconditional support, consider seeking a therapist.

Illness

In the realm of witchcraft and magic, the art of self-care takes precedence over the casting of spells when illness strikes. The wise practitioner understands that tending to the well-being of the body and mind is the most potent magic of all.

In times of illness, the energies that flow through the body may be compromised, making it essential to prioritize rest, nourishment, and self-care. The ancient wisdom of the craft teaches us that the body is a sacred vessel, and attending to its needs is a profound act of magic.

Witches, embracing the cycles of nature and the ebbs and flows of life, recognize that there are moments when the focus must shift from external rituals to the internal sanctum of healing. Casting spells when the body is ailing may divert precious energy needed for recovery.

The magic of self-care extends beyond herbal remedies and soothing balms; it encompasses moments of stillness, mindful breaths, and the gentle embrace of one's own vulnerability. A witch, in tune with the rhythms of life, understands that honoring the body's call for rest and nourishment is a potent incantation for healing.

So, when illness knocks on the door, let the cauldron simmer with healing teas, and may the altar be adorned with symbols of comfort. The true magic lies in the whisper of self-compassion, the balm of a caring touch, and the understanding that, in these moments, the most powerful spell is the one woven for the restoration of the self.

Stop Doing

Letting Others Drain My Energy
Forgetting My Power
Poisoning My Thoughts
Killing My Own Vibe
Fearing The Unknown
Feigning A Smile
Fretting about the Future
Getting Tangled Up With Worry
Forgetting Who I Am
Not Giving Myself Some Slack
Saying Yes Instead Of No
Always Being In Control
Telling Things To Myself, I Would Never Say To Others
Limiting Beliefs
Need to Impress Others
Using Labels
Living in the Past
My Excuses
Letting Society Tell You Anything
Trying to Make Others Happy
Living For Others
Relying On Others To Make You Happy
Doubting Myself
Holding Onto Anger
Comparing Myself to Others
Being Where You Thought You Should Be
Worrying About Not Saying The Right Things
Worrying About Not Being Perfect For Others

Just a little food for thought.

Self Care

Take a Nap

Drink Hot Cocoa

Write in Your Journal

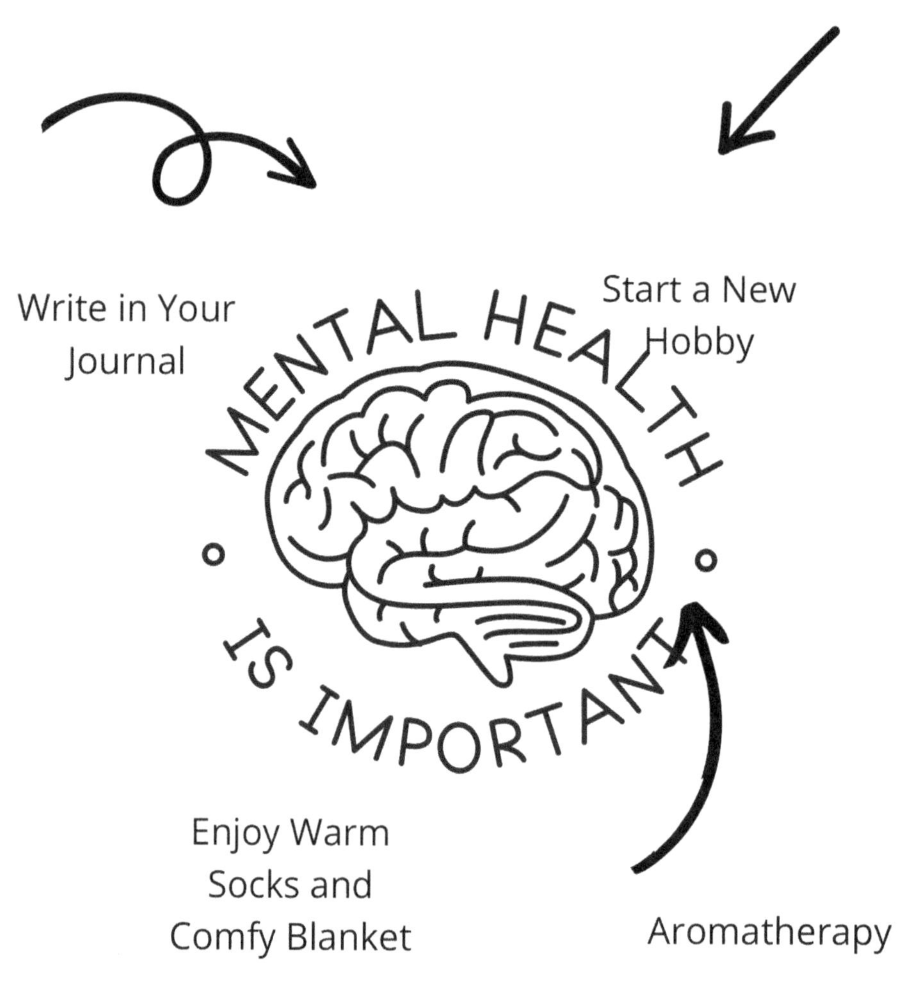

Start a New Hobby

Enjoy Warm Socks and Comfy Blanket

Aromatherapy

Prioritizing Self-Care for Optimal Well-Being

Taking care of yourself is essential for living a happy and healthy life. Neglecting self-care can have a negative impact on both your physical and emotional health. Here are some ways to prioritize self-care:

Practice meditation: Engage in deep breathing exercises for a few minutes to help calm your mind and focus on the present moment.

Choose love and forgiveness: Release past burdens and trauma by forgiving yourself and choosing love over judgment. Opt for inner peace over conflict to build resilience and emotional well-being.

Nurture gratitude: Express appreciation for the individuals and blessings in your life to overcome negative emotions and cultivate a sense of gratitude.

Prioritize happiness: Choose happiness over being right in difficult situations and explore spirituality to achieve inner peace and tranquility. Trust your intuition to transform your life positively.

Remember, taking care of yourself should always be a top priority. By prioritizing self-care, you can become the best possible version of yourself and find happiness, peace, and love in your journey.

5 Herbs for Cold and Flu

GARLIC: boosts the immune system, antimicrobial, + helps to move congestion.
ECHINACEA: stimulates the immune system + helps to shorten the duration of a cold or flu.
ASTRAGALUS: rebuild the immune system + strengthen your body after fighting off germs.
THYME: opens the sinuses, thins + moves congestion, antimicrobial.
GINGER: soothes an upset tummy or nausea, antiviral

Headache Tea

Healthy Elixers

Cold & Flu Elixir

2 Tbs. Fresh Orange Peel (or 1 tablespoon dried)
1 Cup Calendula Flowers (or 2/3 cup dried)
1/2 Cup Fresh Rose Hips (or 1/3 cup dried)
1/2 Cup Fresh Elderflowers (or 1/3 cup dried)
Honey
1 Tbs. Fresh Ginger or 1 teaspoon dried
2/3 Cup Dried Elderberries

Calming Quartet
Tension Tea

1 part skullcap
1 part chamomile
1/2 part motherwort
1/2 part rose

Soothing
Sleep tea

1 cup dried chamomile (base herb)
1/2 cup dried lemon balm (supporting herb)
1/4 cup dried rose petals (synergist herb)
1 tablespoon dried lavender (synergist herb)

Kitchen Spices
Cough Syrup

⅓ cup dried or ½ cup fresh thyme aerial parts
⅛ cup anise, fennel, or cardamom seed
1 cup (8 fl oz) water
½-2 cups (6-25 oz) raw honey

High-C
Immune Boosting Tea

1 part hibiscus
1 part rosehips
½ part lemongrass
½ part lemon peel
¼ part cinnamon

A Prayer to Say Before Bedtime

As I prepare for sleep, I let go of all energies that don't belong to me. May no negative forces remain here. I invite protection and peace to assist me in settling down for the night. May my spirit be guarded by my Sacred Guides until the break of dawn. So be it. Amen.

Wishing you blessings, light, and love.

CHAPTER 30

Welcome to the enchanting world of Yule, a season brimming with magic, warmth, and ancient traditions that beckon us to celebrate the cycles of nature and embrace the mystical energies surrounding us. This section of our Yule book delves into the crafts and magical celebrations that elevate this sacred time of year into a tapestry of wonder and connection.

As we embark on this journey, discover the power of choosing a word for the year, a guiding beacon that will illuminate your path and infuse your days with intention. Enter the world of Witch balls, time-honored talismans that weave protection and positive energy into the fabric of your space. Immerse yourself in the aromatic allure of simmer pots, blending fragrances that scent the air and invoke the season's spirit.

Explore the ancient symbolism of mistletoe, frankincense, and myrrh, and learn how these botanical treasures have been revered for centuries in various magical traditions. Engage in the art of reflection as you contemplate the past year and set intentions for the one ahead. Dive into the joy of gifting, discovering the enchantment of presenting carefully chosen tokens that carry both meaning and magic.

Indulge your senses in the alchemy of baking magical cakes and cookies, infusing each creation with love and intention. Transform your sacred space by adorning and energizing your altar with Yule-inspired decorations. Join the feast of Yule, where the season's bounty is celebrated with gratitude and communal joy.

Immerse yourself in moments of serenity through meditation, allowing the quietude of the season to deepen your connection with the spiritual essence of Yule. Warm your heart and senses with delightful cider recipes that embody this festive time's comforting essence.

And, let us not forget our animal companions—loyal friends who share in the magic of Yule. Discover ways to extend the enchantment to them, ensuring that the bonds between humans and animals are strengthened during this season of love and connection.

May this section serve as a guide, inspiring you to infuse your Yule celebrations with the richness of tradition, the beauty of crafts, and the transformative power of magic. Embrace the season's enchantment, and let the magic of Yule fill your heart and home with light.

Yule

 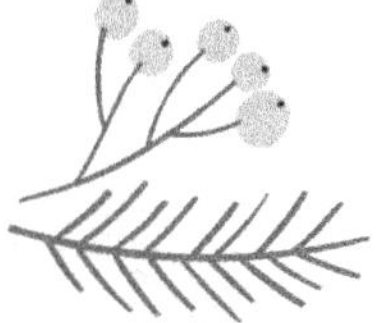

CELEBRATION

- ☐ Bake Cakes and Cookies
- ☐ Decorate Your Altar
- ☐ Meditation
- ☐ Remember your Animal Friends
- ☐ Reflecting
- ☐ Gifting - Natural Items
- ☐ Make Witch Balls and Bells
- ☐ Decorate a Yule Tree
- ☐ Make Natural Tree Décor
- ☐ Feast with Family and Friends
- ☐ Drink Mulled Cider
- ☐ Wassail Recipes

Yule

CELEBRATION

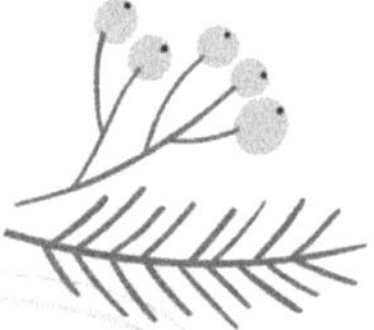

- [ ] Simmer Pots/Potpourri
- [ ] Mistletoe, Frankincense, and Myrrh
- [ ] Explore Lore and Magic
- [ ] Choose a Word for the Coming Year
- [ ] Burn a Yule Log
- [ ] Make a Yule Candle
- [ ]
- [ ]
- [ ]
- [ ]
- [ ]
- [ ]

Yule Log Cake (Bûche de Noël)

Ingredients:

Chocolate Cake
3/4 cup of all-purpose flour
1/3 cup of Hershey's Special Dark cocoa powder
1 tsp of baking powder
1/2 tsp of salt
4 large eggs, divided
3/4 cup of granulated sugar
5 tbsp of sour cream
1/4 cup of butter, melted
1 tsp of vanilla extract

Mascarpone Whipped Cream Filling
1 1/4 cups of heavy whipping cream, cold
3/4 cup of powdered sugar
1 tsp of vanilla extract
1/8 tsp of salt
8 oz of mascarpone cheese, softened but still chilled*

Whipped Chocolate Ganache
8 ounces of semi-sweet chocolate, finely chopped
1 cup of heavy whipping cream
Sugared cranberries, optional*
Sugared rosemary, optional*

Directions:
1. Preheat oven to 350°F. Line a 17×12 inch jelly roll sheet pan with parchment paper. Make sure the parchment paper sticks up at least an inch above the sides of the pan on all sides. You'll use the parchment paper later to lift the cake out of the pan and roll it up.
2. Set aside the flour, cocoa, baking powder, and salt in a medium bowl.
3. In a large bowl, combine the egg yolks and sugar and whisk together until well combined.
4. Add the sour cream, melted butter and vanilla extract and whisk together until well combined.
5. Add the dry ingredients and gently whisk together until well combined, then set aside.

Yule Log Continued

6. Add the egg whites to a large mixer bowl and whip on high speed until stiff peaks form.

7. Gently fold about 1/3 of the whipped egg whites into the chocolate mixture to loosen up the batter.

8. Add the remaining egg whites and gently fold together until well combined.

9. Spread the cake batter evenly into the prepared pan and bake for 10-12 minutes, or until the top springs back when touched and a toothpick inserted comes out clean.

10. Remove the cake from the oven, immediately lift it out of the pan using the parchment paper, and place it on the counter.

11. While the cake is hot, use the parchment paper the cake was baked in and start at the shorter end of the cake to roll it up slowly. Set the cake aside to cool completely.

12. When the cake has cooled and is ready to be filled, make the filling. Add the heavy whipping cream, powdered sugar, vanilla extract, and salt to a large mixer bowl and whip on high speed until soft peaks form.

13. Add the mascarpone cheese to the whipped cream and whip until stiff peaks form. It will happen fairly quickly.

14. Unroll the cake roll very carefully, looking out for areas where it may be sticking to release it. You can use an offset spatula or something similar and run it along the parchment paper as you unroll the cake to help remove it as it unrolls.

15. Spread the filling evenly onto the unrolled cake, then roll it back up without the parchment paper.

16. Wrap it up in a plastic wrap with the seam side down and refrigerate for at least an hour to firm up.

17. Make the chocolate ganache. When you're ready, decorate the cake and the chocolate in a medium-sized bowl and set aside. Heat the cream in the microwave just until it begins to boil, then pour it over the chocolate.

18. Allow the chocolate and cream to sit for a few minutes, then whisk until smooth. Let the ganache cool to room temperature (or cooler; you don't want it too warm/thin), then transfer it to a large mixer bowl.

19. Whip on high speed until lightened in color and thick enough to spread.

20. To decorate the cake, use a large serrated knife to gently cut off a piece of the log about 3 inches in length. Cut with a slight diagonal.

21. Use some of the chocolate ganache to attach the small log to the side of the larger log.

22. Spread the remaining chocolate ganache over the cake, then use a fork to create bark-like lines. Decorate with sugared cranberries and rosemary (instructions in notes), if desired.

23. Refrigerate the cake until ready to serve.

Eggnog Cookies

Ingredients:
2 cups of all-purpose flour (scoop and level to measure*)
2 tsp of baking powder
1/2 tsp of salt
1/2 tsp of ground nutmeg, plus more for topping
1/2 tsp of ground cinnamon
3/4 cup of unsalted butter at room temperature
1/2 cup of granulated sugar
1/2 cup of packed light-brown sugar
2 large egg yolks
1 tsp of vanilla extract
1/2 tsp of rum extract
1/2 cup of eggnog (not low fat)

Frosting:
1/2 cup of butter at room temperature (I used 1/4 cup salted and 1/4 cup unsalted
butter)
3 - 5 Tbsp of eggnog
1/2 tsp of rum extract
3 cups of powdered sugar

Directions:
Preheat oven to 350°F (180°C). Whisk together flour, baking powder, salt, nutmeg, and
cinnamon in a mixing bowl for 30 seconds and set aside.
 In the bowl of an electric stand mixer fitted with the paddle attachment, whip
together butter, granulated sugar, and brown sugar until pale and fluffy.
Mix in egg yolks one at a time, blending just until combined after each addition. Mix in
vanilla extract, rum extract, and egg nog. With the mixer set on low speed, slowly add
dry ingredients and mix until combined.
Scoop dough out by heaping tablespoonfuls and dropping it onto Silpat or parchment
paper lined baking sheets, spacing cookies 2 inches apart.
Bake in preheated oven for 11 - 13 minutes. Allow it to rest on a baking sheet for
several minutes before transferring it to a wire rack to cool. Cool completely, then
frost with Eggnog Frosting and sprinkle tops lightly with nutmeg.

For the Eggnog Frosting:
In the bowl of an electric stand mixer fitted with the paddle attachment, whip butter
until very pale and fluffy. Add in rum extract and 3 Tbsp eggnog and mix in powdered
sugar. Add additional eggnog to reach the desired consistency.
Tip
Cookies previously listed 2 1/4 cups flour (spooned and leveled method). When using
the easier scoop and level method, this is only 2 cups to equal the same amount. If
you'd like cookies to be a little thicker, add 2 extra tablespoons of flour.

Yule Sun and Moon Cookies

Ingredients:
1 cup of butter at room temperature
1 1/4 cup of sugar
2 teaspoons grated lemon peel
1/4 teaspoon of salt
1 1/2 cups of all-purpose flour
1 1/2 cups of ground blanched almonds
1 teaspoon of vanilla extract

Icing:
2 cups of sifted confectioners' sugar
1 teaspoon of vanilla extract
2 1/2 tablespoons of water

Directions:
Combine the butter and sugar in a mixer bowl and cream together until fluffy and light.

Add grated lemon peel, salt, flour, almonds, and vanilla. Mix well.

Place dough in a covered container and place in the refrigerator for several hours (or overnight) until chilled.

When ready to bake, preheat oven to 325 degrees F.

Roll dough out to 1/8-inch thickness. Cut with a crescent and sun cookie cutter. Reroll scraps and cut again (you may need to re-chill the dough to make it workable).

Place the cutouts 1/2-inch apart on an ungreased baking sheet. Bake at 325 degrees F for 8-10 minutes or until done. Remove from oven and let cool on the baking sheet for 1 minute, then remove to a cooking rack.

To ice the cookies, combine the confectioner's sugar, vanilla, and water until smooth. Add additional water if needed. Spread the icing over the tops of the warm cookies.

Alternately, sprinkle warm cookies with powdered sugar instead of icing them.

Yule Altar

Creating a Yule altar is an important part of the celebrations.

As I was typing this, I kept going back and correcting, changing, editing, and researching until I came up with this. Your altar is your personal business. I can give suggestions, but it falls on your shoulders, and what speaks to you now, if you change it up the next day, week, or month, it is totally cool. You Do You, Boo!

A representation of your deity, Spirit Guide, Animal, Angel, Archangel, or Being, and if you don't have any, no big if you don't.
Maybe some candles. I like the fake battery-flickering ones.
The four elements
Cup, chalice, goblet, or solo cup (seriously)
filled with wine, juice, spring water, or your coffee from the morning

Then you go nuts with bottles, herbs, crystals, rocks, feathers, stuffed animals, money, offerings, tobacco (watch the kids and dogs), a book, family pictures, ancestors, knick-knacks, and special possessions from family living or deceased. Whatever makes you happy. Blessings.

Meditate

Types of Meditation

Guided
Process guided by vocal instructions
Often Breath focus and visualization
Perfect for beginners

Metta
Cultivates lovingkindness
Component of self and others
Enhances compassion

Walking
Active, movement-based
Focus on linking breath with movement
For those who sit frequently

Sound Healing
Auditory component
Typically supine
Drums, Singing Bowls, Etc.

Yoga Nidra
Yogic sleep
Guided form of deep meditation
Induces a state of mindful sleep

Chakra
Works with the energy centers of the body
Seeks to balance opposite energies
Single chakra or whole system

Mantra
Mental repetition of a word or sound
Linked with the breath
Rewires neural connections

Transcendental
Standardized, systemized
Repetition of word/phrase
Oneness with Universe

Apple Bird Feeder

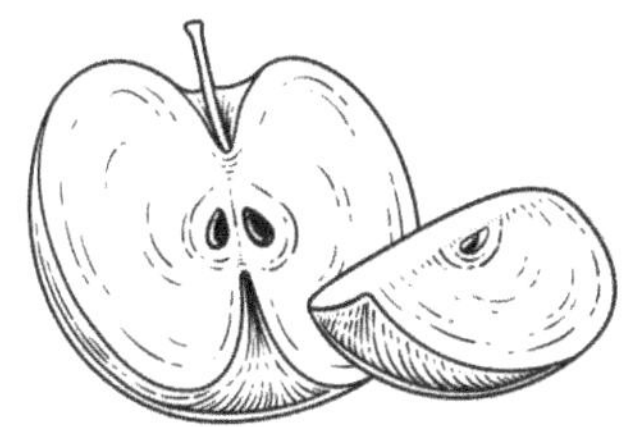

Ingredients
2 cups of Birdseed
2/3 cup of water
2 Packets of Unflavored Gelatin
4 apples
8 small screws
Twine

Directions
Bring Water to a boil, add gelatin, and stir until completely dissolved.
Mix the Birdseed into this mixture.
Cut the apples in half lengthwise and hollow out the insides with a spoon or knife.

Fill each apple with birdseed mixture, set it on a sheet pan, and put it in the fridge for 1-2 hours or until firm.
Poke a screw into the top of each apple and tie a piece of twine to it.
Hang outside for all the birds to enjoy!

Pine Cone Bird Feeder

Ingredients:
Pinecones
Creamy Peanut Butter
Birdseed
Twine or String
Optional: screws

Directions:
Spread Peanut Butter all over the pinecone. You can also put your peanut butter in a separate the bowl and dip or roll your pine cone in it.

Pour your Birdseed into a separate bowl.
Dip peanut butter-coated pine cone into bird seeds.
Put a small screw into the bottom of the pinecone and tie Twine around the screw for hanging your pine cone bird feeders.

Optional: Tie twine directly to the pinecone

Edible Treat for Wild Animals

Some suggestions for food for the Wild Animals

Homemade popcorn and fresh cranberry garland.
Sliced oranges, apples, pears, carrots, or parsnips hung on strings.

Cookie cutter birdseed ornaments.

Orange birdseed ornaments.

Pinecone bird feeder with peanut butter or lard (fat).

Bird Feed

Some suggestions for food for the birds

Cereal
Cooked rice (ideally brown)
Soaked dog kibble
Wet dog or cat food
Fresh coconut in the shell
Baked potatoes
Suet blocks bird cake
Raw peanuts/ walnuts/ others Raw sunflower seeds
Wild birdseed
Bread is better than nothing but is very low in nutritional value.

Squirrel and Bird Feed

Ingredients:
2 tablespoons of peanut butter
2 tablespoons of uncooked oats
2 tablespoons finely chopped walnuts (or any nut you have) 1 tablespoon of
yellow cornmeal

Directions:
In a small bowl, microwave the peanut butter for 20 seconds
add in dry ingredients
scoop out and make into ball form
Let cool and harden
Place in feeder

Birdseed Ornament

Ingredients:
2 cups of Birdseed
2/3 cup of Water
2 Packets of unflavored gelatin fun cookie cutters
Straws
ribbon or twine
Cooking Spray

Directions:
In a small saucepan over medium heat, combine water and gelatin. Mix well until the gelatin is dissolved.
Remove from heat and stir in the birdseed until well incorporated.
Line a cookie sheet with parchment paper. Spray cookie cutters with cooking spray and set them on the pan.
Fill the birdseed mixture into each cookie cutter. Make sure to pat down as you go and continue to fill until you reach the top of the cookie cutter.
Next, insert a straw. (This will make a hole so you can hang it).
Refrigerate for about an hour or until the gelatin is set.
Remove cookie cutters and straws. Add ribbon/twine.
And hang!

Orange Bird Feeder

Ingredients:
Large Orange
Twine
Birdseed

Directions:
First, Bring Water to a boil, add gelatin, and stir until completely dissolved. Next, Mix the birdseed into this mixture.
Cut the apple half lengthwise and hollow out the insides with a spoon or knife. After the center is hollowed out, fill each apple with birdseed mixture, set your apple bird treats on a sheet pan and put them in the fridge for 1-2 hours or until firm.
Poke a screw into the top of each apple and tie a piece of twine to it.
Hang your apple bird feeders outside on a tree or fence for all the birds to enjoy!

Bird feed Wreath

Ingredients:
3/4 cup of flour
1/2 cup of water
1 envelope of unflavored gelatin
3 tablespoons of corn syrup
4 cups of birdseed
*Bundt pan or mold
Nonstick Spray
*If you want to fill your bundt pan, you'll need to double the ingredients.

Directions:
Spray your bundt pan/mold liberally with nonstick spray.
Mix the gelatin packet with hot water until dissolved.
Stir in the flour and corn syrup until mixed with the gelatin, then add your birdseed and combine.
Pour or scoop your mixture into your pan or mold, pressing down with the back of a spoon. If
you're using a wire ring in the middle of your mold, add half your mixture, then the wire, and top the wire with the seed.
Place your mold in the refrigerator or somewhere cold (I placed mine on the porch) to set it up and firm it up.
After 24 hours, unmold your seed wreath.

Natural Bird Feeder

Ingredients:
1 egg carton (made from paper/recycled materials, not plastic)
11 cups of birdseed
Twine or String
Hole Punch

Directions:
Fill each space with birdseed.
When the egg carton is filled, punch a couple of holes into each side.
Push your twine or string through each hole.
Hang outside on a tree.

Wishing Candles
A Yuletide Tradition

In honor of the winter solstice, lighting candles during the Yule festivities is customary. Take a piece of paper, write down your wishes, and roll it up. Insert the paper into the gaps between pinecones. Finally, throw the pinecones into a fire and watch your wishes come to life.

Creating a Wish Jar
Manifest Your Intentions

Here's how to make your wish jar. Write your intention on paper, add 3-5 drops of eucalyptus or peppermint oil, and include gemstone crystals such as black moonstone, which symbolize new beginnings.

Discover Your True Desires
Through Pendulum Magic

Pendulums are powerful tools that can help lead you to the right answers. To determine the best course of action for your desires, try using a pendulum made of clear quartz.

Self-Reflections

What are my intentions for the Winter Solstice and the rest of the winter season ahead?

Self-Reflections

What are some obstacles that might stand in the way of these intentions?

Self-Reflections
What enlightened action steps can I take towards my intentions?

Self-Reflections

How are ways I can honor the cold and dark season of winter?

Self-Reflections

How can I embrace the dark periods in my life with more love and compassion?

Self-Reflections

Do I resist the dark and stillness?

Self-Reflections
What has the winter brought in lessons?

Self-Reflections

Self-Reflections

Self-Reflections

Self-Reflections

Self-Reflections

Self-Reflections

Self-Reflections

Instant Chai Latte Powder

Makes A Great Gift!

1tsp of Allspice
2tsp of Cinnamon
1tsp of Cardamom
2 Cups of Unsweetened Tea Powder
2tsp of Ginger
1tsp of Cloves
1.75 Cups of Sugar
1tsp of Nutmeg

Yule Bracelet

I know this time of year is usually meant for giving, but why not give yourself

something that will help you throughout the holidays and into the next year?

Black Jade - grounding and emotional healing

Amethyst - balances out emotions

Black Tourmaline - deflects negative energy

Smoky Quartz - protection and clears blockages

Prehnite - strengthens your energy and helps with spirit communication

Labradorite - increases energy flow to all chakras and calms the mind

Selenite- keeps emotions in balance and detaches from drama

Garnet- absorbs negative energies and takes the emotional hits for you

Then I add my favorites (but you can add any ones that call to you):

Moss Agate - grounding, stabilizing, and balancing

Black Obsidian - absorbs negativity and helps to cut cords

Lava Rock - add specific EO for each time you wear it.

If you want to get frisky, why not make these for gifts? Or even better, make it for all

the Aunt Karens in the family so the holiday runs smoothly. Give it at the beginning of

the meeting and see it work its magic.

Blessing Bags for the Homeless

Raisins, craisins, other dried fruit
Headlamp flashlight
Rain ponchos
Flashlight
Can opener (p38)
Quarters for laundry
Feminine hygiene products
Cough drops
Tarp
Sewing kit
Utensils
Ziploc bags

Lip balm
Lotion
Sunscreen fragrance-free
Water-free toothbrush
Band-aids
Apple sauce
Pudding cups
Travel mug
Gift-cards can fill for a meal
Toe/hand warmers
Hat
T-shirts
Tuna and cracker packs
Single-serving snacks like trail mix, nuts, crackers
Beef jerky
Peanut butter cracker packs
Breakfast/protein bars (watch out for melty chocolate)

For easy reference, here are some of the most-requested items (according to homeless advocates and shelter workers):
Socks (this is the #1 most asked-for item)
Gloves
Water bottle
Wet wipes
Toothbrush and toothpaste
Nail clippers
Bandages (large ones, especially useful for blisters)
Comb and/or brush
Face towels
Maxi pads
Chewable multivitamins
Tissues

Things to Consider:
Put yourself in their shoes - what is something you would want to have?
When delivering Blessing Bags, don't do it alone. Make sure you take time to say hello, make eye contact, smile, and lend a listening ear. If you are giving used clothing, make sure it is in good condition. Consider including a kind note and a list of local resources to help them recover.

Witch Ball

Witch Balls originated in the 17th Century and were used to protect the home and ward off evil spirits. Hang this ornament near the front door, a window, or in a corner of a room to provide protection and good luck for the new year. Legend says that the contents distract evil, causing it to investigate, thus becoming entangled with the contents and being trapped.

Material:
Any of the following:
Lavender, Spruce or Sprigs of Juniper, Rosemary, Cloves, Sage, Star Anise, Rosemary, Rose Buds/Petals, Basal, Mistletoe, Cinnamon Sticks, Strip of Paper, Incense Stick, Pen, Twine or Ribbon, Glue Gun (Candle Wax or Wax Seal), Large Clear Glass Ornament Feathers, Bells, Keys, Metal Mystical Moon Charms, Crystal Chips, or Cat Whiskers

Directions:
Remove the cap from the ornament. Cleanse the inside and outside with an incense stick—stuff in greenery. Write out prayers, intentions, or sigils on paper and roll them up into a small scroll. Now fill the ball with all the goodies (You can fill however you please, for the intention you set or with what you are drawn to). Run twine through crap (Knotted Hoop to anchor), and secure cap on with hot glue (or wax). You can now add embellishments as you feel drawn.

Witch Bells

Hang small bells on your doorknob to scare away unwanted spirits.
Then repeat this chant three times:
"Salt from the earth
Stone from the ground
Let the evil flee this home
When this bell rings with sound"

Yule Wish Tree

Creating a Yule Wish Tree Tradition

Looking for a unique tradition to celebrate the upcoming Yule season? Try creating a Yule Wish Tree.

Here are the steps to follow:
Find a small, potted evergreen and a few yards of red, green, and white ribbon. During your Thanksgiving celebration, introduce the tree to your family and friends. Ask each person to tie a ribbon on the tree to represent a non-material blessing they wish to receive during the Yule season, such as peace, rest, or good health.

Bless the tree and place it somewhere with ample light.

When visitors come, explain the purpose of the wish tree and invite them to tie a ribbon on the tree as well.

If you plan on using the tree in a ritual, have each participant create a small ornament that symbolizes their desired strengths, such as self-esteem or goal planning.

On February 1st, remove all of the ornaments and ribbons. Burn the ribbons and scatter the ashes to the wind. Store the ornaments away for next year.

Take good care of the tree during the remaining winter months, remembering to give it plenty of water and love.

In the spring, plant the tree outside on your property or a friend's property to continue the tradition for years to come.

Cinnamon Dough Ornaments

Make festive cinnamon and apple ornaments to fill your home with warmth. Makes approximately 10 ornaments.

Ingredients:
Straw
Rolling Pin
Mason Jar
Supplies
1 cup of ground cinnamon
¾ cup of natural unsweetened applesauce
2 tbsp of white glue

Directions:
Mix your cinnamon and applesauce. Once mixed, add in your glue. The more you knead the dough, the better the consistency will get.

Dust your countertop with cinnamon. Knead the dough into a smooth ball and then roll it out to a 1/2-inch circle. If the edges split, put it back into a ball and re-roll until smooth. Use cinnamon as you might flour to avoid keeping the dough from sticking.

Press evergreen leaves into the dough to create imprints. Roll them gently with the rolling pin.

Use a Mason jar (or cookie cutters) to cut out the shapes around the leaf imprints. Make a hole for the string with a straw.

Use a dehydrator and set ornaments on a tray for 6-10 hours. Alternatively, place them in an oven at 200 degrees for a few hours. Keep an eye on them to make sure they don't dry out or bake.

Thread twine through the ornaments once dry and hang them on the tree.

Storing, Maintaining, and Refreshing Your Cinnamon Dough Ornaments

Storing Your Cinnamon Dough Ornaments
When it comes time to put away your Christmas decorations, storing your cinnamon dough ornaments properly is important to ensure they last for years to come. Even though they are fairly robust, they can still crack and crumble if not handled with care. To store them, wrap each individual ornament in tissue paper and place them in a zip-lock bag. This will help preserve their shape and protect them from damage.

How Long Do Cinnamon Dough Ornaments Last?
Cinnamon dough ornaments can last for many years if stored correctly. However, if you find that your ornaments are starting to crack or fall apart, you can always make a new batch. I like to make a fresh batch every year because I love the scent, and it's also a fun activity to do with the kids!

Re-Scenting Your Cinnamon Dough Ornaments
Over time, you may find that the scent of your cinnamon dough ornaments fades away. You can use cinnamon leaf or bark essential oil to refresh the scent. Since the scent is quite strong, you only need to add 1-2 drops to each ornament. Simply use a dropper to apply the oil to the ornament and let it dry. If you want to try a scent other than cinnamon, great options include allspice, anise, clove, ginger, juniper, peppermint, pine, wintergreen, spruce, vanilla, and frankincense.

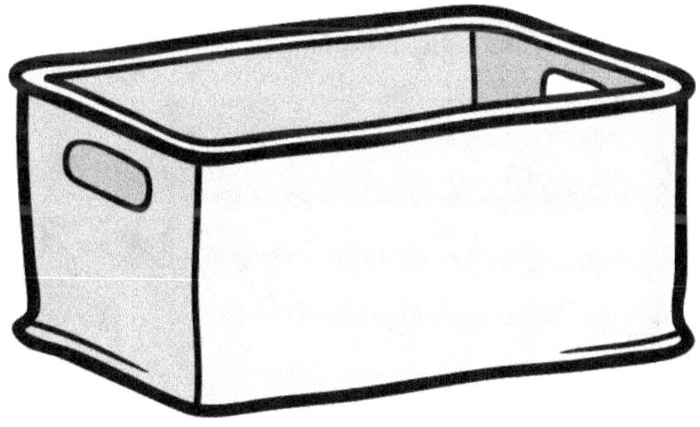

Orange & Clove Pomanders

Ingredients:
Oranges or really any citrus fruit
Cloves, dried
Ribbon (optional)
toothpick

Directions:
If using ribbon, wrap the oranges in it, then tie them with a bow.
Add the cloves at evenly spaced intervals around the orange. I pushed the cloves right into the orange but found it tricky. So I use a toothpick to make a hole, then push in the cloves.

Dried Orange Slices

Orange Drying Options:
Option #1: Bake for 6 hours at 170 degrees, flipping them occasionally to dry evenly.
Option #2: Bake the orange slices at 250 degrees for 3 hours, then hang them when the oranges are still slightly moist to air dry.
Option #3: Air drying. Place them on a baking rack over a cookie sheet to circulate the air evenly.

Uses:
Make Christmas Tree Ornaments.
String them to make a garland.
Add them to a Potpourri.
Add them to a Mulling Spice Mix.
Make them a part of a Christmas centerpiece.
Add them to a wreath.
Hang them on a Christmas mantel.
Use them as a garnish for drinks.

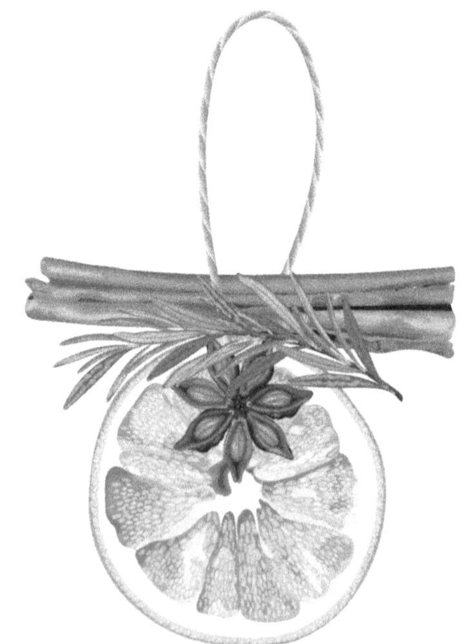

Terrarium Ornaments

Add some life to your artificial Christmas tree with mini terrarium ornaments.

Supplies:
Tweezers
Funnel
Supplies
Clear glass ornaments
Decorative sand or rocks
Found treasures such as moss, lichen, stones, pinecones, bark, and twigs. Dried rather than living items are best.
Ribbon

Directions:
Go out foraging for items to place in your ornament. Keep in mind the size of the opening, and look for items small enough to fit in your ornament.

Using the funnel, add decorative sand or rocks to the bottom of your ornament. This will act as your base. Careful not to make your ornament too heavy.

Use the tweezers to place your found treasures inside the ornament and get the placement right.

Put the ornament cap back on and use ribbon to hang it from the Christmas tree. Hang in front of lights to amplify the ornament.

Store upright in an ornament box. Shake the ornaments to help the sand settle when you pull them out again next year.

Citrus Suncatcher

Citrus brings light and warmth to your life, home, and heart.

Supplies:
Any Dried Citrus (oranges, lemons, limes, grapefruits, etc.)
Twine or string
Toothpick

Directions:
Now, using about 2 feet of twine for 5 or so slices
sew your slices for each suncatcher.
Tip: popcorn, cranberries, cinnamon sticks, rosemary, etc
Hang them from a piece of wood, branch, etc.

Rosehip Garland

Rosehip Ornament Decorating with Roschips can evoke a sense of Earth's abundance and protect against negativity during Winter. Push the thin wire through the dried berries until you create a long enough strand to bend into a desired shape. String a hook or rope to the top and adorn your home or sacred space.

Labyrinth Melking
Use sprigs of fresh rosemary to create mini wreaths, then hang them in the widows of your home.
This will provide protection from unwanted energies while ensuring prosperity flows through your doors.
Add small crystals to enhance the energy.

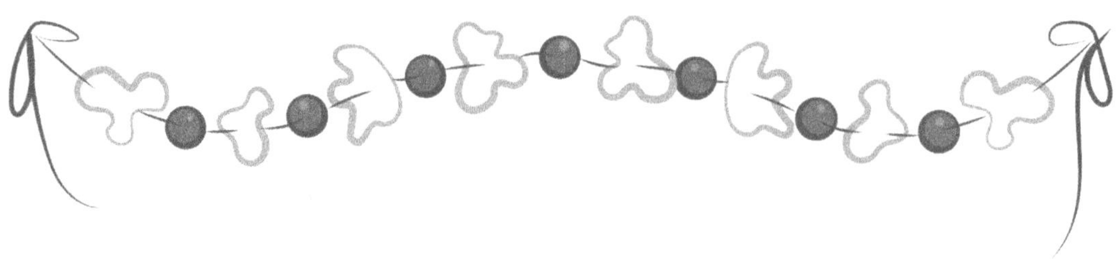

Ice Lantern

Instead of just making clear ice lanterns, you can create beautiful botanical ones with various flowers, berries, or branches. You can even use fir or pine branches, barberry, and rosehip twigs for these ice luminaries. Essentially, anything that you find attractive can be used for this purpose.

Ingredients:
A large container, either plastic or metal
A smaller container
Rocks
Flowers, berries, or branches of your choice

Directions:
Place the twigs between the large and small containers.
Weigh the smaller container down with rocks to keep it in place.
Pour cold water into the large container, filling it completely.
Wait for the water to freeze solid.
Remove the ice candle from the mold carefully.
Place a candle or oil lamp inside the ice lantern and light it up.

Pine Cone Wish

Starting a Yule tradition is a great idea, and here's a cool way to do it.

Get some small pieces of paper and write your wishes for the next year on them.

Roll up the papers and tie a piece of natural twine to the tip of a pinecone.

Dip the pinecone into the melted wax and stick your paper wishes into the pinecone while the wax is still wet.

You can also dust the pinecone with herbs or spices that correspond to your wishes.

Pine Cones

Crafting with pine cones and candy corn is perfect for fall. Add paint and glitter for a festive decoration.

Ingredients:
Pine cones
Parchment paper
Spray paint and glitter

Directions:
First, arrange the pine cones on a parchment sheet and heat them in the oven at low heat for about 30 minutes. This will help kill critters or insects that may have survived the harvest.

Start by painting the first layer using orange spray paint. Make sure you cover the whole pine cone with the color.

After the first coat has dried, take the white spray paint and spray the tip of the pine cone white.

Once the white coat has dried, hold the top of the pine cone and spray the bottom with yellow spray paint. Let the pine cones dry overnight, and then use a Mod Podge and brush to apply the glitter to the cones.

Put the pine cones in baskets or decorate the Mabon altar with them.

Yule Mulled Cider

Ingredients:
1 Bottle of Red Wine
1/3 Cup of Brandy
1/3 Cup of Honey (add more to taste)
1 Teaspoon of Vanilla
1 Orange Cut Into Slices
The Juice of 1 Orange
1 Apple Cut Into Slices
1/3 Cup ofWhole Cranberries
8 Whole Cloves
3 Cinnamon Sticks
4 pods of whole Star Anise

Directions:
Combine all ingredients, EXCEPT spices, into a small saucepan or crockpot. In a separate pan, toast the spices until warm. Add spices to the rest of the ingredients and simmer for 20 min-2 hours.

DO NOT BRING TO A BOIL! The longer the spices simmer the more the flavor will evolve. Strain Spices and serve hot, garnished with a cinnamon stick and an orange slice.

Winter Wassail

Ingredients:
4 cups of apple cider
2 oranges (one juiced and one sliced thinly)
½ cup of pineapple juice
3 cinnamon sticks
Pinch of nutmeg powder
Pinch of powdered cloves

Directions:
Heat apple cider in a slow cooker or saucepan over low heat.
Add ingredients.
Stir to combine. Simmer for 20 minutes. Add orange slices. Serve Hot.

Alcohol Wassail

Ingredients:
4 cups of apple cider
2 cups of cranberry juice
2 cups of orange juice
2 oranges sliced thinly
2 cups of dark ale or brandy
2 cinnamon slicks
2 slices of fresh ginger
1 TBSP whole cloves
1 TBSP allspice berries
1/2 cup of sugar

Directions:
Heat apple cider in a slow cooker or saucepan over low heat.
Add ingredients.
Stir to combine. Simmer for 20 minutes. Add orange slices. Serve Hot.

Pear Cider with Fennel and Orange

Ingredients:
I cup of Pear Juice
2 tsp of Fennel Seed, crushed
I tsp of Orange Peel (dried), chopped
2 Allspice Berries, whole
1 tsp of Brown Sugar
1 tsp of Cinnamon Chips
½ tsp Pure Vanilla Extract

Directions:
Place all ingredients but the vanilla in a small saucepan. Heat until the mixture comes to a boil. Reduce heat to low and partially cover the pan; simmer for 5 minutes.

Turn off the heat, stir in the vanilla, and let steep while covered for another 5 minutes. Strain into a mug.

By SELEFINA.COM

Winter Solstice Tea

Ingredients:
4 Cups of Chosen Water
½ Apple Gala or Fuji work best
2 Cinnamon Sticks
5 Whole Cloves
½ inch Piece of Fresh Ginger
½ tsp of Lemon Zest
4 tsp of Loose Leaf Black Tea
Honey or Brown Sugar as desired to taste

Directions:
Add all the ingredients into a pot and bring to a simmer for about 10 minutes. Remove from the heat and allow to cool for another 5-10 minutes. Strain and enjoy!

Yule Spell in a Mug

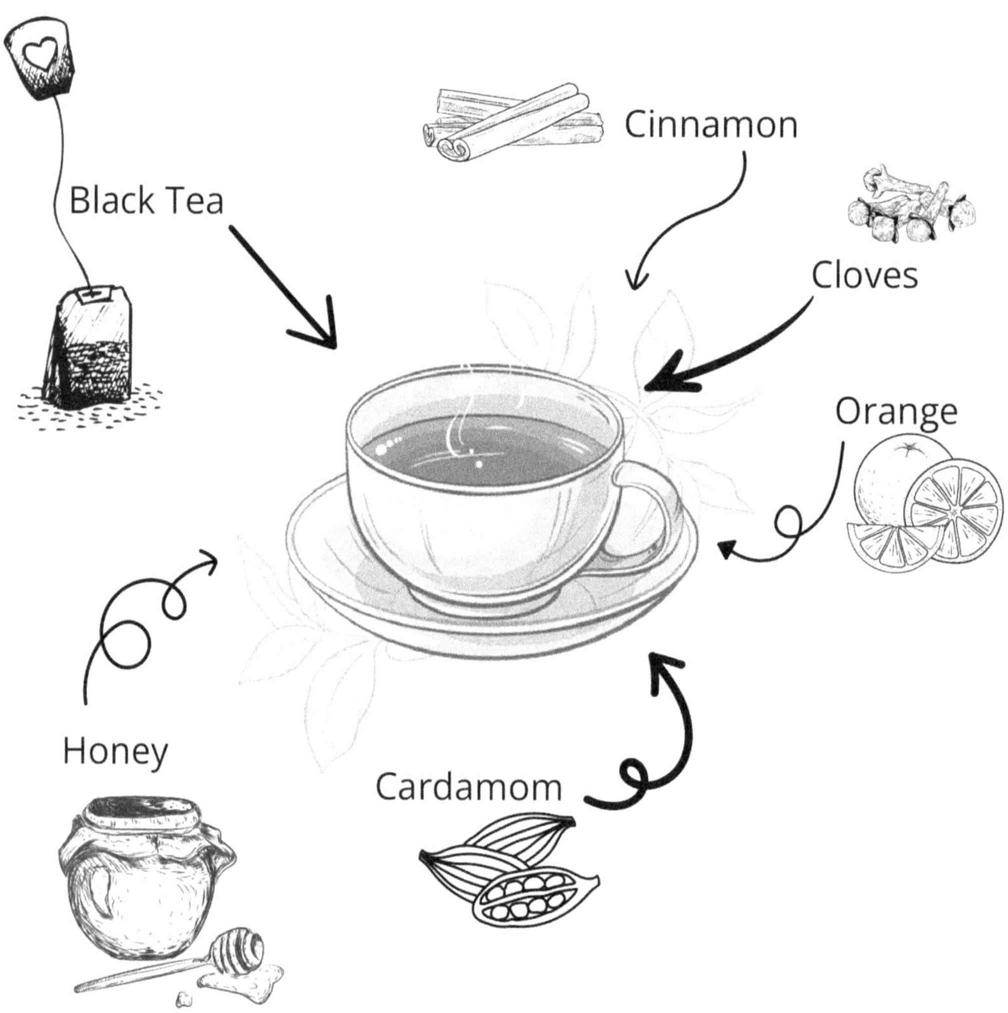

Winter Solstice

Affirmations

I find strength even on the darkest nights
I let go of what no longer serves me
The stillness of winter gives me grounding energy
I am a source of light and warmth in the world
No amount of darkness can dim my light
I release any burdens or negativity
The energy of new beginnings is flowing in my body

Gentle Reminders

Give yourself permission to slow down
Schedule breaks from the holiday hustle and bustle
Appreciate your limits and delegate
Stop comparing yourself to Internet strangers
Find peace and calmness in nature
Spend time with yourself and recharge

Winter Blues

First Aid Kit

Natural Light
Exercise
Supportive network
Energizing
Music
A walk In nature
Getting enough sleep
Hugging your pets
Spend time on hobbies
Decorate your home
Reading

Frankincense

The Ancient Charm of Frankincense: A Resin that has stood the test of time
For over five thousand years, frankincense has been sought after and traded in northern Africa and the Arab world. This magical resin is deeply woven into historical and religious narratives, making its mark in the story of the birth of Jesus. According to the Bible, the three wise men presented gifts of gold, frankincense, and myrrh to the newborn.

Frankincense holds a significant place in both the Old Testament and the Talmud, with Jewish rabbis incorporating it into sacred rituals. Known as olibanum in Arabic, frankincense made its way to Europe through the Crusaders and became an integral part of Christian ceremonies, especially in the Catholic and Orthodox churches.

Interestingly, at the time of Jesus' birth, frankincense and myrrh may have held even greater value than gold. However, with the rise of Christianity and the fall of the Roman Empire, these substances lost favor in Europe, leading to a decline in their trade routes. In the early years of Christianity, incense was forbidden due to its association with pagan worship. Eventually, certain denominations, including the Catholic Church, reintroduced the burning of frankincense and myrrh in specific rites.

In recent years, researchers have delved into the potential benefits of frankincense. A study completed in 2008 found that the aroma of frankincense could help regulate emotions such as anxiety and depression. Lab experiments with mice showed that exposure to frankincense led to decreased levels of anxiety, as the mice were more willing to explore open areas. Additionally, when faced with a hopeless situation, the mice persisted longer before giving up, suggesting potential antidepressive properties of frankincense.

Frankincense has a long history in the world of alternative medicine as well. Ayurvedic practitioners have used it for healing and purification ceremonies for centuries, referring to it as dhoop in Sanskrit.

From its ancient origins to its potential mental health benefits, frankincense continues to captivate and intrigue, weaving an enchanting tale through centuries of culture and tradition.

Myrrh

Step back in time to biblical days, where myrrh takes center stage. It's known as one of the three gifts presented to baby Jesus by the Magi. Spoken of in Matthew 2:11, it states, "They presented Him gifts of gold, frankincense, and myrrh." However, its presence continues beyond. Myrrh can also be found in the Book of Exodus as an ingredient in the "oil of holy ointment" and in the Book of Esther as a purifying agent for women. Even the Song of Solomon describes its exquisite fragrance. Why was myrrh so revered in ancient times? Perhaps because it was considered sacred to the Hebrew people and is mentioned in the Tanakh and Talmud. Myrrh played a central role in Ketoret, a consecrated incense blend used in the early temples of Jerusalem.

Beyond its spiritual aspects, myrrh has also been utilized in Eastern medicine for its rejuvenating properties. Its scent is said to uplift the spirit and soothe the nervous system. In fact, myrrh can even be found in certain toothpastes and mouthwashes in the Western world, thanks to its analgesic qualities.

Not limited to its resin form, myrrh is available as an oil. Embraced by many practicers of aromatherapy, myrrh oil aids in healing coughs, colds, insomnia, pain relief, and boosting the immune system.

Leading alternative medicine expert, Cathy Wong, MD, suggests applying myrrh essential oil directly to the skin or incorporating it into baths with a carrier oil such as jojoba, sweet almond, or avocado. Another option is inhaling the oil's aroma by sprinkling a few drops onto a cloth tissue or using an aromatherapy diffuser or vaporizer. It's important to note that, like any other essential oil, myrrh should only be ingested without guidance from a healthcare professional.

Plant Magic

Experience evergreen trees' timeless allure and vibrant green hue, even during winter. Delve into a captivating legend of the winter solstice that reveals their resilience and unwavering belief in the sun's return.

Discover the historical significance of green during the Yule season, which is celebrated in festivals like Saturnalia and the ancient Egyptian festival of Ra. Embrace the magical properties of green, symbolizing prosperity, abundance, and rebirth.

Tap into the transformative energies of green by adorning your home with evergreen boughs and holly branches. Invite financial blessings and new beginnings into your life. Embrace the captivating allure of evergreen magic this Yule season and harness the power of green in your celebrations.

Mistletoe - Experience peace and harmony by embracing the tradition of kissing under the mistletoe. Discover its mystical connections and the potential for prosperity and fertility.

Birch - Harness the power of rebirth and regeneration with the resilient birch tree. Use birch branches to add momentum and vibrancy to new projects and rituals for fresh starts and new beginnings.

Oak - Find inspiration in the endurance and power symbolized by the oak tree. Connect with deities of victory and triumph while exploring the historical significance of oak crowns.

Yew - Deepen your understanding of the yew tree's association with immortality and the connection to the beyond. Embrace change and welcome new possibilities as the winter solstice unfolds.

Yule Log

Ingredients:
A log about 14 - 18" long
Dried berries, such as cranberries
Pine cone
Dried fruits (cranberries, orange peels)
Cuttings of mistletoe, holly pine needles, and ivy
Feathers and cinnamon sticks
Some festive ribbons - use paper or cloth ribbon, not the synthetic or wire-fined type.
A hot glue gun

Each type of tree is unique and can symbolize different intentions.

Use natural materials only for your bonfire. Go on a nature scavenger hunt for inspiration.
If available, you can go as far as to choose the log based on the magical properties of the
wood, such as oak for wisdom and pine for prosperity.

Birch (fertility, creativity, cleansing, and new beginnings)
Aspen (defeating your fears, divination, spiritual knowledge, and perception)
Oak (intellect, leadership, security, resilience, endurance, and wisdom)
Pine (success, well-being, joy, excitement, and spiritual awakenings)
Ash (wealth, prosperity, transitions, growth, peace, and the strength of women)
Holly (protection, expertise, analysis, and opens your mind to accept revelations (useful for
divination)
Willow (balance, intuition, sentimental feelings, the flow of water, and honoring a
god/goddess/deity)
Yew (ancestry, history, aging, dying, transitions, thoughts, and memory)
Rowan (defense, control of one's actions, protection of animals, growth, and fresh ideas)
Alder (spiritual guidance, creativity, choices, and safeguarding yourself against harm)
Hazel (knowledge, creative inspiration, proficiency, and practicality)

Lore and Magic

Mistletoe

Five days after the first New Moon following the Winter Solstice, priests cut the mistletoe with a golden sickle from a special oak tree and had to catch the mistletoe before it hit the ground. The plant was distributed among the people to hang over their doors for protection against evil in the coming year.

Pagan Tree

Discover the fascinating history behind the Christmas tree. In Pagan tradition, the tree was brought indoors, too. Treats and food were hung from the branches for the spirits to enjoy. Bells were added to chime in the presence of appreciative spirits. Atop the tree, a five-pointed star, representing the five elements, was placed to honor the tree's significance.

Witch Ball

According to folk tales, witch balls would entice evil spirits with their bright colors; the strands inside the ball would then capture the spirit and prevent it from escaping. This protects the home it's hung inside. Witchballs were used to avert the evil eye by attracting the eye's gaze and preventing harm to the house and its inhabitants. Hang it by the front door or in an east window to protect against evil.

Yule Log

Did you know that each type of wood releases its own kind of magick during Yule? Oak brings healing, strength, and wisdom. Ash brings protection, prosperity, and health. Pine signifies prosperity and growth. Holly inspires visions and reveals past lives. Willow invokes the Goddess to achieve desires. After selecting a log, carve the sun or the Horned God on it and place it in the fireplace. Light it at dusk on Yule. As the log burns, visualize the Sun shining within it and think of the coming warmer days.

Pine Cone Magic

Pine Cones can be used for cleansing, purification, and repelling negative energy.
Hang Pine Cones in the home/business to bring success and prosperity.
Hang Pine Cones over your bed to ward off illness during the cold winter months.
A Pine Cone on the altar wards off evil influences and negative energies.
Carry Pine Cones to increase fertility or wear them as a fertility charm.
Carry Pine Cones to maintain strength, health, and energy during old age.
Use Pine cones in rituals to attract prosperity, purify and cleanse a new home, and/or help " stay the course" during difficult times."
Meditate with Pine to help alleviate dark moods.
Burn Pine Cones in your hearth to protect and warm your home.
Throughout history, Pine Cones have been used to symbolize spiritual consciousness, enlightenment, and everlasting eternal life.

Coffee Magic

Adds a boost of power to spells
Use coffee grounds in water to make ink for writing spells
Motivates
Protection
Banishing
Dispels nightmares
Stimulates the mind and creativity
Use as a natural offering
Coffee grounds can be read like tea leaves

Besom Magic

CLEANSING:
It is used to consecrate your magical space before casting a circle or even during doing magic. Then grab a handful of salt, throw it on the ground, and start brushing with your magic broom.

PROTECTION:
In addition, if you feel that you are a target of demonic or psychic attacks when you sleep, them place it under your bed as it will create a magical barrier and protect you effectively from these attacks.

STOP GOSSIP:
If you wish to protect your house from unwanted magic, guests (physical or spiritual), or gossip then place the broomstick across the main windowsill or the front door or across the boundaries of your property,

LOVE MAGIC:
If you have a special partner and you would like to be bonded even more then lay the broom on the floor and perform, "Jumping the broomstick" ritual.

DIY Besom

Brooms or besoms are often used for ritualistic cleansing and purification, particularly during sacred times or handfasting ceremonies. For centuries, brooms have been associated with witchcraft, but do you know why?

Crafting a styled besom broom is a perfect addition to your practice and can be done with just a few materials.

To make a besom broom, you'll need a stick, pine needles, grass, straw, natural twine, and a hot glue gun. Follow these steps:

Gather pine needles around the base of your stick, ensuring that some portions of the stick are entirely submerged in the needles.

Place this configuration on twine and tie it around the pine needles and the stick, making double knots to secure the broom.

To secure the broom further, pour hot glue on the back of the twine knot. Carefully wind the twine around the broom in a circular manner.

To make your besom special, you can decorate it using gemstones, dried flowers, ribbons, or even old jewelry.

Anoint your broom with essential oil and perform your ritualistic ceremony. By following these simple steps, you can create a beautiful and functional besom broom for your ritualistic needs.

Hanging Besom Ritual

Supplies:
Broom
Purifying spray, such as sage. palo santo, or rosemary
3 small nails to secure the broom
Hammer
Step ladder

Directions:
Open your door and begin spraying it. As you do this, repeat aloud or in your mind:

I cleanse my home of all impurities. I return all negative energy to the Earth so that she may recycle it anew.

Use your broom on the doorframe, making sweeping motions towards the outside of your home. While doing this, repeat, aloud or in your mind:

I rid my home of all negativity. I humbly show this energy out of my home so that the Earth may recycle it anew.

Grab your step ladder, hammer, and nail. Close your door so that you are outside of your home. Position your broom above the door so the bristles align with the door's opening direction.

Use the 3 nails to secure the broom above your door.

The broom can be hung to one side if there's no room above the door. You can also place it inside to decorate the home.

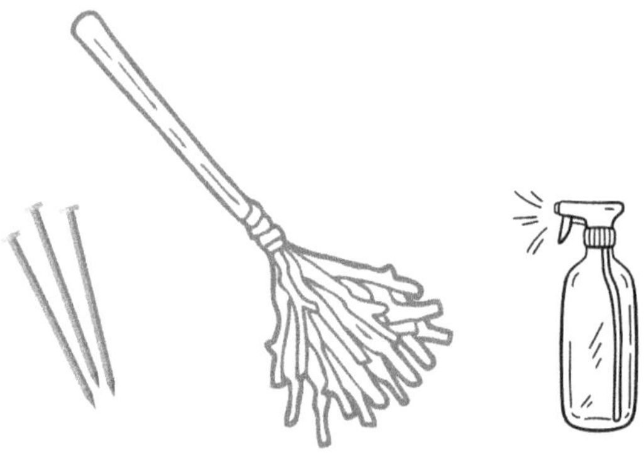

Discover Your Focus
Choosing Your Word for the Year

If you're feeling lost and unsure of what you want to achieve, try this simple process to help you focus. Writing down your thoughts and goals can help you understand what you want to accomplish. By following this worksheet, you can identify ONE WORD to direct your energy and progress towards your goals.

1. Start by listing the areas you want to focus on this year. Keep it simple and don't overwhelm yourself.
2. Determine the theme of your list. This can be a simple description of what you want to achieve.
3. Identify some words describing your theme or how you could achieve your goals.
4. Choose the word that motivates you the most and describe how it will help you.

Abundance	Ease	Hope	Purpose
Adventure	Education	Initiative	Receive
Alignment	Elevate	Ispire	Relax
Ambition	Empowerment	Intuition	Renew
Assertive	Energy	Joy	Resilience
Authentic	Enlightened	Kindness	Romance
Balance	Enthusiasm	Laugh	Self Care
Beauty	Evolve	Learn	Simplicity
Believe Bloom	Fairness	Listen	Spirituality
Bold	Faith	Live	Strength
Boundaries	Family	Love	Support
Brave	Fitness	Magic	Surrender
Breathe	Flourish	Manifest	Transformation
Calm	Flow	Mend	Trust
Career	Focus	Mindful	Unlimited
Caring	Forgive	Nature	Vitality
Centered	Freedom	Organize	Wellness
Change	Friendly	Peace	Worthy
Clarity	Friendship	Performance	Yes
Co-creation	Fun	Play	Zen
Compassion	Grace	Pride	
Confidence	Gratitude	Prosper	
Connection	Growth		
Courage	Happiness		
Creativity	Harmony		
Daring	Health		
Discerning	Honesty		
Discover	Honor		

Dressing Candles

Preparing candles can be as simple or intricate as you desire. Dressing a candle is a way to make herbs adhere to it so they burn as it melt.

Using Oil:
For a decreased spell, rub the oil anti-clockwise.

Sprinkle your herbs on a plate and roll your oiled candle in them to make them stick.

Using Candle Wax:
To use candle wax for your spell and light it.

Allow the wax to melt for a few minutes. Once it starts melting, drip the melted wax onto the candle that you want to dress. Then, use the melted wax to stick the herbs to the candle. You can do this by hand or place the herbs on a plate and roll the candle in the herbs so that they stick to the melted wax.

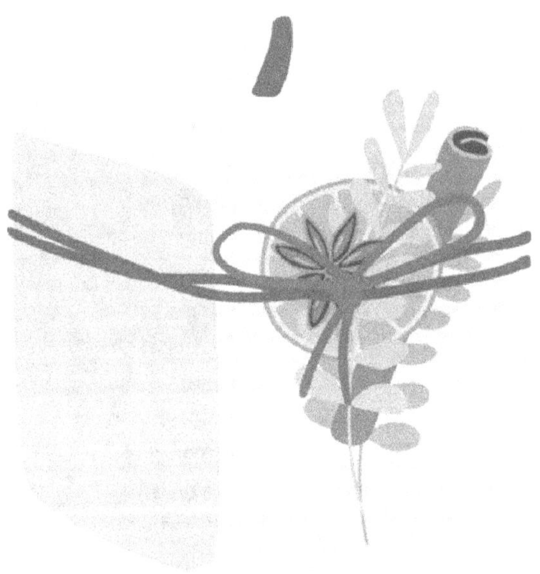

Colors at First Glance

Bringing balance to our lives with color energy is easy. We can do it by wearing our favorite colors, painting rooms in calming colors, or adding different colors to our decor. If we pay attention to the colors around us and how they make us feel, we can use them to improve our lives and increase our vibrations.

Black for banishing, protection, binding, releasing, and defense.

Green for money, prosperity, employment, fertility, growth, luck, abundance, and your Heart Chakra.

Red for strength, passion, courage, action, survival, love, and your Root Chakra.

Yellow for intellect, confidence, travel, movement, joy, imagination, productivity, willpower, and your Solar Plexus Chakra.

Orange for attraction, energy, legal matters, ambition, vitality, opportunity, creativity, inspiration, and your Sacral Chakra.

White for protection, purification, peace, purity, tranquility, and balance.

Blue for healing, peace, forgiveness, communication, truth, calming, focus, memory, and your Throat Chakra.

Purple for spirituality, wisdom, peace, harmony, intuition, psychic abilities, divination, dreams, and your Third Eye Chakra.

But remember to do what feels right to you.
As always: You Do You, Boo!

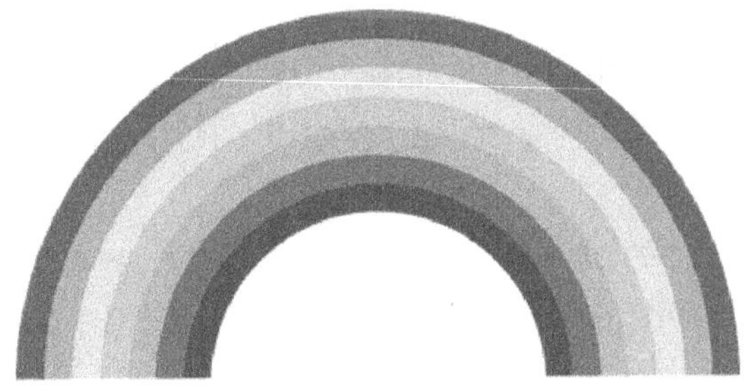

Spell Candle Color

Orange: Courage, creativity, joy, and success. Sunday is associated with orange candles, so burn on that day.

Brown: Grounding, earth element, stability, practicality and focus Tuesday is associated with brown candles, so burn on that day.

White: Peace, healing, protection, divination and purity. Monday is associated with white candles, so burn on that day.

Blue: Protection, creativity, spirituality, harmony, and divine guidance. Thursday is associated with blue candles, so burn on that day.

Yellow: Communication, focus, intuition, and inspiration. Wednesday is associated with Yellow candles, so burn them on that day.

Black: Absorbing negativity, protection, breaking bad habits, breaking hexes and curses, clearing obstacles, and banishing evil. Saturday is associated with black candles, so burn on that day.

Purple: Psychic abilities, divination, clairvoyance, spirit guides, and manifestation. Thursday is associated with purple candles, so burn them on that day.

Pink: Love, romance, self-love, harmony, and compassion. Friday is associated with bink candles, so burn on that day.

Green: Fertility, money, abundance, prosperity, and luck. Friday is associated with Green candles, so burn on that day.

Red: Passion, power, sex, vitality, and desire. Tuesday is associated with Red candles, so burn on that day.

Candle Observance

Flickering Flame

A flickering candle flame often indicates the presence of a spirit, and your request was understood.

Jumping Candle Flame

A lot of energy surrounds your spell; this is typically a good sign and indicates your magic or intention will manifest quickly.

Dancing Flame

Suggests success, but it is likely to coincide with complications. The taller the flame jumps, the more resistance and obstacles you'll likely encounter.

Candle Popping

It signifies that a spirit or ancestor is trying to communicate with you by using candle crackles, sizzles, and pops.

Self- Extinguishes

Indicates your intention or spell has been resolved. Your candle will sometimes self-extinguish if the outcome has already happened before the candle is completely burned out.

Weak Flame

A weak flame will deliver inefficient outcomes, and your intention is up against various complexities.

Types of Candles and Usage

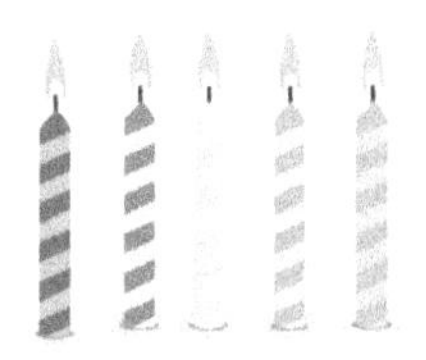

Fast Spells: Birthday Candles

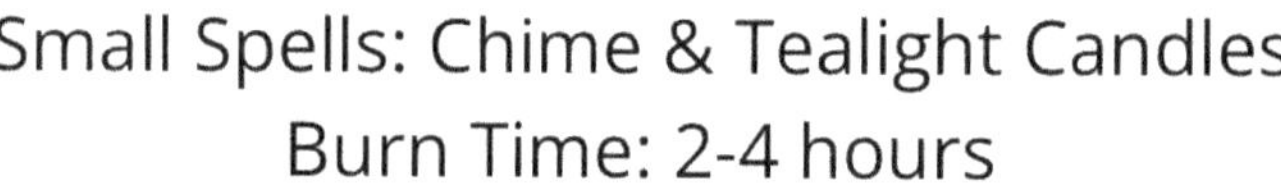

Small Spells: Chime & Tealight Candles
Burn Time: 2-4 hours

Medium Spells: Votive & Taper Candles
Burn Time: 6-10 hours

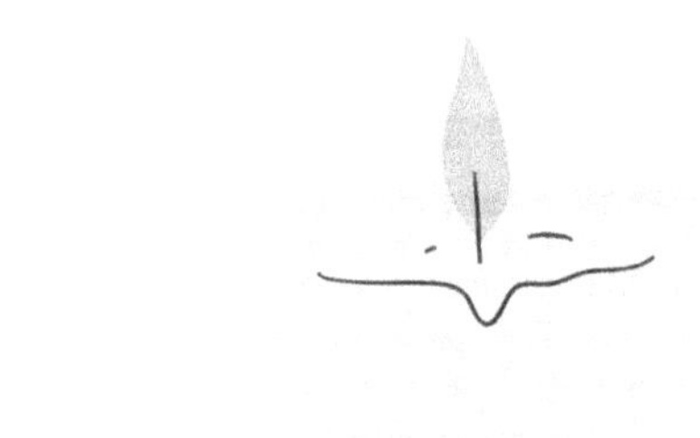

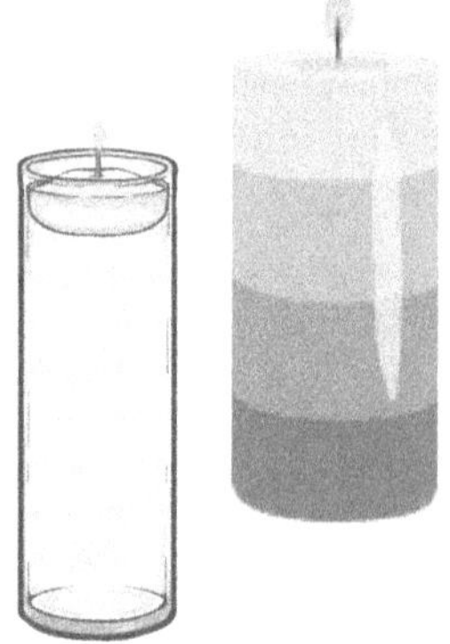

Big Spells: Pillar & 7-day Jar Candles
Burn Time: 12 hours to several Days

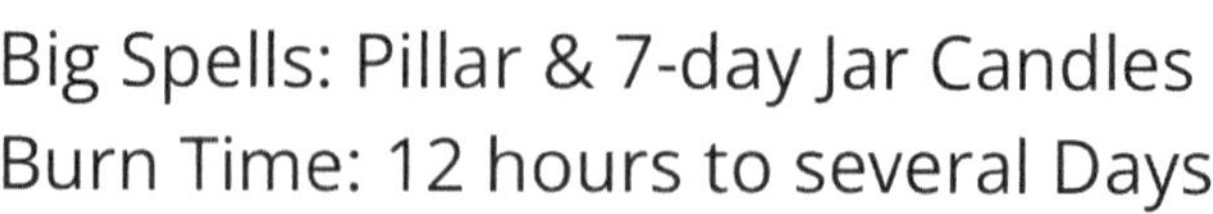

CHAPTER 31

The Role of Prayer in Paganism

The Universal Importance of Prayer Throughout History

From ancient times, people have sought divine intervention through prayer. Ancestors across cultures and locations have prayed to multiple gods, the universe, and the source of all things. Evidence of this can be found in hieroglyphs from Egyptian pharaohs' tombs, carvings and inscriptions from the philosophers and teachers of ancient Greece and Rome, and illuminated manuscripts from Irish monks. The desire to connect with a higher power transcends cultural and geographical boundaries, and stories of prayer's power can be found worldwide. While many prayers were never written down, they have been passed down through oral traditions and preserved in folktales, songs, and legends. Although the wording of these prayers may have changed over time, their message remains the same: we cannot succeed alone, and we require the help of a higher power.

Offerings and Altar Set-Up in Pagan Beliefs

In Pagan faiths, both modern and ancient, it is customary to present a gift to a divine being as a sign of honor and respect. These gifts, known as offerings, are not a bargaining tool ("Here's a pretty gift, can you please grant my wishes now?"), but rather a way to show appreciation, regardless of the outcome of your prayers. For some followers of Wicca, dedicating your time and commitment is just as significant as presenting physical items. Many religions have altars or shrines where offerings can be left, such as candles or flowers in front of a statue of the Virgin Mary at a Catholic church.

Contemplating the Value of Prayer: Does it Have Merit?

Have you ever wondered about the significance of prayer? Is it worth our time and effort? Some claim that if God/Gods/Source/Universe is genuinely divine, they must already know our needs and desires. So why bother asking?

In truth, God/Gods/Source works similarly. However, they don't always understand our wants and needs – and sometimes, what they believe we want and what we actually want are entirely different concepts. That's why it's essential to make our requests known. If you're hoping for divine intervention, you should ask for it. If you don't, the answer will always be "no."

Prayers vs. Spells - Prayer is a plea directly to God/Gods/Source/Universe, the Goddess, Allah, Yahweh, Herne, Apollo, or whomever you believe can lend a helping hand. You ask them directly, "Please help me with..."

Spell vs Prayer

The Difference Between Spell and Prayer

A spell is a command that redirects energy, bringing about a change to align with one's will. While a god or goddess may be called upon for assistance in spell work, it's not always necessary. The power of a spell comes from within the caster, whereas prayer's power comes from the God/Gods/Source/Universe.

Who to Pray to, and How

Regarding prayer, you can direct your words to anyone or anything you please – a god, goddess, or the "Toaster Oven Grand High Poobah." Choose someone most likely to take an interest in your situation. For example, if you seek to protect your home, you might invoke Vesta or Brighid, guardians of the hearth. Or, if you're about to enter a nasty conflict, you may call upon Mars, the god of war.

Others prefer to pray to spirits, such as those of the earth, sky, or sea. Some Pagans also pray to their ancestors, whether as specific individuals or archetypes. Whichever approach you choose, always choose what works best for your tradition.

The Personal Practice of Prayer

Prayer is a deeply individual experience that can be done anywhere – whether out loud or silently – in a church, backyard, forest, or kitchen table. Express what you want to convey and pray when you need to. It's comforting to know that there is always someone who will listen.

Spirituality and Religion

Spirituality and religion are not one and the same. Religions are comprised of attitudes, beliefs, and practices that are centered around groups, while spirituality revolves around an individual's understanding of their place in the world.

Contrary to popular belief, spirituality does not come from religion but rather from within one's soul. It is important to differentiate between religion and spirituality, as religion is a set of rules, regulations, and rituals created by humans to aid in spiritual matters. Spirituality, on the other hand, is not theology or ideology but simply a way of life that is pure and original. It is the connection that exists between us, God/Our Most Highest Self/Source, the universe, and one another.

Understanding Omnism

Omnism is a belief in the recognition and respect for all religions, including their respective gods or lack thereof. Those who practice this philosophy are referred to as omnists, or sometimes spelled as "omniest." In recent years, the term has resurfaced with the growing interest of modern-day omnists who have rediscovered and redefined the term.

Omnism shares similarities with syncretism, which involves combining different beliefs and schools of thought. Syncretism merges or assimilates various traditions, particularly in the theology and mythology of religions, which asserts an underlying unity and allows for an inclusive approach to other faiths. However, omnism can also be seen as a way to acknowledge the existence of different religions without necessarily believing in all they profess to teach.

Many who practice omnism believe that all religions are based on truths, but no single religion can claim to offer all truths. This philosophy emphasizes the acceptance of diversity and inclusivity in religious beliefs.

Cultivating Inner Peace

I will deal with life as it comes; I don't have to worry about it now.

I focus on the peace that life offers me.

All worries, doubts, fears, and anxieties leave my mind, making space for calmness and peace.

In each moment, I have a choice, and I choose peace.

I breathe in stress and worry; I breathe out peace and serenity.

My breath anchors me in the present moment.

Every breath I take fills me with peace.

Peace is my natural state.

I am rooted in inner stillness.

I think peaceful thoughts and enjoy peace in my life.

I am calm and relaxed in every situation.

I choose peace over doubt and fear.

I welcome peace into all areas of my life.

CHAPTER 32

Journal Prompts for Self-Reflection and Shadow Work

Journaling prompts can be an excellent tool for self-reflection by helping you delve into your thoughts and emotions. Expressing yourself through journaling can be therapeutic and provide clarity and understanding of your experiences without fear of judgment.

The versatility of journaling prompts is a significant advantage. You can customize them to your unique needs and interests and use them to explore any aspect of your life. Whether it's your relationships, career goals, personal values, or simply gaining a better understanding of yourself, there's a prompt that's perfect for you. You're free to choose the prompts that speak to you and follow your authentic path.

Remember, there's no right or wrong way to engage in self-reflection. This is a personal journey, and the insights you gain are unique to you. Embrace the process, trust your instincts, and allow yourself to be vulnerable. Your journaling practice will mature over time, and each entry will bring you closer to a deeper connection with yourself.

Self-Reflections

What does my yes feel like?

What does my yes feel like?

Self-Reflections

What does my no feel like?

Self-Reflections

Who is my future self?

Who is my future self?

Self-Reflections

What is my full potential?

Self-Reflections

How would I like to feel? How can I experience more of that feeling in daily life?

Self-Reflections

What are my greatest gifts/talents? How am I cultivating them in my life and the lives of others?

Self-Reflections

What is my proudest achievement?

Self-Reflections

What is the biggest obstacle I've overcome?

Self-Reflections

What masks do I wear for the world, for my
partner, kids, parents, etc?

Self-Reflections

What are my "worst" (self-sabotaging, unhelpful) traits?

Self-Reflections

How much do I judge others daily? What do I judge them for? What are the judged traits and behaviors mirroring back to me?

Self-Reflections

What was the overall theme of this year?

Self-Reflections

What is one belief, habit, or pattern I can release that would transform my life?

Self-Reflections

What areas of my life need to be released from external influence?

Self-Reflections

How judged do I feel daily?

How judged do I feel daily?

Self-Reflections

What am I being judged for? Are these judgments real or imaginary projections?

Self-Reflections

Self-Reflections

Self-Reflections

Self-Reflections

Self-Reflections

Self-Reflections

Self-Reflections

Self-Reflections

Self-Reflections

Self-Reflections

Self-Reflections

Notes

Notes

Notes

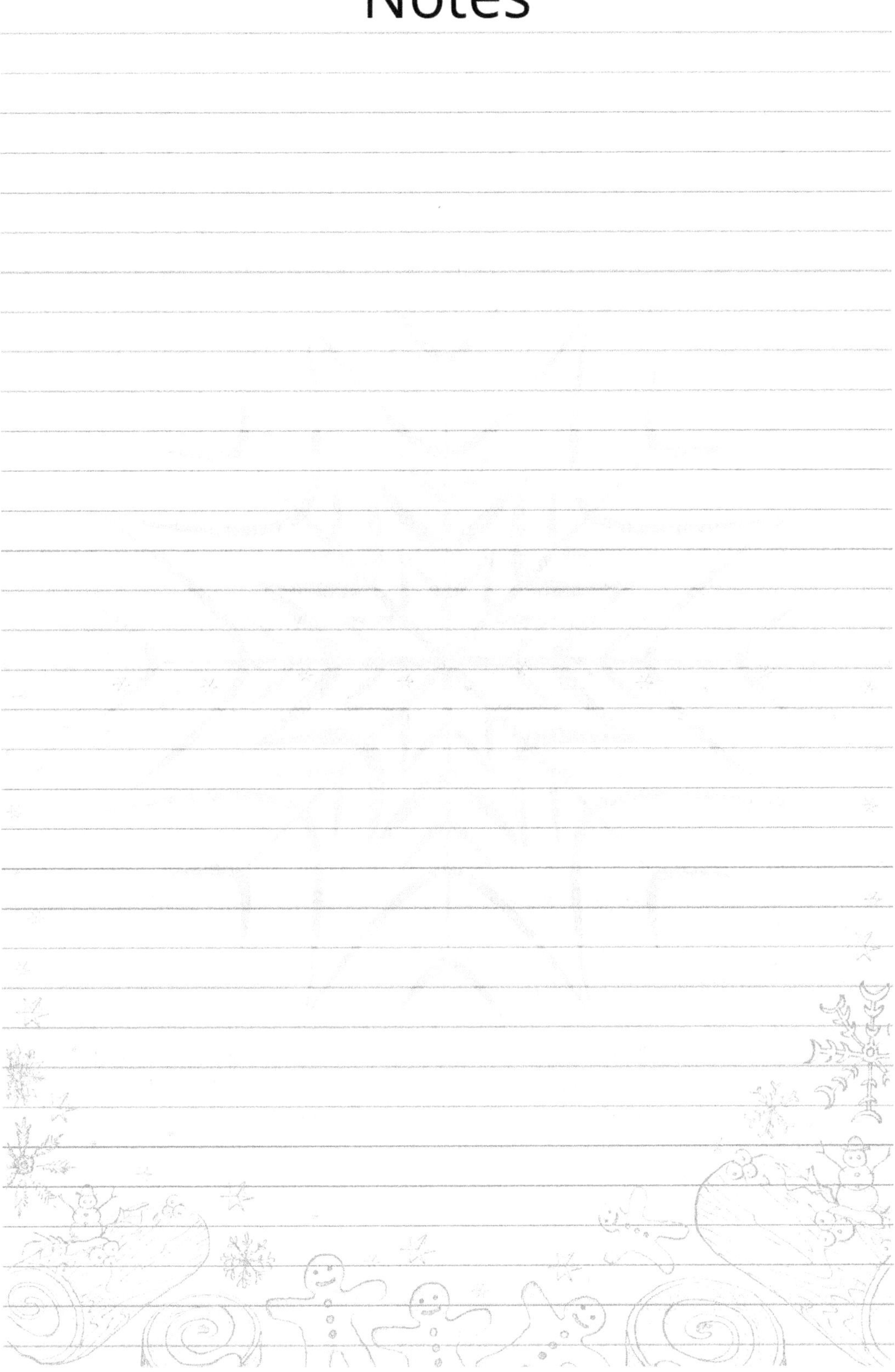

Cutting Energy Cords

If you're looking for ways to cut energy cords, try these techniques:

Visualize All the Cords Coming Back to You

When trying to cut cords, you're often thinking about yourself or someone or something else. To test this exercise, visualize yourself calling back your golden light from what you're trying to cut cords. Imagine all of these golden threads entering your core. When you're finished, do something empowering to seal the energy, such as doing at-home exercises or enjoying a nourishing snack.

Intuitively Ask the Holder of the Cord to Let Go

Center your energy field and identify where you feel the most energetic cord is coming from. Ask this source, with claircognizant or clairaudient inner thought, to release this cord from you, watch it be let go, and come back to you. Some people like to imagine a golden energy scissor cutting the cord, with the cord on your end coiling back to you. Do something nourishing to seal the energy after seeing the cord entirely return to you clairvoyantly, like visualizing a light ball surrounding your energy field. If you're doing this technique for a client, ask your Spirit or Guides for one nourishing thing they can do.

Blue Grid Visualization

This technique seals your energy field with healing light. Imagine a blue electric field cage glowing around you, then visualize any old links or dangling cords twisting or dropping from the energy field. Imagine the old cord pieces breaking off and washing away at your feet, back to the nearest waterway. Then, visualize a glowing blue light grid across your energy field until you feel clear.

When you're finished, visualize a golden light in your core, your Solar Plexus. Bow to yourself or your guides, and offer gratitude for the energy you used to visualize, sense, or think through these shamanic energy exercises. Finally, imagine your palm chakras and heart shining golden light.

Did it Work?

After cord-cutting, you should experience a sense of balance and inner peace. You may feel more focused on a particular project and experience contentment, which is the typical energy state of most soul bodies on Earth.

However, if you continually think about a certain person or situation even after cord-cutting, you may have a karmic relationship with them. In this case, deeper energy work may be needed.

To achieve longer-lasting results after cord-cutting, repeat the above process for up to 21 days or explore other techniques such as "How To Cut Cords Energetically" or "3 Easy Steps To Spiritual Cords Cutting."

For optimal results, try cord-cutting during a full or new moon, representing release and setting new intentions.

Usually, energy entanglements sort themselves out with continued intent, deeper energy work, or when doing energy boundary work. Give yourself and the other person or situation three days to settle after using any cord-cutting technique.

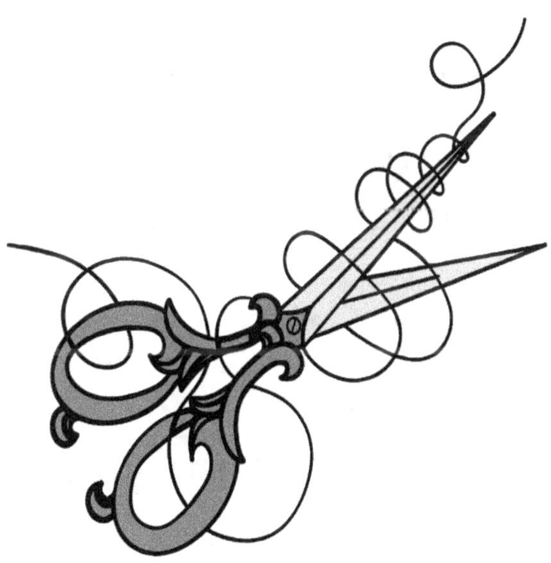

A Mantra for Cord Cutting

With a full heart, I release you from your place in my life – forever grateful for our shared memories. May your chosen path bring happiness and joy.

I now reclaim the energy that was taken from me and release any energy that I gave away. May I be free from any lingering attachments that bind us.

May all cords be cut, transmuted, and dissolved, and may all energy return to its rightful sender with power, peace, and forgiveness.

Let this process be completed and sealed now with the comforting power of acceptance. So it is.

Reference

The Complete Book of Correspondences Sandra Kynes

The White Goddess Graves, Robert Guiley, Rosemary Ellen. The Encyclopedia of Witches and Witchcraft

The Complete Grimoire: Magickal Practices and Spells for Awakening Your Inner Witch by Lidia Pradas

Heal the Witch Wound: Reclaim Your Magic and Step Into Your Power by Celeste Larsen

Cunningham's Encyclopedia of Magical Herbs (Llewellyn's Sourcebook Series) (Cunningham's Encyclopedia Series, 1) by Scott Cunningham

Psychic Witch: A Metaphysical Guide to Meditation, Magick & Manifestation Mat Auryn

Llewellyn's Practical Magick (11 books)

Encyclopedia of World Mythology and Legend

The Encyclopedia of Celtic Mythology and Folklore Monaghan, Patricia.

Astronomer's Stars Moore, Patrick

Self Care for Witches: The Art of Healing and Self Love through Witchcraft by Blair Blackmore

The Door to Witchcraft: A New Witch's Guide to History, Traditions, and Modern-Day Spells by Tonya A. Brown

Seventy-Eight Degrees of Wisdom: A Tarot Journey to Self-Awareness (A New Edition of the Tarot Classic) by Rachel Pollack

Everyday Tarot: Unlock Your Inner Wisdom and Manifest Your Future by Brigit Esselmont

The Ultimate Guide to Tarot Card Meanings by Brigit Esselmont

Intuitive Tarot: 31 Days to Learn to Read Tarot Cards and Develop Your Intuition by Brigit Esselmont

Everyday Tarot: Unlock Your Inner Wisdom and Manifest Your Future by Brigit Esselmont

Reference

A History of Magic, Witchcraft, and the Occult DK

The Modern-Day Witch (11 books) by Shawn Robbins, Leanna Greenaway, Lisa Chamberlain

Witchcraft for Daily Self-Care: Nourishing Rituals and Spells for a More Balanced Life by Michael Herkes

The Untamed Witch: Reclaim Your Instincts. Rewild Your Craft. Create Your Most Powerful Magick. Lidia Pradas

Paganism: Pagan holidays, beliefs, gods and goddesses, symbols, rituals, practices, and much more! An Introductory Guide by Riley Star

Buckland's Complete Book of Witchcraft   Raymond Buckland

The Modern Witchcraft Spell Book: Your Complete Guide to Crafting and Casting Spells (Modern Witchcraft Magic, Spells, Rituals)
by Skye Alexander

Scott Cunningham—The Path Taken: Honoring the Life and Legacy of a Wiccan Trailblazer by Christine Cunningham Ashworth

Herbalism for Witches: 3 Books In 1-Guide to Herbal Apothecary and Plant Witchery+Magical Herbs for Spiritual Healing and Sacred Heart+Manifest Your Spiritual Wellness with Spells and Herbal Magic
by Ruby Goldwin

Protection and Reversal Spells: The Witch's Self-Defense Guide Against Curses, Hexes, Negative Energies, Harmful Spirits, and Psychic Attacks. Create Your Own Shield with the Most Powerful Magic!
by Alyssa Vera

Book Reviewing for Independent Authors: A Personal Experience
As part of my company, I have been reviewing books for Independent authors for a period of five years. I've had the opportunity to meet and interact with some really incredible people. One of those individuals was Rev. Pamela Irene Flowerday, who reached out to me with her book, "Ask Yourself: Understand and Unlock Your Psychic Power for Personal & Planetary Healing." Her writing style was absolutely incredible, and I was blown away by the content. I highly recommend this book, and if you're interested, check out my reviewer page at Robinsreview.com for a short Q&A with the author. (sorry not a shameless plug)

The author, <u>Rev. Pamela Irene Flowerday</u>, wrote Ask Yourself: Understand and Unlock Your Psychic Power for Personal and planetary Healing.

After completing some of the exercises in the book, I was astounded by the wealth of knowledge I had gained. The book helped me to identify and trust my inner knowing, and I was inspired by Rev. Flowerday's insightful content. With this newfound understanding of my intuitive abilities, I was able to embark on a path of profound spiritual growth and personal transformation.

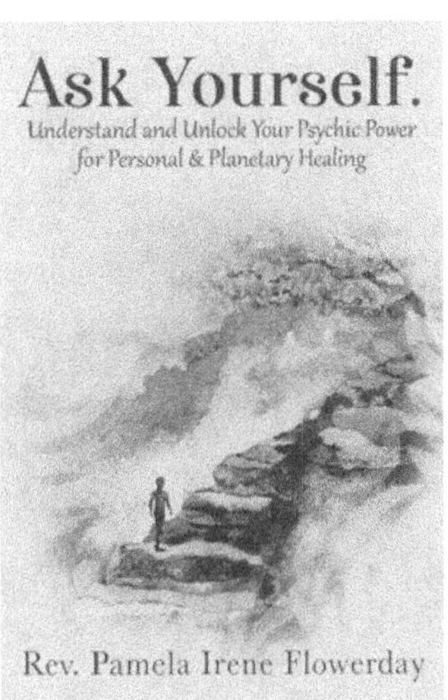

Mystic Mind Community

Why Join The Mystic MindCommunity?

We bring together spiritual people who are seeking more connection, the ability to share their own experiences, and learn from online Challenges, Live Events, Courses, and each other!

The concept for building this Spiritual Social Network is so we can grow together in a supportive, inclusive, and fun Spiritual Metaverse covering a wide range of spiritual resources.

The Mystic Mind Podcast

The Mystic Mind Podcast is a creative exploration to help support you in your intuitive and spiritual development journey and add a little fun!

I mean, we have to have fun on this journey, right?

As a professional Energy Healer and Spiritual Teacher, I share some of what I've learned along the way during my spiritual development journey for over a decade. In this podcast, you will find shows on Intuitive Development and/or reflections, Angels, Divination, Energy Work, special guests, interviews, and more.

Also, have you joined our Mystic Mind Community?
Mystic Mind is available on
Spotify
Anchor fm
Amazon Music
Apple Musi
DCNW Podcast:
Spotify:

Colby Parrish

(727) 831-8077

Facebook: The Wondering Fool - Spiritual Advisor
Instagram: Thewonderingfool333
TikTok: TheWonderingFool333

Hours of Availability
Tuesday through Saturday 11 am - 8 pm EST

Service Menu
General Psychic Readings
30 min/$60
45min/$90
60min/$120

Tarot - Oracle - Lithomancy
3 Card Single Message
Pull/ $20
Couples Readings
40min/$80
Personal Monthly
Forecast/$120
Numerological
Chart/$150

Available for private parties and events!

He is my spiritual adviser, so I highly recommend him and his services!

Jamie Wareham

www.lightworkerpath.com
Email: lightworkerpathsite@gmail.com

Service Menu
Reiki + Sound Healing Sessions
Soul Coaching Sessions (spiritual life coaching)
Intuitive Development
Mentorship Programs
Reiki Level 1,2 & 3 Attunement
Certification Courses
Spiritual/Energy Development Classes

She is a fellow writer who co-authored "The Voyage & The Return: The Path to Self Discovery." Moreover, I've taken her classes, and they were interesting and helpful. She's super knowledgeable about energy work, angel spirit guides, meditation, and reiki healing.

Here is a profound quote from her book "Some of the best teachers are ones who have journeyed into the heart of darkness and come through it all like the powerful Phoenix they are! A rebirth into something else, something stronger, something that yearns to help others through their own forms of darkness."

Elemental Magic
For all of your metaphysical needs

elemental-magick-inc.myshopify.com
948 4th Avenue Coraopolis, PA 15108
Phone Number: (412) 741-1428

Facebook Group Elemental Magick
Instagram Elemental Magick Inc

We are a women-owned metaphysical business that has been operating since 2015! Located in Coraopolis, Pennsylvania, we provide some of the best quality crystals in Pittsburgh with a personal service guarantee every time you shop. Our products include candles, books, incense, and items from local artisans, including Gaias Grace.

Hours of Operation
Sunday: CLOSED (Sunday Funday Facebook Live 7:00 pm EST)
Monday: CLOSED
Tuesday: CLOSED
Wednesday: CLOSED (Witchy Wednesday Facebook Live 7:00 pm EST)
Thursday: 12 pm - 6 pm
Friday: 12 pm - 6 pm
Saturday: 12 pm - 6 pm

Odie's Curiosities

Handmade High-Quality Jewelry Available on Facebook

Discover beautifully crafted handmade items, including reiki-charged jewelry that is hand-strung with care. With a specialty in Mala beads, this Facebook store offers stunning and unique pieces you won't find anywhere else.

Contact through Facebook Messenger

Whimsical Cauldron and Crafts

www.whimsicalcauldronandcrafts.com
Email: Whimsicalcauldron2019@gmail.com
Facebook: Whimsical Cauldron and Crafts, LLC

They sell crystals, minerals, specimens, jewelry, herbs, sage, etc.
They also feature other vendors and their merchandise.

I have purchased almost everything they have for sale and can confidently say they are a great small business for high-quality crystal needs. They have always been kind and patient, especially when I first learned about crystals. If they didn't have something I was looking for, they would get it for me.

Emerald Coast Alternatives

emeraldcoastalternatives.com

Welcome to Emerald Coast Alternatives, your online herbal tea shop. We aim to provide accessible, effective, and affordable herbal tea blends that help you feel better and enjoy life more. Our teas are delicious and effective in managing symptoms of anxiety, PTSD, PMS, insomnia, inflammation, and headaches. We donate one Herbal Tea "Care Package" monthly to a Recovery Center in the USA. Thank you for choosing Emerald Coast Alternatives as your trusted herbal teas and self-healing tools source.

Follow them and learn more about what their products can provide on TikTok @freespirit.beauTEA

Enhance your Health with The Plant Cemetery Herbal Subscription Box!
MONTHLY HERBAL HEALTH & BEAU-TEA SUBSCRIPTION BOX
$10 OFF YOUR FIRST BOX with Code: PlantBox10
FREE SHIPPING ON ALL PRODUCTS!

Although I am not typically a tea fan, I absolutely adore the tea from this company. I purchase it frequently and have even signed up for their monthly subscription box.

I just wanted to express my deepest gratitude for your unwavering support. It has been an absolute joy to share this journey with you, and I hope you've enjoyed it even half as much as I have. Every single like, follow, share, and review means the world to me. If you're feeling particularly generous, I would be truly moved if you could take a moment to spread the word about my books by leaving an honest review. Together, we can make this world a brighter, better place. Thank you from the bottom of my heart for everything.

Thank you!!
Robin

Discover a world of possibilities at KIPS Publishing LLC. Books have the power to transform lives and expand horizons. And we are proud to bring you some of the most captivating, informative, and inspiring books you can imagine. Now, with just one scan of our QR code, you can access a whole library of books from KIPS and discover the best of what we have to offer. So take advantage of this exciting opportunity to take your reading journey to the next level. Scan now and open the doors to a world of knowledge, imagination, and inspiration!

 Scan here for the latest release
from Robin Ginther Venneri
and KIPS Publishing

Thank you so much for your support!

If you enjoyed this book, then kindly leave a review on Amazon and on any of your social media accounts, and please tag me on them.

Blessings to You and Yours,
Robin Ginther-Venneri

Questions, concerns, and ideas can be directed to KIPSPublishingllc@gmail.com.

How to Support Indie (Independent) Authors:

Review their books:
Like & comment on their posts:
Share their in-story or about pages:
Preorder their books. You know you are going to buy them anyway!
Recommend them to other readers:
Email or message about a book of theirs you loved:
Follow them on social media.